Silks, Soaks and Certainties

Silks, Soaks and Certainties

Bob Butchers

Blenheim Press Limited
St Albans

First published in 2008 by
Blenheim Press Ltd
35 Market Place
St Albans
Herts AL3 5DL

ISBN 978-1-906302-04-7

Typeset by TW Typesetting, Plymouth, Devon

Printed and bound by CPI Antony Rowe, Eastbourne

To Marian, Lesley and Guy
for whose love I am ever grateful.

CONTENTS

ACKNOWLEDGEMENTS

Without a computer it would have been difficult to have produced this book so I had to rely on the help of my family even though I was able to do some work on a laptop kindly loaned by my grand-daughter Joanna. Her sister Emma was responsible for turning my pages of scribble into computer print while their father, David, was a great help with scanning photos and other technicalities.

Proof reading was done by my son Guy, who also gave valuable advice on other matters. It was he, with Quark skills and his sophisticated computer set-up, who advanced the contents to what I understand to be book format. Colleagues on the *Daily Mirror*, Dave Mitchell and Roger Plummer, who were there in my days, made contact with the picture library and their help was invaluable. It resulted in Tony Schipani searching and finding negatives of treasured pictures taken in the early seventies, one of which I did not know existed. I have never met Tony but his willing assistance is very much appreciated.

My cousin, Paul Lucas, worked tirelessly on the colourful cover, getting it to a design that we all approved. He also came up with the title and in case you may wonder, the word 'soaks' refers to the many drinkers that crop up in the book. It was also very kind of Gay Kindersley to write the Foreword which brought back happy memories. Stewart Nash kindly allowed me to include two photographs from his book *The History of Plumpton* and thanks also to Plumpton racecourse.

An amusing article from *Private Eye* and a verse by Mary Lascelles in a greetings card are included and I trust they will have no objections. Similarly I trust that Judy Middleton will have no objection to my using a photograph of the 'Bottleneck' from her excellent book *Lewes* which gave me joy and brought back even more happy memories.

I offer my heartfelt thanks to all of the kind folk mentioned and finally to my wife Marian who washed so many dishes, and glasses, unaided, while I was engrossed in my writing.

A young Gay Kindersley

FOREWORD

by Gay Kindersley

The name of Butchers was part of the racing scene for over a century and came to a close when Bob retired as 'Newsboy' of the *Daily Mirror*. My connection with the family was through Don Butchers who trained my horses successfully for many years. He was Bob's uncle and at a later date became his stepfather.

He and Bob were very close so it was not long before we met while riding exercise at both Lewes and Epsom and, of course, frequently on the racecourses. Bob has written in some detail about Don's riding and training careers and I would like to say how our association began. My first horse with Don was Tight Knight in Lewes and early in the morning I used to cycle the eight miles from my East Chiltington home to muck out before riding at exercise. I would return in the evening to 'do my two'. Before riding Tight Knight in a race I went to Canada to work as a 'roughneck' on a family oilrig and was then offered a good office job in Calgary. However, Tight Knight was engaged in a selling chase at Newton Abbott in a few weeks' time and as my heart was in racing I left Canada and the horse gave me my first winning ride.

Don and I always got on very well together, he as a guide, mentor and friend. I bought a stable in Epsom and Don moved there to train a dozen horses for me, including the 1963 Grand National runner-up, Carrickbeg. He also helped me to be the leading amateur in 1959/60. He never ever praised me when I rode a winner but always told me in no uncertain terms when I had ridden a bad race. Bob tells in the book how this sort of approach was par for the course in bygone days.

Bob and I have been great friends for a long time but as we get older our paths do not cross as often as we would like. His book tells of racing and some characters of yesteryear and how his ambition to be a jumping jockey was ended shortly after it had begun. I know how heartbroken he must have felt.

INTRODUCTION

An attempt to be an author in one's eighties is, I guess, not the usual trend. The advantage is that there is so much more to put into print. The disadvantage is that it is that much harder to remember.

When I retired from the *Daily Mirror* in 1985, I had spent almost 39 years as 'Newsboy', the chief racing correspondent. It was then that I made two definite decisions. The first was not to follow fashion and write a book. The second was not to go near Newmarket again.

The first decision has been reversed, while living deep in Suffolk virtually reverses the second decision. No doubt I have changed in the last twenty-odd years so goodness knows how I, and most other things, have changed compared with the previous sixty years.

To be honest I think the reason for writing this book is to recount and wallow in the gloriously happy times I enjoyed with that noble beast – the horse. Whether directly or indirectly he has played a big part in my life and I have aimed to relate the pleasure that horses have given me.

I also recall some of the characters that were central to or on the fringe of racing. The four years I spent in the RAF during the war and then my career as a journalist do not match my truncated youth and retirement years for happiness. If the events are not in chronological order, I beg forgiveness. It could be due to laziness in research, loss of memory or oncoming senility! You will find no 'purple prose' but simply reality. For me it is like living my life again.

Bob Butchers
Suffolk
2008

1

THE EARLY PART

Somebody said that life begins at forty and if that is so I have completed the second round. Hopefully it does not signal a second childhood as that is something I consciously try to avoid. Of one thing I am certain: I have learnt more in my second forty years than I did in my first. Sadly, that does not become apparent until you reach eighty. What is more, the learning process continues.

The following pages are not so much an autobiography as a stroll through the life of an ordinary individual and his family. Life rarely runs smoothly but I have no complaints, even though mine includes six years of war. Disappointments, there have been many, but regrets very few. The world would be a happier place if everyone was lucky enough to have been dealt a similar hand. Unfortunately that is not the case and I am too cowardly to face up to the tragedies of life but have the greatest admiration for those brave souls who do.

The reference to six years of war should not be taken out of context because my four years in the RAF were more of an inconvenience than anything else. Like so many families, the Butchers clan lost a member in the Great War but there were happier days when the name was prominent in the racing world for more than a century.

The way racing is now run bears little resemblance to how it was before the war and a few years after it. I am not the one to say whether the changes are for the better but I know which periods were the most enjoyable and that should be easy for you to guess. People of my age tend to look back and remind themselves of happy days and become convinced that they were better than present-day life. I suspect it is a case of looking back through rose-tinted glasses.

There are references later on to what, in days gone by, were regarded as innocent wrong-doings that in today's world of racing would certainly result in huge fines and suspensions. Nobody can argue with that; after

George Butchers

all I campaigned in the *Daily Mirror* for more inquiries. My stance was prompted by one flat race season when there were just three inquiries into the running of horses. This was taken seriously by the Jockey Club and I, together with David Phillips, the racing editor, entertained the then Senior Steward, Lord Leverhulme, to lunch to discuss the matter. The outcome was a directive for local Stewards to be more vigilant. In my opinion the pendulum has probably swung too far in the opposite direction these days. The past and present eras are as different as chalk and cheese.

Despite some adverse headlines, racing is probably as lily-white as it can be considering the huge amounts of money involved. Commerce and finance are probably a lot less lily-white and a probe by a governing body would surely unveil some scandalous goings-on.

'Avoid talking about politics and religion' has for long been sound advice. In my case the topics of corruption in racing and the fox-hunting issue come under the same heading. Both subjects have complexities that are seized upon by the fanatical 'for and against' parties.

Having spent virtually half my life as racing correspondent of the *Mirror* my face became familiar to quite a lot of people. The *Mirror* and

2

the *Daily Express* are the only two daily papers that, for a short time, sold over five million copies a day. It was estimated that each copy of the *Mirror* was read by an average of three people per household.

With my picture appearing daily it was inevitable that I was recognised but that did not mean a thing and quite often was embarrassing. The only publicity I craved was to see headlines in the racing press such as 'Bob Butchers rides three more winners'. A number of circumstances made sure that was never to be.

I suppose the best way to start my story is from the beginning. It is not all about me but the Butchers family. The way we were brought up was different and so was the environment. No doubt I fall into the category of 'old-fashioned'.

My grandfather, George Alexander Butchers, began the family connection with racing in the 1880s. It is now almost certain that we have reached the end of the line, as has the even larger family of Smyths, even though no individual of that family had twelve children.

With several early deaths in the family it was with Don Butchers that I had the longest and closest association even though he died at the age of 56. When I was a small child it was Don who would bring me a saddle, bridle and whip so that I could use the back of the settee as a horse. Because we were so close I know the details of his career and have devoted many pages of this book to him and hope they are of interest.

2

DIVIDED FAMILY

For me, it all started in Lewes, the county town of Sussex – a place I still adore and greatly miss. I was born at home in De Montfort Road, in what was an extremely well-built semi-detached abode within spitting distance of my grandfather's stables. I mention this because the pair of houses stood on their own and had the sort of interior finish that is not seen in the equivalent structures these days. They had solid brick throughout and real wood. They were made to last but the pebble-dash exterior is very much a no-no these days. Recently we went to look at the house when it was empty. The interior had had structural and modernisation work, probably for the better, but sad.

The Black Horse stables, so named because they were next door to a pub of that name, were in the centre of the upper part of town. In between the stables and the pub was an alleyway that housed not only the side entrances to both the stables and the pub but a farrier by the name of Ted Rainbird, who did all the shoeing, and a well-used gentleman's urinal. I was fascinated by the farrier and spent ages watching the process from measuring a horse's hoof to the fitting of the shoe. From there it was down a flight of steps to our house which, incidentally, cost £500 the pair when first built. Before the steps from the stables were constructed they were crudely cut out of the bank with a handrail alongside.

An early memory was looking out of a bedroom window and seeing two men with their sleeves rolled up having a bare-knuckle fight on the bank, undoubtedly after the pub had closed.

My father, Leslie, took over the stables from his father, George Alexander, but sadly they were demolished before the war and an ugly new building was occupied by staff of the Inland Revenue.

At this point I will clarify the family structure. Grandfather George was a son of a coachman in Rye near the Sussex-Kent border, a town best known for the Mermaid Inn set in a picturesque cobbled street and as being the home of the late Spike Milligan.

George moved to Lewes with his wife Isobel and they had twelve children – a not uncommon feat in the days before TV took over from 'an early night'. Isobella died at the age of fourteen and the surviving girls were Mabel, Hilda, Violet and Edna; the boys came in the shape of George Frederick, known as Fred, Ernest, Joseph, Leslie, Reginald, Alec and Donald.

Three of the boys went directly into racing and became jockeys. Fred was reputed to be among the best jockeys of his day. Slim and debonair, he was six feet tall – an unusual height for a jockey. He left for the First World War with the Household Brigade and the depressing words to his mother that he was too tall to be missed by enemy fire. Sadly, Fred's prediction became reality as he was killed on the Somme in November 1916, though his death was not notified until 1917.

My father, Leslie, also fought in that war and served in Mesopotamia, now Iraq. He suffered gas poisoning and frequently had enormous boils on his back so a retired doctor, Dr Sadler, came to the house to treat

Father with Fay and Bob

5

them. He used a milk bottle and steam, which acted as a suction pump to remove the unbelievably large cores.

The poisoning eventually caused my father's death in the spring of 1939 at the early age of 42. I remember the sequence of events all too vividly. My mother had taken me and my older sister Fay to the Southdown Point-to-Point at Ringmer. When we returned home my father had taken himself to bed and was in a delirious condition. Phone calls to our GP were unanswered for several hours but he was taken to the Lewes Victoria Hospital late that evening. A dreaded boil had developed inside his ear and in the space of 48 hours he was dead – a legacy of his war service. The family feel sure that the use of modern day drugs would have saved him and perhaps the more immediate service of a doctor might have helped. The official cause of death was septicaemia.

The fourth member of the family to enter racing was Donald Charles Victor. He and my father were close, as were mother, Fay and myself. It is during this period that confusion arose. Some years after my father's death, my mother Elsie, daughter of a well-known Sussex miller, married Don. No doubt some people construed this as the culmination of an on-going affair. I know they were wrong, but that is neither here nor there.

More importantly, Don and Mother consulted me and my sister Fay on the matter of their getting married and we gave our blessing without hesitation – in fact we were hugely delighted. Don, having been my uncle, now became my stepfather and a better father would be hard to find. That observation does not reflect badly on my real father who was kind and loving and to whom I was getting really close when he died. Incidentally, the family friend, Dr Sadler, was a witness to the marriage.

As my appearance on the racecourses, both as a would-be jockey and journalist, overlapped Don's career as jockey and trainer, many people inquired about our relationship. That needed a quick answer, which was 'brother'. There was no reason to give a long-winded explanation.

Four of my other uncles – Joe, Reg, Ern and Alec – were athletes of some ability. Three athletic brothers worked in local government while Ern became a mechanic. They were members of the Brighton and County Harriers, which boasts as its most famous member the runner Steve Ovett of Olympic fame.

3

BEAUTY AND THE BEAST

I was born on 2 July 1924 and although I have the solitary Christian name of Robert, it would have been Richard but for a lapse of memory. The christening took place at St Anne's Church opposite the family stables. A last-minute discovery was the lack of a godfather, quickly remedied by snatching Joe Reed, one of our trusty stable lads, from our nearby yard.

It was not long before ponies were introduced – the second being a Shetland. After twice whipping round and dumping both my father and Don it was declared to be unsuitable. I can't remember much about the first pony except that at the age of around two, I fell off and was taken to hospital with a suspected broken leg. Luckily, the X-ray showed otherwise.

There was a gap of a few years before a jet-black mare named Phoebe became my intended mount. She was sleek and pretty, despite her bobbed tail, with a distinct air of superiority. She was stabled with the old riding-school master Fred Marshall, who gained fame locally as the trainer of Plum Jam, a horse that became a Plumpton specialist ridden by Bert Carter and had a race named after him at the near-Lewes course.

However, back to Phoebe. She was headstrong, nappy and a bit too much for a youngster – and the cause of me losing interest in riding. I think my father may have been a little disappointed but he did nothing to rekindle the flame. Eventually, at the age of around twelve or thirteen, I did burst into flames at the sight of a young girl riding on the Lewes Downs with a couple of others who I assumed were her younger sister and mother.

At about the same time, Tom Masson arrived to train at Barn Stables and my father was down to just a couple of horses. Masson was new to training and became friendly with my father. The outcome was an invitation by Masson to bring the two horses to Barn Stables and

Leslie Butchers

familiarise him with the administrative side of training, including the entering of horses for races. Among the Masson imports was a fairly big skewbald pony and it was Masson who suggested to my father that I should start riding again. By this time I had discovered the name of the pretty girl I had been admiring.

To start riding again gave me the possible chance to see the girl more often and hopefully at closer quarters. She turned out to be a blessing in disguise. I made friends with the skewbald pony immediately. My confidence was restored at once and within the first week I was on my first racehorse. I had the 'horse bug' in a big way and it was down to the pretty girl I had never met nor spoken to. Belated thanks to Angela Kelly. Despite the puppy-love, I still remember that Rockleigh was the name of that first racehorse I rode at exercise.

It was at about this time that Lewes trainer G.S. (Jock) Langlands took an apprentice from a family of horsemen. His name was Ken Mullins and his brother Alf was already a jumps jockey with Jock. Ken was still a schoolboy and we both went to the County Grammar School but had other priorities – riding racehorses. What is more, we both had

Tom Masson on the skewbald that started me riding once again

permission to miss assembly as our riding duties did not end until around 9.30 in the autumn and winter months. I remember well the first winner Ken rode and also recall him later showing me the inscribed watch he received from Sir Malcolm McAlpine, the owner of his winner, Truckle, at Lingfield. He was champion apprentice in 1939, 1941 and 1942 with scores of twenty-nine, nine and seven respectively. The lower scores were due to the racing being severely restricted. Increasing weight forced Ken to join the jumping boys and he proved to be one of the very best. We had a lasting friendship and I rode against him on several occasions.

The two Rees brothers lived in Lewes and rode for George Poole – a top trainer of jumpers, who won the 1921 Grand National with Shaun Spadah ridden by F.B. Rees. The following year L.B. Rees won the Aintree race on Music Hall. Incidentally, Shaun Spadah was owned by Sir Malcolm McAlpine and as well as giving the jockey an annuity, he gave a shilling to all the schoolchildren in Lewes. Fred was champion jockey five times, and in 1924 rode 108 winners when the totals were amassed from 1 January to 31 December, making him the first to record a century.

The Grammar School Christmas party. The girl on the right with the hair ribbon is Patsy Rees with Bob opposite while the first two girls on the right are Marika Foster, later Leader, and sister Fay

Fred Rees had three daughters, Joyce, Peggy and Patsy. I had previously been at the Grammar School, known locally as the Red Cap Grammar for obvious reasons. Patsy was in my class and I had a crush on her, which I thought was a secret until F.B. asked, in a jocular manner, if I was 'hanging my hat up' to Patsy. Plenty of blushes then and when I next saw her in the classroom.

It is worth recording that F.B. Rees rode in a flat race as an amateur against professionals when that was permitted. The trainer of a horse ridden by the great Australian Brownie Carslake said there was only one danger in a race at Brighton and that was being ridden by 'a mug'. After being beaten in a close finish, Brownie's only remark was 'that Rees is some mug'. He was a stylist and as a jumping jockey had only one serious accident, a broken leg towards the end of his career.

L.B. Rees had a larger brood: Richard, a vet, Michael and Bill, both top jockeys, and three girls, Deirdre, Diane and Marigold, each of whom died at a much too early an age.

10

On the Lewes Downs with Alan Oughton

Diane was married to the jockey Alan Oughton, who later trained at Findon. Alan, one of my great friends, died of cancer as a young man and Diane took over the training. After her death, their son David was the governor. David had some National Hunt rides before he started training. He was an ambitious young man and when things weren't going to plan, he applied for a trainer's post in Hong Kong and was one of the leaders there for many years. David brought over Cape of Good Hope to run at Royal Ascot 2004 and he finished second in the King's Stand Stakes and third in the Golden Jubilee Stakes four days later. On both occasions it was a tight finish. He came back to win the Golden Jubilee in 2005 when the Royal meeting took place at York while Ascot was being rebuilt.

Alan and Diane's other child was Gay and she is a charmer married to Newmarket trainer James Eustace.

The boys of L.B. Rees, minus Bill who was a toddler, with Ken Mullins and me, knocked about together. Knocked about is an appropriate phrase as I produced a pair of boxing gloves and along with Richard, Michael and Ken staged a tournament in the front room of L.B.'s house. The details are hazy except for me giving the smaller Ken Mullins a few thumps that were followed by tears. Ken was much braver as a jockey.

All of these pre-war friendships carried on and still do with the survivors and with the offspring of those who have sadly departed. Those Lewes days were memorable and so were the twelve years I was in Lewes after the war when married to my teenage sweetheart Marian. We still had the same friends and, of course, some new ones.

Other activities in those days included visits to the Geerings' farm. The family consisted of three sets of twins and a single child. Tony was the only boy who was naturally spoilt. The girls were a fun bunch and the youngest was Peggie who married 'Towser' Gosden and is the mother of the present trainer John. Peggie was another boyhood love but a trip to the variety show at Brighton Hippodrome was as far as any romantic attachment went. We were both in our early teens and, yes, her name is spelt PEGGIE.

In those days the groups of youngsters made their own pleasures, which did not involve vandalism. The nearest we came to that was chalking squares on the road to play hopscotch or daring to knock on doors and running away. Boredom is often put forward as an excuse for wrong-doing these days but we were having too much fun to be bored. Obviously the change of lifestyle is a major factor and the biggest is the onset of television and other electronic devices.

George Poole with L.B. Rees (L), F.B. Rees (R) and Minnie Poole (sister)
(W.W. Rouch & Co Ltd.)

It was a magical pre-war existence providing you came from a family who were employed or at least where the man had work. When I see pictures of those days I find it strange that I was part of it, especially the streets without cars. It is also strange to remember that we wore those sorts of clothes. If I could have had one wish about the world we live in, it would be a return to pre-war days but without the impending war and, as importantly, not the sort of hardship that so many had to endure.

I thought some of my early cars looked stylish until I see photographs of them. Pop-up direction indicators were sufficient to put your car in the ultra-modern category. In pre-war days we wore what we called 'Sunday-best' clothes on certain occasions. In my case, it was worn to have Sunday tea at Grandma's house. It was a weekly ritual and a large chunk of her family sat round a very large table spread with all manner of things. If there were any winkles available they were there but most of all I remember caraway seed cake which I tried once but never again. Grandma Butchers was a creature of habit who always shopped at the Co-Op and went to Chapel wearing a variety of hideous hats.

4

FATHER OUT OF LUCK

Pre-war Lewes was a town full of horses. The number in training then was over four hundred but now there is hardly a horse to be found. On a recent visit to the town I found nothing but houses built on the stable yards and it caused me sadness. At each site I just visualised how it had been and those people connected with that stable.

I went to 'the foot of the hill' which is how we knew the first area of grass after entering the South Downs from the main road. The area was used to break-in yearlings, for grazing and for the assembly of trainers' strings. Now the grass has been neatly mown, several trees planted and there are noticeboards saying, 'No horses allowed on this area.' It makes no difference now but had it been done pre-war or during the early years of war, there would have been an outcry and undoubtedly four hundred equine trespassers.

When there was this large population of horses, the gallops were cared for by 'Old Mo' and a helper. Mo Henty had respiratory trouble from the First World War and had to have an outdoor job. The air on the South Downs was sufficient for an army of men. His equipment was carried in a wagon drawn by a trusty old steed. The gallops were, I believe, leased by the trainer George Poole but whatever the arrangement it was he to whom the gallop fees had to be paid. Riding a hack, George popped up all over the place but usually when the second and third lots emerged for exercise. He was quick to pounce on any lone rider or on any small group, blasting out: 'What's that horse you're on, Tommy?' He called every lad Tommy, and checked on his list of horses to make sure it had been paid for. His gruffness disappeared in later years and he was an interesting companion. Like my grandfather, he did not drive a car but had a vehicle with a chauffeur. My grandfather eventually dispensed with his Austin 6 and travelled by train or with his jockey sons.

George Poole trained at Astley House which was just across the road from the Downs and thus within 100 yards of the Lewes prison walls. It was a lovely yard with a number of cage boxes in a covered area from which there was a door to his house via the billiard room. I know this because the unmarried George had his sister living with him, as well as her two children: Eunice, known as Peggy, and Peter May. There were plenty of outside boxes looking out onto a large grassed area with a sandbed. Peter was my friend but Peggy was another of the opposite sex that attracted me, secretly more than Peter.

It was during the summer holiday that Mrs May decided we should camp on the downs and 'Old Mo' was instructed to transport a bell tent and a churn of water to the site. During our stay on the campsite Tom Gates, secretary, amateur rider and later trainer, used to lead the retired Grand National winner Shaun Spadah to see us.

One sunny morning, Peter and I were supposedly hunting butterflies among the gorse bushes. In fact we were experimenting with cigarettes at the age of about seven, when Tom Gates shouted, 'Who wants a ride on the old horse?' I whipped the top off my fag and shoved it in the hip pocket of my khaki shorts. While trotting around in circles with Tom holding the lunging rein I felt a pain behind my hip – the fag was still alight. As if it was yesterday, I can remember Mrs May applying Milton to the burn which left a scar a couple of inches wide. I lost touch with Peter May before the war, but at Plumpton races a few years ago, a man came up behind me and said, 'How's that scar?' I knew before I turned round it was Peter but would not have recognised him except for that remark.

It was nice to sit on Shaun Spadah who is buried in the corner of the paddock of Lewes racecourse, and the ashes of his jockey, F.B. Rees, were also scattered there. I can claim to have ridden the first three in the Grand National. My placed mounts were Carrickbeg who finished second and Eagle Lodge who finished third, ridden, of course, at exercise

When Shaun Spadah won the 1921 Grand National he was winning the second leg of the Spring Double which in those days was given great prominence. His win on the Friday was preceded on the Wednesday by the Lincolnshire Handicap which was the first leg of the double in which his stablemate Senhora was second at 20/1. She was beaten two lengths by the 33/1 shot Soranus. My 1921 book *Form in a Nutshell* tells me that Senhora carried just 6st 13lb and with Tommy Weston riding 'refused to struggle'. Considering that Poole was not really known as a flat race trainer it would have been a wonderful 253/1 double to pull off.

Riding Grand National 3rd. Eagle Lodge with Jimmy Lindley on Tudor Jinks
at Lambourn

There were plenty of George Poole stories including an amusing incident told to me by his then secretary, Tom Gates. He was never tolerant of the authorities and on receiving a letter from Weatherby's, secretaries to the Jockey Club and the then National Hunt Committee concerning some trivial matter, he replied:

> Dear Sir,
> Your letter that was before me is now behind me.
> Yours sincerely,
> George Poole.

This was confirmed by George when I was with him on a train to Folkestone. He was a different man in retirement and an amusing companion. I never called him George to his face, nor did he call me Tommy. He had several secretaries/amateur riders over the years as well as many would-be jockeys. Ray Pulford was among the amateurs while Colin Richards was among the pros. Colin was the younger brother of Sir Gordon and Cliff. He later became the long-serving travelling headlad, and occasional jockey, for Herbert Blagrave.

His beautiful yard has long been demolished and became first a large garage and showroom, but not before it was a depot for horses required for the military during the war. These horses were referred to as 'remounts' which were replacement horses. The garage has since been replaced by offices.

A recent visit to the old Lewes racecourse made me readjust my mental picture as it has now been made into two or three training establishments. Despite the many changes it was still beautiful to be on those Downs.

My father is reputed to have been a fairly useful jockey who, despite going to scale at below eight stones, mixed flat racing, hurdling and steeplechasing. He was certainly competent enough for my grandfather who at the time was also using the services of the leading jockeys Bill Stott and Bill Speck.

The first clear memory I have of my father was when an ambulance pulled up in front of our house in De Montfort Road. Father was on a stretcher, having broken his leg at Chelmsford. Our house had seven or eight winding steps with a fence either side. The ambulancemen tried every possible way to get the stretcher to the front door without success and there were moments when Father seemed likely to be unshipped from the conveyance. Finally he was put back in the ambulance and the attendants showed their versatility by removing the fence. During his recovery he frequently had visits from the two Bills, Stott and Speck, for card schools while Len Lefebvre was another visitor. After a riding and training career, Len was one of the admirable team who compiled the invaluable *Raceform* and *Chaseform* publications. My sister Fay and I would often leave our beds and look through the bannister rails and be fascinated by the goings on.

Father, whose apprenticeship was shared between his father and Senator J.J. Parkinson in Ireland, was accident prone and in addition to snipping off the tip of a finger with a carrot-slicing machine he rebroke a healing collarbone by stretching across to open a car door. When I used to look through the *Horses-in-Training* at that time I discovered that the Senator had more than double the number of horses than any other trainer. I was quite upset when that publication went up from sixpence to a shilling.

Father gave up riding to take over the training from his father and the stable luck held for a little while but then a sorry fate overtook what was probably the best animal he ever had. This was Sir Charles Pulley's home-bred filly Another-In-Law. Plenty of promise had been displayed in home gallops by this highly-strung filly and she ran well enough, although unplaced, in her first race to suggest she would win a £1000 two-year-olds' race at Gatwick on her next attempt. With George Bezant riding, she duly obliged and my father began to have thoughts about the following year's One Thousand Guineas. However, such thoughts were short-lived, for not so long after that encouraging victory, Another-In-Law snapped her fetlock while cantering on the Downs. How strange to be mentioning £1000 events as something special but that is how it was.

It seems that my father made the best use of the material at his disposal and he was a good judge of just how well, or poorly, his horses were likely to run in any particular event. He showed extraordinary judgement on one occasion with the result that a well-planned coup was brought off. The horse concerned was And How, a tall and powerfully built gelding, also owned by Sir Charles Pulley. This horse had not been on a racecourse until he contested a maiden hurdle race at Lingfield in the January of 1933, when four years old. Ridden by Don, he did not perform too well and there was only slight improvement when he ran at Hurst Park the next week. Later the same month he ran without distinction in a race won by the smart Story of Eden at Windsor.

And How goes on to win at 33/1

Whereas Don had not been too impressed with his three rides on And How, my father, who used to ride the horse in all his work, had a much higher opinion of this hurdler's potential. Undoubtedly the horse continued to improve with experience because my father told Don that he was running him in the Ashford Novices' Hurdle at Kempton on 1 March, and that he thought him sure to win. Don could not follow this line of reasoning and was equally mystified by my father's optimism, uncommon for him, when he gave him a leg-up on the day and again stressed his confidence.

There was a field of twenty for the race and the result was an easy four lengths win for And How at the not insignificant price of 33/1. To his last day Don could not fathom out my father's confidence but even more extraordinary was the way the animal was backed.

A certain professional man had placed a sizeable commission at starting price, and arrived to see the horse win. And How was freely offered at 50/1 and his team took this big price to units of a few pounds. As soon as the odds had contracted to 33/1 after this 'nibbling' he called off his men so as not to spoil the starting price. Such a practice would be practically impossible these days but that is exactly what happened in this case and all concerned were highly delighted. If you wonder why trouble was taken to have a small 'nibble' at the 50/1, it was simply because it would have been a crying shame to have missed such a price when And How would almost certainly have been returned as 33/1 others in any case. Unlike the present day, not many horses were returned at bigger odds.

Exactly three weeks after landing this useful 'touch', And How went to Lincoln to run in his first race on the flat. With Joe Marshall riding him in the Kesteven Plate, he won at 5/2. He ran a respectable sixth in the following season's Imperial Cup at Sandown but after three more hurdle race wins he showed signs of a leg weakness so Father put him in a selling hurdle at Newbury. And How won this at 4/1 and was bought for 150 guineas after the race by Mr C.V. Tabor, the trainer. It turned out to be a cheap buy for the horse didn't break down and went on winning for several seasons. It looked as though my father got that one wrong.

My thinking for Father's confidence before that Kempton win is that And How was sired by Sansovino who won the 1924 Derby in the heaviest going known at Epsom. I'm sure the fact that the Kempton going was also very heavy had a lot to do with his confidence. And How

Don Butchers

had feet as big as dinner plates and was ideally suited to the conditions. Well done, Dad!

My father was not a heavy backer but he used to spend a lot of time studying the form book. This no doubt helped him to assess his own horses with a fair amount of accuracy. He did do all his local friends a good turn, however, by insisting that they backed Bois Roussel for the Derby.

The landlord of the Pelham Arms, the headquarters for racing folk in Lewes, was a particularly close friend of my father, as he was to me and other members of my family. It so happened that this likeable landlord, Guy Laker, had already had a bet in the Derby but my father absolutely forced a bet of £66 to £1 on to him because he was so sure of the outcome. Bois Roussel won at 20/1 but, as in the case of And How, nobody knew the reason for such confidence. It was not as though my father was in the habit of making these predictions but you can be sure that he and Guy Laker marked this happy occasion with a visit to Brighton for an oyster feast at English's.

When my father was training he had horses for the family friend Dr Sadler, whom I have mentioned earlier as the treater of father's boils. He owned the Dreadnought Garage in Brighton, which was a large covered area simply for parking cars at, if my memory serves me right, the cost of sixpence. The garage was next to the Seven Stars pub and a stone's throw from the Bodega Bar and Restaurant. Both of these venues were the haunts of various members of the racing fraternity that included some punters from well-to-do families whose tastes varied from Champagne all round to days when everything went on the slate. I know from a reliable source they all honoured their debts, even if it took a bit of time. These people really were characters and a quote from a Rod Stewart hit, 'Crazy She Calls Me', probably sums up these likeable men. The appropriate lines are, 'The difficult I'll do right now, the impossible will take a little while.'

Back to our friendly Dr Sadler, who as an owner was no luckier than my father as a trainer. He had an old horse called Prince Alloway who was a poor 'doer' and not often inclined to do his best. Father gave him the benefit of the doubt and regularly supplemented his diet with half-a-dozen eggs and a bottle of port.

It was after Prince Alloway had been beaten by Gift Scheme in a selling chase at Wolverhampton that the winner was bought by Dr Sadler for 140 guineas. She fell in her first two races and failed to exert herself in the following three outings.

Hopes of winning with Gift Scheme were indeed gloomy but at her next attempt, although not a wholehearted one, she consented to win a really atrocious selling chase at Plumpton. There was relief all round, and almost joy, when a solitary bid of 50 guineas meant she would be moving to fresh pastures.

Now emerges a classic example of how foolish horses can make one appear. This mare went to be trained by Harry Whiteman. With an unknown and inexperienced amateur, Mr W. Corry, riding she won four selling chases off the reel at Plumpton, Windsor, Gatwick and Sandown while her efforts to complete a nap-hand for Mr Corry failed by only a head in another race at Gatwick. Whatever such happenings go to prove I don't know but no doubt similar unpredictable incidents will accompany racing until its close. My theory is that Gift Scheme, who took a strong hold, was always in control and that's how she liked it. It would seem that my poor old Dad got that one wrong, too.

My father's training career failed to flourish and it was not until his death that it was discovered he had not kept up insurances. Don told me that my father was too proud to ask for help.

21

5

WHISKY GALORE

Senorita is the only other of Dr Sadler's horses that I can recall. She will always be remembered in the family for giving Don Butchers one of his worst falls. She appeared to have her race at Plumpton well won when she stood back too far at the last hurdle and somersaulted on top of Don. I accompanied him to Lewes Victoria Hospital. He had several broken ribs and a punctured lung. It was not a pleasant journey even though it was only six or seven miles.

The Plumpton meetings are indelibly on my mind and it was here that the then retired Jock Langlands had one of his many mishaps. Having enjoyed his favourite pastime of having a few drinks, he decided to leave before the last race. Unfortunately for Jock, the runners in the previous race had only just passed the winning post while he was crossing the course some fifty yards ahead. There was a slight collision, which left Jock lying in the mud but otherwise unscathed.

This kindly and amusing gentleman – and I mean gentleman – managed to fall down a large hole in Lewes High Street and received nothing worse than bruising. Perhaps the most farcical incident occurred when Fred Rees and Jock were driving home from Brighton after a night out. Luckily it was when there were very few cars on the roads. Fred Rees was driving when he mentioned there were two lights in the distance. As the lights drew closer, Fred was unclear as to which side he should steer. Jock, ever thoughtful and intelligent, advised Fred, 'Play safe and go between them.' Not good advice when the lights turned out to be on a double-decker bus which they thankfully noticed in time. Jock was a character and thank goodness there weren't so many cars around in those days.

It was also misplaced advice by Jock that cost him and L.B. Rees £100. They were drinking in the bar at Gatwick before a two-runner race. The favourite was 100/8 on, so Jock suggested they invest £100 between them as the £8 winnings would pay for a few more rounds. The result, of course, was a shock defeat. It was only a short while ago that I tripped and fell headlong into a very large and deep puddle. I was soaked through to my underclothes and during a ten-mile journey home I was reminded of dear old Jock.

It was another such character by the name of Charlie Weston, a long-suffering punter, who caused alarm at the Pelham Arms in Lewes, a pub that I'm sure you must know by now. The landlord could smell burning and left the bar to investigate. It did not take long to trace the source. Believe it or not, the smell was a cigarette burning through the fingers of a comatose Charlie Weston. It was, of course, not the only time he had his fingers burnt!

Otto Marcus was another character. He was a German Jew who used to train near Berlin and then became a bloodstock agent. He bought a house near the Downs in Lewes and it was almost opposite our abode, after we had moved from 'Hylton'. I mention this because Otto was in the habit of calling on us when he was drunk. If any of us noticed him coming up the garden path, we were told not to answer the door and to lie low. I'm afraid the same instruction applied when a pair of persistent door-knocking nuns were spied.

Otto was a dapper little man who walked the length of the High Street every day. He always wore a double-breasted suit, white and brown 'co-respondent shoes' and a trilby hat and carried a walking cane. He was a short man, probably no more than 5ft 3in, so had to look up to most people when in conversation. Otto overcame this disadvantage by pulling his victim down by the lapels or any other available tab. If you were unlucky enough to be grabbed by him you knew that it would be some time before you could break free. Crossing the road was the best plan if you saw him in time. Women received the same treatment as regards the tugging. Topics of conversation covered a wide range but invariably included some individual which led to Otto summing up with his favourite expression, 'Nice fellow but no f—— brains.'

On one occasion Otto came into our local in a heavily inebriated state and being a bit of a nuisance. Our tolerant landlord escorted him to the front door and returned to his place behind the bar only to be confronted by Otto returning via the back door. This caused good-hearted laughter all round.

I had to suffer the 'Otto treatment' in Newmarket. He had already been drinking at the races but insisted I join him for a drink in the

Subscription Rooms. He was drinking Kummel, a German liqueur, one after the other until closing time and it had been dribbling down his chin and congealing. Amazingly he was still upright but a little unsteady as I guided him to his lodgings. He had no key and there was no answer when knocking on the door. I made my get-away when Otto started throwing stones at the windows.

Otto was not a bad man when sober, and his drinking bouts were only occasional. He had a sweet wife named Elsa and a son, Klaus. Being a Jew he had no time for Hitler and I'm afraid there were sad times ahead. Early in the war, he went on a spree with one of his friends. Returning home from a country pub they were stopped by police at a road block. This was normal practice and the police asked to see in the boot of the car. Otto was only a passenger but would not be left out and engaged the policeman in conversation. 'What nationality are you sir?' the copper enquired. 'I'm f—— German' was the reply and poor Otto was arrested for questioning and both he and his son were interned in Canada for a time. It was really a bit sad, as I know they were obviously anti-Hitler and all he stood for.

Old Tom Fitton was another Lewes fixture who was a trainer both before and a few years after the First World War. He used to train his horses in mackintosh sheets and cover long distances to get them hard and lean. He was not alone in doing this but I suspect the modern racehorse so treated would not survive.

Tim O'Sullivan, the Irishman and not the Australian Tim of a later era, was a bachelor who was invariably drawn towards the Pelham Arms. There was no bathroom in his digs so he was invited to use the pub facility. Guy was busy and some time had elapsed before he realised Tim had not reappeared. Knowing Tim had had a skinful when going upstairs for his bath the landlord thought he should see if everything was in order. No need to worry, Tim had not drowned but was just sleeping like a baby in a bath full of cold water.

Tim was a shrewd trainer but sometimes sailed close to the wind. Don Butchers used to ride several of the horses including the selling plater Buchil. Tim wanted to get her rehandicapped to a lower rating and gave her, via the jockeys and not often Don, several easy races which, as now, constitutes a non-trier. However, Buchil was saddled with 12st 7lb in one race, ridden by Don. The instruction to 'not finish in the first four' was followed by added information as the horses were going onto the course. Tim said: 'And by the way, as she is small I've left the leadcloth off.' To

24

the uninitiated, I should explain that the leadcloth housed flat pieces of lead to make up the allotted weight. As Don was light, in this case there would have been between 14lb and 21lb in lead.

Don was at the point of no return. The real trouble was that as the jockeys returned to the weighing room after the race they were greeted by one of three instructions from the clerk of the scales. He would shout, 'Placed horses only, first four weigh or all weigh.' Luckily in this case they were not all required to weigh and Don had a few harsh words with Tim for putting him in such a career-wrecking position.

The likeable Tom Gates, mentioned earlier as George Poole's secretary, was a delight and would not do a bad turn to anyone. He was the opposite to many in the area and in the first part of the war he became a special constable as well as being a trainer. Unfairly, in my view, he was confronted by his superior and admonished because he had made no arrests and not even reported any wrongdoings. That was how Tom saw his life. He was a bit like Sergeant Wilson in *Dad's Army*, but more manly. Tom died of Parkinson's disease well before reaching old-age. The world would be a better place if there were more like Tom.

Before going out to ride in my first chase at Plumpton, I was told 'to kick my mount into the water jump'. Evidently I took this to the extreme and it was old-time jockey and trainer Jimmy Hare who helpfully told me I had shown too much daylight between my legs and the saddle. Such constructive criticism should always be taken on board. Mind you, I was very small and the saddle was very big so I was probably kicking the flap of the saddle. It is Jimmy who was almost a fixture in the boozer but this time the White Hart. Every night he and his wife were dressed in their finest and stationed just inside the door. Only a few feet away was Fred Rees and they were separated by a bench but I never saw any of the trio sitting or speaking. Fred's sole companion was a glass of whisky which was replenished at regular intervals. Jimmy was private trainer to the notorious East-Ender Horatio Bottomley who dealt in tens of thousands of pounds. He was a journalist, a promoter of dubious financial schemes, a lay lawyer, gambler and an MP. Bottomley was said to be the greatest con-man of his time. He died penniless in the public ward of a London hospital.

The bar at the White Hart was ruled over by 'Greenie' and I really mean ruled. She was known, loved and sometimes feared by clients over a wide area. Fred Rees was one of her favourites and she would say: 'Now then, Mr Fred, you've had enough. It's time to go home.' What's more,

Fred always obeyed. There was a fine oil painting of 'Greenie' hanging in the bar and I believe it is there to this day. It was outside this White Hart that the Martyrs were burnt at the stake. How well would some of the whisky-filled clients have burnt if finding themselves in such a situation?

Going back to Fred Rees, known to some as Dick, he served in the Royal Flying Corps (RFC) during the Great War. I was fascinated when he told me that as a gunner he sat in the plane using just an ordinary rifle. What a shame that this brilliant jockey could not win his battle with the bottle.

6

DISTRACTIONS

As I said in my introduction, getting events in the right order is not guaranteed but I do know this episode came early in the war years. The owner of the Shelleys Hotel in Lewes was Martin Heriot and it was by far the smartest joint in town. Martin was aristocratic, a natty dresser and the possessor of a very noticeable cast in one eye. He also spoke with a voice that suited his bearing and sense of humour. He married Peggy Rees, who was the middle daughter of F.B. Rees, and was seldom seen behind the bar of his establishment. Actually it was not a bar as such, more of a dispensary.

It was usually on Sundays that he had to spring into action and on one such day a very old and wealthy bookmaker from Brighton entered with a youthful-looking floozy. On asking what she would like to drink there followed moments of indecision while Martin was drumming his fingers impatiently. Eventually she asked for something long and soft to which the mischievous Martin replied: 'We haven't anything long and soft and if we had you wouldn't like it.'

He was really a very pleasant man but was sometimes overtaken by his wit. As you may have gathered, Martin was of independent means and would ask people to leave the hotel if he disliked them. This he did when a cross-eyed man upset him but he softened the blow by saying, 'As one boss-eyed man to another, I am asking you to leave.'

You may get the impression that Martin was difficult but it was not so. He was great fun with an immense sense of humour. If you need convincing, try to imagine the scene when a kind and likeable lady walked in a bit tipsy and, after refreshing herself with another drink, decided to do a handstand in view of the regular clientele. I will not reveal the lady's name and less likely am I to relate Martin's remark. A good evening was had by all and this regular customer made 'What The Butler Saw' seem a little tame. I had the task of giving this lady a lift home when her legs were not working very well. She was, as a front seat passenger, delighted to show how she was able to touch the roof lining of the car with both feet.

Old Tommy Dunn, as distinct from his son Tom, had many good days as a jockey but I didn't know him then. He was, apparently, one to celebrate extravagantly and in the Shelleys he once set fire to one of those lovely white £5 notes to light his cigar Not surprisingly, Tommy was not too affluent in latter days and was employed by the Press Association to supply the Lewes runners for the papers.

The mention of a fiver reminds me of our many visits for dinner there. If we took a couple of guests the cost would be four dinners @ 12s. 6d., a bottle of Moet and Chandon Champagne @ £1 10s. 0d., and a five shilling gratuity which totted up to £4 5s. 0d. There was fifteen shillings left over and you could buy many, many drinks for that.

It was at around this time that Professor Happy, pronounced without the H, was lurking, and he was an occasional Shelleys' customer. He was no spring chicken and drove a large open-top car, usually draped with a girl. He was very short, moustached, dressed in a dandy-like fashion and of Baltic extraction. He owned a club a few miles from Lewes, and for reasons I can't remember, I was welcome to visit there and take any guests. At this time I was married to Marian, and I took guests quite often. It was a fine house full of antiques and young Bill Rees, who became one of the Queen Mother's jockeys, made his first visit memorable by knocking over his glass of light ale. It was on a table displaying valuable objects and I know there was an antique crib board, which had to have its peg holes emptied. The Professor was a bit of a mystery man but it was well known that you had to guard your woman or you would find that she had been invited to see his boudoir. It was, however, for another reason that my means of entry could have been vital.

One of our close friends was Marika Foster, who together with her brothers lived near the Rees family in Lewes. Marika married Jimmy Leader and there were no secrets between us. Jimmy was in the police and rose to the rank of Assistant Chief Constable of Sussex. We shared many happy occasions outside Jimmy's area and he always regretted not being able to join in such things as after-hours drinking on his patch. It was not so much his own presence that worried him but the fact that others would be uncomfortable. Jimmy was a lovely man in every way and his daughter and our daughter went to their first schools together and are still close friends. It was my friendship that nearly caused us to mix business with pleasure.

On the loose at the time was Alfred Hines, who had been serving a prison sentence for what was called 'The Maples Robbery' and all police forces were on the look-out. It was gone midnight and I was in bed when the phone rang. It was Jimmy and he said: 'I don't know how to go about this but we've had a tip-off that Alfred Hines is holed up in Professor Happy's club.'

He knew I had access and asked if I could go over and keep my eyes open. The face of Hines had appeared regularly in newspapers and was instantly recognisable. Jimmy's concluding words were: 'Sorry about this, but give it some thought.' Marian was awake and we were in a bit of a state as to whether it would be too risky and perhaps turn nasty. I was wondering whether to get dressed when the phone rang again. It was Jimmy with good news for me. He said: 'It's totally unfair to ask a friend to do what I asked, so we've decided to raid the club.' Raid the club they did, but alas no Alfred Hines was to be found.

It was at Lewes racecourse that the 'razor gangs' were finally broken up but years before Jimmy was on the scene. At that time there was the Sabini mob and one of them, Harry, was a regular at the races after the war. I knew him well and it was hard to believe he had ever been anything but a kindly man. On one occasion I had my binoculars stolen from the luggage rack of a race-train. I mentioned this to Harry who said he would get them back for me. Sure enough, true to his word, he returned them to me a couple of days later. He said: 'I have told the boys to leave you out in future.'

The wide-boys and petty criminals were well known to regular racegoers and it was after racing at Newbury that I was having a drink with Richard Baerlein of the *Guardian* when his binoculars were stolen from a shelf. Luckily Richard saw the culprit and gave chase. He pressed charges and while waiting to appear in court the thief, well known to me, attended a meeting and asked if I would give him a character reference even though he knew I was with Richard at the time. He certainly scored top marks for optimism.

My dear friend Jock Langlands is back on the scene. He knocked on the door one evening and asked if he could come in for a glass of water as he had a heavy cold and was not feeling too well. He actually drank his water and explained how he had been caught drink-driving a little earlier. He asked if I would be a witness in court to say he had been in for a glass of water that evening and I agreed even though I did not know what bearing it could have on his case. I liked the man and was sorry for the way his life had turned out, with a broken marriage and a daughter he seldom saw.

The day of the court case duly arrived and I gave my evidence and answered questions honestly. In the summing up the judge said: 'You have heard the evidence of Mr Butchers, who seems a reliable witness.' That was all I could do but Jock was found guilty and before announcing his verdict the judge had access to previous convictions. The final words of the judge were, 'In view of your twenty-eight previous convictions for motoring and drinking offences, I am disqualifying you from driving for life.' Poor old Jock, but almost certainly for the best. I can't remember whether or not I had put whisky in that glass of water.

Just one more incident that never ceases to tickle me. Monty Koski was a tubby regular at the races who didn't walk but waddled with his feet aiming in the 'ten-to-two' direction. He was the son of a Brighton milliner and obviously didn't have the need for a job. He was always fighting a losing battle with the bookmakers and was approached by one to whom he owed money. When Monty asked the bookmaker if he was worried he replied that he was. 'Well,' said Monty, 'there's no point in two of us worrying,' and with that remark he waddled off into the betting jungle.

Plumpton in the late nineteenth century (Racing Illustrated). *Note the bowler hats*

7

FOOD FOR THOUGHT

George Alexander Butchers, my grandfather, had a long and successful career in racing. Born in Rye in 1866, he served his apprenticeship with a Mr W. Bell at Findon and then moved to J. Gatland's Alfriston stables. He rode his first winner at the age of eighteen in the year that St Gatian dead-heated with Harvester in the 1884 Derby.

Turning back the clock is something that nobody can do but perhaps if my grandfather was alive, he would be thankful he was training in the past and not now. It was possible then to keep owners and staff perfectly happy and make sufficient from the training fees to live without worry. My grandfather certainly did so and his betting amounted to only a very few wagers a year, always on his own horses and with £25 his absolute maximum. I understand that not many of his bets were losers and, what is more, the odds had to be just about right as well. Ike de Costa, from Brighton, often placed bets for people and would ring Grandad if he suspected he had a likely winner. However, his calls were made when he knew Grandad would be out and that my naïve Grandma would spill the beans either directly or indirectly.

It was at Plumpton in 1888 that he performed a real feat of horsemanship to win on Bonnie Scotland. In recovering from a bad mistake early in the race he pushed the bridle over her head, leaving just the bit in the mare's mouth. The partnership made up the lost ground and won the race amid much applause. On returning to the paddock, George received not only another ovation but the proceeds collected from the mainly bowler-hatted crowd. The latter fact I noted in the picture opposite.

Even before dismounting, a heavy gambler, known as the 'Jubilee Plunger', thrust ten £5 notes into the jockey's hand. How would that go down with the authorities today?

Although still a jockey, George started training in 1893 at the stables attached to my favourite pub – the Pelham Arms. He then had a spell as a private trainer to Mr E. Palehampton at Rottingdean before returning to Lewes. After two years at Heath House he moved to the Black Horse Stables which became his permanent base, except for the wartime interruptions.

In 1917 George took over the Nunnery Stables at Thetford in Norfolk. It is now the Nunnery Stud owned by Hamdam Al Maktoum and is a luxurious set-up. Grandfather went as a private trainer to Madame Varipati and turned out sixty-five winners in three seasons, including some major events of the time. Ann Wilkinson researched the pedigree of Desert Orchid and discovered that his sixth dam, called Darklein, was trained by George at Thetford and ridden by son Leslie to win a selling race at Lincoln.

He returned to the Black Horse Yard after Madame Varipati was killed in a car crash, and resumed his association with Sir Charles Pulley who had horses with him from the very start. After giving up riding my father, Leslie, became George's right-hand man until taking over the training in 1931.

Apart from Sir Charles Pulley, the owners included Mr Tommy Walton from Brighton. He started with a fruit and vegetable shop and his aim was to have a hundred of them. This ambition was achieved and included a shop at Victoria Station. His sea green and chocolate colours were carried to many wins. The mention of chocolate reminds me that a confectioner from Eastbourne named Mr Panto also had a horse in the yard. Yet another in the food business with a horse was Bill Harris who had an SPO shop in Brighton – SPO is sausage, potato and onion, and very nice it is too.

It was an era when discipline was the order of the day. The head lad was Joe Keogh who ruled with an iron fist. Frequently I would pop round to the paper shop to get the five o'clock edition of the *Brighton Argus*. This was as a youngster and my interest was to see the late racing results and the Sussex cricket score stamped on the 'fudge' or late news column. After checking the results and noting how many runs Jim Parks and John Langridge had made in their opening partnership, I would go into the stables and watch the lads doing their two. Any chat between me and the lads earned a rebuke if Joe was in the vicinity.

Johnny Coltman, owner of the Clarence Restaurant in Aldersgate Street, was a great friend of Grandad and his winners included English Fare, Soldiers Fare and Ballyroge. After buying Hand from Heaven for 720 guineas, he changed the name to English Fare, a form of advertising even in the twenties.

George on his old pal, Zarane

The best known of his horses, though, was undoubtedly Zarane. This big, plain horse was the type that everyone would wish to have in their yard. Zarane did not race until he was a six-year-old but he won a dozen races, while trained by Tom Leader, before my grandfather gave 860 guineas for him on Mr Coltman's behalf at a Gatwick public auction. The old horse proceeded to win three flat races and six more hurdle races and then the owner gave him to my grandfather as a sixtieth birthday present. He had run three times on the flat for Tom Leader without success, but as an eight-year-old he won his only three flat races for my grandfather. In the first of them, at Folkestone, he was the 10/1 outsider of three runners; he beat a hot favourite in his second outing and only in his final flat race did he start favourite, at even money, when ridden by my father, Leslie.

When my grandfather became the owner of this old warrior, then thirteen years old, he was raced in the weight-for-age selling races simply because he was unhappy in retirement. Zarane went on to win eight 'sellers' in my grandfather's chocolate and orange colours, and it cost a total of 1,690 guineas to buy him back at the subsequent auctions. As a sixteen-year-old, Zarane failed to win and a few days before he was due to run in his next race, he dropped dead while my grandfather was riding him at exercise on Lewes Downs. This grand horse, the cut of a chaser, was schooled over fences but twice refused to jump the open-ditch, and, being so highly thought of, was not asked to do so again. To give you an idea of his ability, he was third in the 1924 Imperial Cup at Sandown, carrying top-weight of 12st 7lb. Giving close to 21lb to Noce d'Argent and Spinney Hill, he was beaten by a neck and half a length, with the 'mugs', Frank Wootton and George Duller, riding the first and second respectively.

Such genuine and capable horses do not come into a trainer's possession too many times during a career. Zarane was everything one could ask for and I have little doubt that he would have made quite a name for himself as a chaser if sentiment had not played its part. Probably with a few 'reminders', the old horse would have relented and jumped those open-ditches without fuss but this was one horse to whom my grandfather was prepared, and satisfied, to give in to.

Zarane became more of a pet in his latter days and his wins in the selling races did not show a profit. As a fourteen-year-old, it cost 470 guineas to buy him in after he had won by twelve lengths at Sandown, while the same season, it cost 370 guineas to retain him following a six-length win at Newbury. There was, however, no intention of letting him pass into different ownership.

Mr John Coltman, who gave him to my grandfather, was a lucky owner and after the last war had success with a good horse called Delirium, trained by Jack Leach. One of the most important winners on the flat trained by my grandfather was Marechal Strozzi, who won the Esher Cup for Sir Charles Pulley. The Esher Cup was a major race in those bygone days.

I read in my grandma's scrapbook that George retired because 'I've had enough of it'. He had several operations and would sit in his breakfast room having a puff of his pipe. In those pre-war days, trainers were allowed to give their horses a stimulant and in full view of the spectators my grandfather often administered a sizeable quantity of whisky to one of his horses as a 'soother'. He was, however, an honest, quiet and extremely popular man. I can vouch for his quietness. On those Sundays when we visited him for tea he would just sit, smoking his pipe and listening. When, however, on the rare occasions he chose to speak, everyone listened because it was bound to be something worth hearing. Although very kind, he was strict with Don as an apprentice. 'You've got a tongue in your head,' he said to Don as a boy after he had inquired where he should change trains for a certain meeting.

On another occasion when he came down for his early morning tea he found Don sitting with his feet in a bowl of water. It happened that Don had fallen asleep on the last train from London and had been carried on to the terminus at Eastbourne. Don walked the sixteen miles back to Lewes but the only words of sympathy he got from his father consisted of 'Hurry up, you've got ten minutes to get to work.' A clean living, non-swearing man, he did, however, have a fine sense of humour. An old-fashioned maid, Daisy, complete with cap and apron, had a habit of bending low when she cleaned the grates and on numerous occasions my grandfather had spotted a hole in her voluminous pair of bloomers. The day arrived when he could bear it no longer, and pulling a ten-shilling note from his waistcoat pocket said: 'Here, Daisy, get yourself some new knickers. I'm fed up with seeing your backside.'

After Grandfather's retirement, my father took over the Black Horse stables in 1931. Even so my grandfather took a lively interest in the yard and still used to be called on to administer the physic 'balls' to horses. It was reckoned he could do this job by hand as quickly and efficiently as anyone in the business. His advice was often sought, and having been used to an active life, there was seldom a morning or evening that passed without him paying a visit to the yard.

Despite his retirement, my grandfather kept a horse in training. This was Llandreamer whom he bought at public auction for £25. He was the first racehorse I sat on and not only for a photograph. There was a quiet path running behind the rear entrance to the cemetery. It was a cul-de-sac about three hundred yards long and I would trot Llandreamer to the end and back with my father standing on guard. Don had won on him when he was trained in Lewes by Tom Fitton. Although Norman Abbot was the first winner trained by my father, Llandreamer quickly followed suit, and as on three subsequent occasions provided a family success for he was owned by my grandfather, trained by my father and ridden by his brother Don.

Apart from his continued interest in my father's horses, he would enjoy a walk and a chat with the other trainers in the town. A love of flowers, and he knew a bit about them, and a half a pint of beer in the Pelham Arms just about completed my grandfather's interests in retirement. He died peacefully in Don's arms from a heart attack at the age of seventy-two.

Bob on Llandreamer at Black Horse stables

The eldest of grandfather's twelve children, Frederick, was, as I have said earlier, killed in France in 1916. According to reports he was quite a live spark and most certainly a brilliant jockey in his day. After serving his apprenticeship in Ireland plenty of success came his way on the flat until increasing weight, he was a six-footer, forced him to ride steeplechasing. In this sphere he was even more successful and in his first year, 1907, as a jumping jockey he was third in the Scottish Grand National. Towards the end however, he was riding in steeplechases on a saddle weighing only a pound. Apparently, Fred was a gambler and a large bet on one of his certainties came unstuck when beaten by one of his father's horses.

In his first season as an apprentice and as a small boy Fred, as he was known, rode Happy Slave in the Duke of York Handicap at Kempton in 1903 and was beaten by a head by the mighty Sceptre. The following season, he rode Coxswain in the Derby. Starting the extreme outsider of eight runners at 100/1 he finished unplaced to St Amant. The only other Butchers to ride in the Derby was my father, Leslie, who in 1927 partnered Parker. This colt, owned by the famous comedian Charlie Austin who used to portray PC Parker on the stage, started at the astronomical odds of 1000/1. Don, when in his prime as a steeplechase jockey, was due to ride Buxton in Blue Peter's 1939 Derby but had to forego the mount owing to a broken collar-bone.

Happy Slave and Parker both made news in their day. In 1903 Sceptre was four years old having the previous season won the One Thousand Guineas, Two Thousand Guineas, Oaks and St Leger. She was fourth in the Derby and Eclipse Stakes and had started the season by finishing second in the Lincolnshire Handicap – an almost unbelievable perform-ance. Thus defeat in the Duke of York Handicap at Kempton seemed out of the question even though this great filly is reputed to have been lame on the morning of the race and subsequently had to race in soft going wearing heavy working shoes. Ridden by Otto Madden, this filly was shut in several times but when she got clear she made up a lot of ground and snatched the race by a head. Sceptre was giving 40lb to Happy Slave and I imagine all racing enthusiasts at that time were delighted that the filly just succeeded.

The outcry in recent years of too many moderate horses running in the Derby would certainly have had justification in the year 1927 when Parker was allowed to start in the Epsom classic won by Call Boy. The record of this colt is worth recalling. As a two-year-old he was badly left at the start of his only race – a maiden at Sandown. He started the following season by finishing sixth of nine runners in a maiden apprentice race at Gatwick, and then was next to last in a moderate nine-runner race at Lewes. That was the record of Parker before he ran as a 1000/1 shot in the Derby. In a field of twenty-three, it amazes me how he managed to finish in front of Gordon Richards on Chichester Cross, and the other 1000/1 chance Stampede, who graced the British turf just this once.

In his only other flat race after the Derby, Parker ran last in a maiden event at Folkestone. An unsuccessful debut in a three-year-old hurdle race at Fontwell in the autumn was followed by an equally dismal performance in a selling hurdle at Hawthorn Hill and thus ended the racecourse appearances of what must surely have been one of the most moderate colts ever to have run in the Derby.

A few years before Father died, we had moved to our house adjacent to the Downs and the 'Front Hill Gallop'. Father and Don had semi-detached houses built and I could never make out why they constructed a pair unless it was for economic reasons or simply because it was quite usual then. We lived in ours and Don let his out as he was still living at home. It was a nice house with the front garden extending over the roof of the garage. The architect was the slightly eccentric 'Chicken' Worsfield who sported a beard and it was not unknown for him to answer the door scantily dressed. When he broke an ankle I have heard it said that he once answered his door with nothing but his crutches.

The house had a veranda with an expanse of bare walls but Father and Don declined Chicken's offer to adorn them with murals of nude ladies. The short drive into the garage was at an angle, which proved a blessing. It was quite usual in those days to be trusting and Father had left the garage unlocked and the ignition keys in the car, a Hillman Minx. On going out one morning the car was wedged over a small wall and it transpired that the awkward angle had thwarted two prisoners who had escaped from the nearby jail and attempted to steal the car.

It was on the Front Hill Gallop that a Gotha biplane landed in August 1940. This German light aircraft came to a standstill one hundred yards from our house and was quickly approached by some of our neighbours who were in the Home Guard. The pilot, Leonard Buikle, claimed to be lost and had flown in the opposite direction from his French base and landed in England instead of Jersey as intended. There was plenty of enemy activity in the skies above the south coast.

It was quite usual to see doodlebugs heading for their target. I remember a summer morning when I was riding on my own, probably third lot, when a doodlebug came overhead and not too high. Just where it struck I know not but after a short while RAF planes used to intercept them and tip their wings and send them back over the Channel.

Another incident involved a Messerschmitt which came second in a dogfight with one of our planes. It nose-dived into a field three or four hundred yards from our house at a spot named Hope-in-the-Valley. The hole in the ground just a few yards off the main Brighton road remained for many years and for all I know may still be there. Perhaps I will look the next time I visit. So many names are simply taken for granted when you are brought up amidst them. Our gallops were known as Front Hill, Hurdle Hill, Middle Hill, Balmer, Inside the Racecourse, the Rails, the Well and Summer Gallop.

Other landmarks included Honeysuckle Valley and Bonnie Scotland. The last named was a succession of very steep banks. It ended in the village of Offham, which reminds me of some unusual pronunciations. Oh, such happy memories.

Offham is pronounced Oaf-ham and Balmer is Ball-mer while the nearby village of Falmer is pronounced Fal-mer. Lewes is usually pronounced correctly but there are a few who call it Loos. While on this topic, I am amused by the racecourse commentators who pronounce the racehorse Odiham as Odd-ee-ham. It is O-dee-am and I know because I lived there for many years as did one of the part-owners, David Brooks. Such examples are, of course, found in every county but fascinating nonetheless.

8

RUNNERS AND A RUNAWAY

Don was the last of the three racing brothers to ride and while the remaining four sons did not enter racing they were all mad keen on other forms of sport – running and football in particular. At one period Ern, Joe, Reg and Alec all played in the same Lewes Football Club side, which was fairly powerful in the Sussex County League, and Joe was capped for the county. These four brothers also formed a relay team, which not once tasted defeat.

Of these, Ern took running less seriously but Joe had few superiors in the south of England as a half-miler. He could clock something under two minutes for the half-mile, which was good going in the days when they were not so record conscious and, of course, ran on grass. The occasion for which he used to get himself in really peak condition was the championship race. He held the title for four years but in none of these races was he hard enough pressed to return what could have been a quite extraordinary time. He devoted his retirement to athletics, in the capacity of a starter.

Reg, part-time secretary to Tom Masson, and Alec who did similar duties for 'Towser' Gosden, were sprinters. Alec usually returned 10.4 seconds for the hundred yards even though he would not train as seriously as he should. Reg worked harder in training and ran his hundred yards in 10.2 seconds although on one occasion at Redhill he clocked 'even' time. They all belonged to the Brighton County Harriers and successfully 'farmed' most of the local sports meetings. Three special display cabinets held just a few of the trophies and prizes in my grandmother's drawing-room and believe me, she was as proud when her athletic sons won as she was when Grandfather or her racing sons had a win.

Of these four athletic sons, Alec alone had the urge to enter racing. His father was the decider, however, and a career as a jockey was not the choice. He remained interested in racing though but like so many other people, he awaited that elusive fortune from the bookmakers that would set him up as a second Aga Khan! At the beginning of the last war, Alec still had a desire to get himself in the saddle and, despite his total inexperience, persuaded Tom Masson to allow him to ride out with the string. The horse chosen for Alec was the old entire Boozers Gloom who was by Gainsborough out of Take A Glass. I was behind Alec as the string made its way to the Downs. We all had a good laugh when Alec got too close to the mare he was following and Boozers Gloom immediately mounted her. The old horse must have thought it was his birthday.

Although Boozers Gloom was docile, he would occasionally whip round and that was how Alec was unshipped. I remember the string returning home on a beautiful sunny morning with Alec, another lad and me in casual conversation when a pheasant flew out from the gorse bushes. That bird scored a hat-trick with all three of us hitting the deck. Fortunately, we all held on to our mounts. Having been unseated a couple of times in the first week, Alec good-heartedly decided that he was 'too bloody old to start this lark'. I'm sure, however, that Alec would have been unhappy had he not satisfied his urge.

Alec had always had the spirit of adventure and his days at the races have undoubtedly given him immense pleasure. He is the subject of many amusing incidents connected with racing on and off the course. We all have an 'Alec' in our circle: the only one to whom such things could happen! Alec, jokingly I hope, used to tell his friends that neither Don nor I would ever tip him a winner but both were certain to send the biggest bloody wreath available when he died.

Reg had never possessed the same desires. He has, however, dealt most efficiently with racing administration for many, many years and could quite truthfully be described as the perfect secretary for a trainer. Like all true sportsmen, he hates to give in but some years ago was forced to admit that increasing years and a bigger waistline made him ineffective over a hundred yards.

Although no 'flying machine', in three heats and three finals I was unbeaten over a hundred yards in school sports. A few beers prompted Reg to challenge me to a hundred yards race on the road, with me giving him a start of yards for years. This amounted to twenty-two yards and in his courageous attempt to prevent me forging further ahead he fell and cut his knees. It probably goes without saying that his last race took place under street-lighting after our local hostelry had closed its doors.

Another 'would-be' rider had a lucky escape. He was a member of air-crew on leave and a relative of a friend of both Tom Masson and me. He said he could ride but suspicions arose when he turned up at the yard next morning wearing flying boots. I was surprised that he was allowed to be mounted but I think Masson was relishing this adventure.

When the string started an initial canter it was immediately realised that the airman was out of control and being run away with. His mount knew one of the ways that we used to go home which was through a housing estate approached by a narrow cutting from the Downs. Now comes the almost unbelievable, and possibly life saving, episode. As the pair reached the cutting so too did a couple of workmen carrying a long ladder. They completely barred the way and a sudden halt sent the airman flying between the animal's ears. The partnership was severed and only then was the most horrifying discovery revealed. The airman had one flying boot wedged tightly in the stirrup iron. He was freed by the workmen and was no doubt pleased to return to his wartime flying duties.

Jockeys and racing lads seem keen on most sporting activities, particularly boxing and football. Before such things as television came along as a form of distraction even more attention was given to these activities. The jockeys' football match between Epsom and Lewes used to be quite an attraction while Don helped to form a club at which boxing tournaments took place. The sudden death of the club's chairman brought the end of the club but while it was in being, Don was persuaded to have his one and only fight. He was matched against one of my grandfather's lads, Charlie Southey, and officially won by a knockout in the first round. It is thought by many to this day that Charlie was bribed to 'lie down', but Don still prefers to think that it was his Dempsey-like right that put his opponent on the canvas.

Sport of all kinds certainly played a big part in the Butchers family, and with so many in which to participate there was hardly time for discontent or boredom. I am pleased that my son, Guy, played rugby to a good standard and that his stepson and younger son show more than a little promise as footballers.

Don Butchers, as a jockey, had a career spread over twenty-one years but a hair-raising experience before he ever rode in public might easily, and certainly in these days, have stopped him in his tracks. When not quite fourteen years old, and apprenticed to his father, he was taken for a ride that nobody would forget. It was a rainy morning when he rode Whyte Warbler in her work on a gallop that runs parallel with the five furlongs of Lewes racecourse. With her nose pointed towards home, Don was unable to pull up at the end of the work ground and the wet reins did not help him in his task. On the mare went, past the back of the prison and on to the main road.

For those unfamiliar with Lewes, I can tell you that it is quite a long way from the foot of the Downs to the bottom of the town. Whyte Warbler galloped through the shopping centre at the top of the town, down St Anne's Hill, through the bottleneck and the High Street until she came to the War Memorial. This marks the top of two very steep hills, one of them, School Hill, leading to Cliffe Bridge, and the other a slightly less steep one-way street which finishes at the Fire Station and Corporation yard. Having already narrowly missed a variety of vehicles, Don was relieved when he managed to steer his mount down the quieter and less steep Market Street.

There was, however, no sign of easing up on Whyte Warbler's part until she saw the huge red doors of the Fire Station staring her in the face. Swerving violently away from these, she found herself in the Corporation yard with only a pile of kerbstones between her and the River Ouse. Stopping suddenly she deposited Don on the stones and stood looking down at him. Neither Whyte Warbler nor Don were any worse for the experience but a mile and a half gallop down a main street is not what any rider would choose if having any regard for his life or limb. The 'bottleneck' that I mentioned was wide enough to take only a single vehicle and is now controlled by traffic lights.

That adventure caused quite a stir in the town and it was the only occasion that the well known local milkman, 'Grunter' Leney, was seen to run with his laden handcart. A few months later Don had his first public mount on Flaxen Boy at Lewes but had to wait until early the next season before Borjom, trained by his father, gave him his first win at Leicester. Increasing weight made it obvious that he would have to switch to hurdle-racing and as a sixteen-year-old he had his first ride over hurdles at Chelmsford. It was a Lydie Whyte filly, a half-sister to the runaway Whyte Warbler, then un-named and later known as Pure Caress. In those days a jockey riding ten winners under any Rules lost the right to claim an allowance. Having scored six times on the flat, Don had only four wins to go before riding on equal terms with such men as Duller, Rees and Wootton. In December 1929 he won his first hurdle race on Dandy Dennis and others flowed fairly regularly.

The bottleneck in Lewes

Leslie on Pure Caress

Story of Eden (Don) on the way to victory

Don ended that first season over hurdles with sixteen wins, a highly respectable total in those days for a mere boy. Not only was he a stylist but he rode cheeky, Piggott-like, races against the 'cracks' and he was retained to ride in the 1930–31 season for Jim Bell, as his jockey, George Duller, was retiring. The Bell-Duller combination had been highly successful and their six Imperial Cup wins included a hat-trick by the brilliant Trespasser. Among the string for Don to ride were a trio of three-year-olds, Story of Eden, Telegraphic and Sea Rover, owned by Sir Malcolm McAlpine. Jim Bell had his own ideas about schooling youngsters and they were first of all galloped between two wings without a hurdle to jump. The next step was to gallop over hurdles lying flat on the ground. The hurdles were raised in stages until they were up to regulation height and always the schooling was carried out at a good gallop. These particular youngsters did not race until they were four years old in the New Year. Story of Eden was the first to appear and he beat an odds-on favourite by a neck at Windsor at 20/1. He went on to win easily at Sandown and Newbury, after which he was saddled for the Imperial Cup, carrying 12st 11lb, which was a colossal weight for one of his age.

45

Before this race, Jim Bell insisted on Don being a partner to another of his peculiar whims. His instruction was for Don to ride on a three pound saddle, which meant him having to carry two lead cloths. No explanation was given but Story of Eden started favourite at 2/1 and after jumping the last hurdle in the lead, weakened to finish seventh. The next to be produced was Telegraphic. Starting at 5/1, he won by a short head at Kempton but on his second venture at Lingfield he was equipped with blinkers and Don, wearing spurs, was told to keep at him from start to finish. To disobey Jim Bell meant instant dismissal, so Don rode as instructed with the result that Telegraphic finished eight lengths behind the winner in third place. His other race that season was to be the International Hurdle at Gatwick. For this important event, the blinkers and spurs were shelved and ridden entirely differently he scored easily by three parts of a length. The workings of Bell were a mystery but after Story of Eden and Telegraphic had made winning debuts there was still Sea Rover to come and rumour had it that he was by far the best of the trio.

Sea Rover had been beaten a short head, with Gordon Richards riding, in the Royal Standard Stakes at Manchester, runner-up in the Column Produce Stakes and third in the Newmarket Stakes. These performances had encouraged his trainer to run him in the Two Thousand Guineas and Derby. Thus he came to hurdling with a tall reputation. His debut at Gatwick was eagerly awaited and he duly obliged by winning in a canter at 5/2 on. In his only other race that season, however, he showed little fight and was beaten at Liverpool.

Despite these successes, Don was not retained for the following season until things went wrong. Then he was given £200 to ride the Bell horses for the rest of the season. One of his mounts was another of Sir Malcolm McAlpine's, Pickpocket, a colt who had been second to Sandwich in the Chester Vase. That was not bad form for a prospective hurdler as Sandwich went on to win the St Leger after having been third in both the Derby and the Eclipse Stakes. Pickpocket, with Gerry Hardy riding, had been third at Sandown but Don had his first ride on him in the Lancashire Hurdle at Liverpool. Here the trainer instructed him to join the leaders at the final hurdle and win by half-a-length. The race was run at a crawl and Don finished up making all the running and winning by a couple of lengths. Although Pickpocket was a heavily backed 6/4 favourite, Jim Bell was white with rage when Don returned. Despite protests from the delighted owner, Bell continued to tear the jockey to shreds for disobeying his orders. By the next season, Bell, whose illness forced him to spend his summers in Iceland, reduced his string and George Duller took over several of the horses. You have probably guessed by now that in those days to question the reason for anything was like pressing the self-destruct button.

Gerry Hardy, who had previously ridden Pickpocket, was a tough nut whose riding career came to a premature close. He had 'done' a certain jockey in a race, which I believe was at Fontwell, and was the victim of 'pay-back time' in a race at Plumpton. He was pushed into the wing of a fence which in those days were of very solid wood and suffered compound fractures of his leg. It was the last race of the day and Gerry was lying on the ground for twenty minutes before the course doctor was located. It was a sad sight to see him walking around with the aid of a couple of sticks when he was able to attend meetings again. With no patrol cameras and unprofessional stewards such occurrences were not uncommon even though few had such disastrous endings.

9

HIGHS AND LOWS

After Duller's retirement from riding it was his ambition to train an Imperial Cup winner. In 1930, his first season, he had his wish. He saddled two for Mr Victor Emmanuel: the 100/7 chance Rubicon II, ridden by Steve Donoghue's brother Pat, and the 25/1 War Mist with Don riding. Jim Bell ran Porthaon and he and his former jockey watched the race together. It must have been a thrill for both as the horses neared the line. In the end, Rubicon II beat Don on the other Duller horse by a short head with Jim Bell's Porthaon a head away in third place followed closely by the favourite, Residue. Don rode in all but three of the Imperial Cups that took place in his riding career but, while he failed to win one, swears that War Mist failed only through being squeezed for room after the last hurdle. An objection was pointless as the two horses were in the same ownership. The winning jockey, Pat Donoghue, was, of course, always overshadowed by his famous brother.

You may think a great deal of emphasis is placed on the Imperial Cup but in pre-war days this race together with the International Hurdle at Gatwick and the Liverpool Hurdle were more sought after prizes than the Champion Hurdle. The fact that Jim Bell won six Imperial Cups among other important races stamps him as an outstanding trainer even if a little unorthodox. Never did he ask a jockey to give one of his horses an easy race. The jockeys rode his horses to win all the time but Bell had his own methods of producing his animals in superior condition on the chosen day.

Don jogged along after Bell's death but no new retainers came his way so he decided to take a job in Denmark during the summers of 1936 and 1937. In both seasons he was top jockey over obstacles and runner-up to Alf Gordon on the flat, his wins including the Danish and Swedish Derbys on Cavallo. Just before he left on the first of these trips abroad he had his first ride in a steeplechase. Hitherto, he had confined himself to hurdle-racing because he was a stylist and his employers wanted him

48

Don wins on the Aga Khan's Dharampur. The other jockey is Staff Ingham

Danish and Swedish Derby winner Cavallo (Don)

that way. It was at Hawthorn Hill that Matt Feakes was injured and unable to ride Cragsman II. He and the trainer, 'Jock' Langlands, suggested that Don would get more opportunities if he rode over fences as well as hurdles so he agreed to start there and then.

Although Matt Feakes was the stable jockey, Don had ridden several winners for Langlands, including Styx River, who landed a 'starting price' gamble at Leicester. Styx River had failed in eight hurdle-races spread over three years, so it was not surprising to find the stable jockey, Feakes, riding the recent winner and stablemate, Troutwal, in the same event. Troutwal, in fact, opened up favourite for the race but a long delay at the start enabled money to get back to the course from London and Styx River ended favourite at 3/1 with Troutwal drifting dramatically to 7/1. It was unfortunate that something went wrong with the commission but nothing went wrong in the race for Styx River cantered home a six lengths winner. Strangely, it was Langlands who gave Don his first win over fences when he returned from Denmark. He did not return until mid-October for the 1937–38 season and had to wait until 1 December before gaining his initial win on Pompous at Newbury. Things looked black but a sudden change of fortune transformed this into his most successful and eventful season with forty-eight wins earning Don third place in the jockey's table.

After that win on Pompous on the first day of December the winners started and within seven days he had five more which included a treble at Gatwick, sparked off by Two Royals – his first steeplechase success. Don started the New Year with fifteen wins and tons of hope. His immediate hopes were so high that he went to Plumpton's meeting on New Year's Day expecting to ride five winners. The first two, Worthy Down and Lutin III, obliged and the next one, Senorita, seemed set to do likewise until falling at the last hurdle. Don's injuries were several broken ribs and a punctured lung as I have referred to in a previous chapter. The two other horses that he was due to ride were Peaceful Walter who was second, while George Duller withdrew the automatic odds-on favourite, King Carnation, from the final race as Don could not ride.

That serious injury came when Don was at last in real demand and I think it must have been this fact that enabled him to make such a quick recovery. Exactly twenty-five days later he resumed at Newbury, and although beaten by a head on his first mount, was soon back among the winners. Plenty of good rides came his way and one of them was Macaulay. His first ride on this chaser, trained by Peter Thrale, was at Hurst Park where they beat the odds-on Golden Miller by five lengths with Airgead Sios another eight lengths back in third place. Incidentally,

Golden Miller leads Airgead Sios and Macaulay in an Optional Selling Chase

that Hurst Park race was an Optional Selling Chase, in which horses carried weights according to the amount for which they would be offered for sale if winning. Those not offered for sale carried top weight, which suited the class horses.

Later, in the King George VI Chase at Kempton, Airgead Sios gained his revenge by a head after a desperately exciting duel. It was virtually a duel because the third horse, Morse Code, was eight lengths behind. Next on the agenda was the Cheltenham Gold Cup in which Golden Miller, Airgead Sios, Morse Code and Macaulay were all to meet again.

At this time Golden Miller, the idol of the crowds, had won five successive Gold Cups and would probably have made it six had not the previous year's race been abandoned. However, he was a 7/4 favourite to make it six on the trot this season despite having been beaten by Macaulay at Hurst Park. The old champion certainly turned the tables on Macaulay but was unable to hold the challenge of the younger Morse Code. Don feels that the tremendous struggle that Macaulay had with Airgead Sios at Kempton had left its mark, a point of view borne out by the Gold Cup running of Airgead Sios who finished a tired fifth.

Another top-class ride for which Don was booked was Beachway. Mr J.V. Rank's hurdler was in the Lingfield Cup but at Kempton the day before, Don broke three toes when falling off Mesmerist at the last hurdle. I say 'fell off' because that is what happened. With a chance of winning if Mesmerist gained ground at the last hurdle, Don asked him to stand back. Unfortunately he overdid this and his jockey went spinning between the horse's ears and landed on his toes. That evening Don had his left foot toes strapped by his doctor and also cut a hole in his racing boot to prevent any pressure on his broken bones. Although in obvious pain, Don walked on his heel and disguised the injury to the best of his ability.

Mrs Pat Rank was a heavy gambler in those days and this was to be one of her plunges. It was also her wish that Beachway won as narrowly as possible for the sake of future handicapping. Don took Beachway round on the inside, dreading that his injured foot would come in contact with the rails, but all went well and Beachway justified hot favouritism by winning, hard held, by half a length from Elmstead. Staff Ingham, on the runner-up, was far from pleased, not because he was beaten but because Don's tactics had meant him giving Elmstead an unnecessarily hard race. Don won the very next race on Balladeur, one of twenty winners he rode for Gosden that season, but perhaps his most extraordinary success came a little later on Flagg in the Liverpool Hurdle, a race he had won two years earlier on Armour Bright.

Beachway, with Jack Fawcus riding, was favourite and fell in this Liverpool race in which Flagg won at 8/1 much as trainer, Willie Carr, and owner, Mr John Hamer, had anticipated. There were few others, however, who could possibly have visualised success. Flagg, a grey entire horse with a flowing mane and tail, had previously raced as Clifton-treschic and his record was far from good. He had won his first two races as a three-year-old over hurdles but in the next seventeen outings managed to win just one small race at Derby. Before the weights for the Liverpool Hurdle were published the trainer asked Don if he would accept the mount. It was possible that Don might be needed for Beachway or a couple of others in the race so he could not give an immediate reply. When, however, it became evident that he would not be required for anything else in the race he accepted the ride on Flagg as he had to be at the meeting in any case.

Don had not previously ridden for Willie Carr and, to say the least, considered him an optimist when the riding orders were given. He was told to take Flagg into the lead after passing the winning post on the first circuit and then make the best of his way home. This, Don reckoned, was all right in theory but how about the ability of the horse to co-operate?

Don followed the instructions and at half-way was flabbergasted when he could not hear the sound of the other runners behind. He did not want to look round and at the same time reassured himself that it was impossible to take a wrong course. Flagg maintained his merry gallop and without his rider ever hearing the hoof-beats of another horse passed the post an easy eight lengths winner. The local Stewards were as amazed as the jockey and the whole business being beyond their comprehension referred the matter to the Stewards of the National Hunt Committee. Don, never having been on Flagg before, was an unhelpful witness but the far-seeing Stewards accepted the trainer's explanation. Willie Carr was often referred to in the press as the man who trained his horses between the Bolton tramlines. He was not related to W.H. Carr, the Royal jockey, known as Harry.

At this particular Liverpool meeting Don had his only ride in the Grand National. This was on Didoric who fell at the fourth fence but in other seasons he had several mounts in other steeplechases at Aintree. In 1939, he performed a very unusual feat on the course. With the Foxhunter's Chase taking place, only five races were open to professional jockeys. Three of these were flat races and the other two were steeple-chases but Don rode in all five. He was unplaced on the two-year-old, Miss Contrary colt, the name of his dam as unnamed two-year-olds were allowed to compete then, fourth on Kingsland in the Champion Chase, third on Iceberg II in the Liverpool Spring Cup, third on Jolly Toper in the Stanley Chase and won the last flat race, the Maghull Plate, on All's Fair. It is a unique achievement particularly as he had ridden in two hurdle races at the meeting on the first day after having ridden in four races at Lincoln's opening-of-the-flat programme earlier in the week.

With a little luck Don might have ridden a Grand National winner. Bruce Hobbs, at seventeen, was the youngest jockey ever to win the Grand National and his victory on Battleship in 1938 cemented him as one of my heroes. Trainer Reg Hobbs had Flying Minutes in the big Aintree chase in addition to the diminutive entire horse, Battleship. The trainer's son had elected to ride Flying Minutes while Don was booked for Battleship – a son of the famous American racehorse, Man O' War.

Unfortunately, Flying Minutes broke down during his preparation and Bruce switched to Battleship who mastered Royal Danieli by a head in a controversial finish. The doubt arose over the decision of crack Irish jockey Dan Moore to bring Royal Danieli towards the stands' rails and race wide of his rival. There was no photo-finish camera then and controversial judgements were not uncommon.

During this very successful season, Don also rode for the late Aga Khan, one of the few winners to carry the famous chocolate and green hooped colours over hurdles. His win was on the four-year-old Dharam-pur, who won a useful race at Newbury at 100/8 after having shown little interest in the proceedings of his previous race. The colt was trained by George Duller but Don had to be content with the honour for no present was forthcoming for that success. In those days there was no automatic percentage for winners or places as there is now.

Another prominent owner for whom Don rode that season was Miss Dorothy Paget. His solitary win in her colours had been on Tulip Time at Fontwell the previous season and his last mount for her turned out to be Publicity at Windsor. On this horse he was beaten a length and a half by Henri's Choice after receiving little co-operation from his mount. Don told this gambling owner that her horse was untrustworthy, a remark which caused Miss Paget to become very annoyed. 'How dare you speak of one of my horses like that?' she replied, and Don was never employed by her again. Honesty may be the best policy, but there are

War Mist (Don) leads over the last in the Imperial Cup

many cases, such as this, when it is not. Incidentally, the winner, Henri's Choice, was running again after having broken his neck in a fall.

The mention of the eccentric Dorothy Paget reminds me of the time she rang her then trainer Fulke Walwyn, to say she wanted her jockey, Frenchie Nicholson, sacked. When Fulke told the jockey he had the sack, Frenchie replied: 'And you can tell her I have got it full up.'

It is a wonder DP did not sack Charlie Smirke when that cheeky chappie was seen to put his arm around her ample waist in the Newmarket parade ring!

It seemed that Don had become firmly established at the top of his profession, quite rightly but belatedly most people thought, and all appeared set for another good season. In August 1938, he went to Ireland and became the first jockey to land the Galway 'double' on Symaethis and Serpolette. The English season started with a win, and then at Wye in September he rode all six favourites at the meeting. Three wins, a third and a fourth was his record before riding the 3/1 on chance, Berks and Bucks, in a four-horse race. This one was cantering over his rivals when he fell but the season had started well enough, for a win at Ludlow on Spinner brought his score to five wins from only sixteen mounts. Then with September not yet out, he suffered that which every steeplechase jockey dreads – a bad fall whilst schooling. Such an accident means no compensation from the National Hunt Accident Fund as it has not taken place between the time of weighing out and weighing in for a race. Don's accident occurred schooling a young horse for Gil Bennett at Polegate. The horse collided with the wing and Don broke a leg. This proved a troublesome affair for the broken bone overlapped after being set. While fully conscious, a hole was bored through his heel and a wire inserted. In this manner his leg was stretched by traction and the bone put in place.

The process of mending was lingering on too long and also becoming costly. Finally Don went to Bill Tucker in London for he was the man who specialised in getting sportsmen back to work with the least possible delay. At a later date it was he who manipulated the 'famous knee' of cricketer Denis Compton. He had made a special high boot for Don and had him walking on his injured leg in practically no time at all. It was, however, 27 February before he found himself in the winning enclosure again.

Any jockey knows the difficulty of getting going again following a serious injury. The stables for which you were riding have had to make alternative arrangements and a similar force of circumstances has often been responsible for a jockey receiving the opportunities that have for long been denied him. That season ended with Don riding fourteen winners but it could so easily have been the year for him to have headed the jockeys' table. He had more success at cribbage. He moved into our house while recovering as it was more convenient than living with his ageing parents. Don and I played endless games of crib and I actually recorded the results of each game. Although the scores escape my memory, I know the total of games ran into four figures, with Don just having the edge.

10

UNCONSCIOUS WIN

The outbreak of war rather than injury spoilt the next season but Don managed to ride nine winners before being called into the Army. Two of his wins were on novice chasers trained by men for whom he rode only the one horse. The first of them was Interlaken, trained by George Beeby. He had refused to jump an open ditch when schooled at home but Don was told this and offered the mount on him at Newbury. Interlaken did not put a foot wrong in the race and won by several lengths. It was, however, the only steeplechase he won and the only occasion on which Don rode him.

A little later in the season he rode Sandy's Choice for Tom Coulthwaite. This had been an unsure jumper and Don finished fifth on him at Haydock. In their next outing the result was a comfortable win at Wolverhampton and this was responsible for his starting favourite for the Stanley Chase at Liverpool. Although completing the course he finished a very tired fifth. When winning on both of these horses the runner-up was Iceberg II, on whom Don had finished third in the Liverpool Spring Cup. Lord Sefton's horse won flat races, hurdle races and chases. He scored in the Broadway Novices' Chase at Cheltenham, the best race of that kind at that period, and then made a name for himself as a sire of jumpers.

Don had only a few chances to ride during his time in the Army but did get to Cheltenham to partner Flying Mascot for George Todd in a selling hurdle race. So unused to handling Don's name-board were the number-board workers that they put my name in the frame instead. Flying Mascot was at 6/1 but as soon as a loudspeaker announcement notified the change, the odds dropped immediately to 2/1 and Flying Mascot finished up an eight lengths winner at 11/10! So much for the difference between D. Butchers and R. Butchers.

Don had several good rides after the war, including Vidi, who was beaten three quarters of a length in the Champion Hurdle by Brains

Trust, but his most brilliant riding at this time came on Swanee River. This American-bred colt was, during his flat career, owned by Mr J.H. Whitney and trained by Captain Boyd-Rochfort. He won at six furlongs but failed to stay any further. On two or three occasions he ran in seven furlong races at Newmarket and was literally cantering in the lead until weakening up the final hill. Like many sprinters he was a hardish puller and when Major J.B. Walker bought him and sent him to Ray Pulford this trainer decided to make him into a hurdler. In his first season he ran unplaced, and unfancied, three times but he coasted home in a moderate Wincanton race when running for the first time the next season. This, I might add, was by design.

Swanee River won that race at 5/1 and landed a big starting price gamble and the plan was to win three more successive handicaps at Windsor against stronger opposition. In the first of them he was tackling a really smart hurdler named The Diver. It was indeed a joy to watch Don's handling of the headstrong Swanee River. He dropped him in right behind the field, which in itself was an achievement on this hard-puller, and got him switched off. There he remained until three hurdles from home where he was allowed to improve his position just a little. At the second last hurdle he was still several lengths behind the leaders, but safely over that, Don pulled him out of the heels of the horse he was tracking and let him sprint.

These may sound obvious tactics but carrying them out was not easy on this horse. When he began to sprint he did so in a manner that those who saw him are unlikely to forget. Don is certain that he has never been so fast over a hurdle in his life, and truly observed that had Swanee River hit the last hurdle he would not have stopped rolling until he reached the winning post. He beat The Diver with ease by a length and a half at 2/1, carrying the life savings, amounting to £18, of a hut-mate of mine in the RAF. Unfortunately, he worked in the cook house and I found it impossible to refuse the regular supply of cheese which he thrust upon me with the compliments of the Air Ministry.

The scene was set for a repeat performance at the next Windsor meeting but Don broke his ribs when Tower Knowe fell with him in the previous race. Fred Rickaby was substituted but found the settling-down process on a strange horse more than a little difficult. The result was a sapping of Swanee River's practically non-existent stamina. He came with what appeared a winning run after the last hurdle but swerved violently through tiredness and was beaten a short head by Le Cure. Exactly a fortnight later, Don, with his ribs strapped, rode Swanee River in the third of the Windsor races. This time Pelorus came from Ireland and was fully expected to win. Right up till the 'off' there was nothing to choose between the pair of them in the betting but a load of money from the London offices arrived just in time to make Swanee River favourite at 13/8. Don rode him as before and that final sprint made the Irish horse look like a park hack. In a few strides Swanee River had opened up a six lengths lead and won, pulling up, by that distance. While in the RAF I rode Swanee River in a school over hurdles and he was certainly an impressive horse to sit on.

Swanee River ran in the Liverpool Hurdle and was going well when he fell three hurdles from home. The following season he was sold to Lord Mildmay who raced him at the West-country meetings where he was capable of winning even if this gallant rider found himself unable to settle him. Swanee River won seven lowly hurdle races with Lord Mildmay riding and when he changed ownership again finished up by gaining his last win in a selling steeplechase at Haydock. He was the type of horse that used to win hurdle races many years ago when the pace was sedate. Nowadays, it is extremely difficult to win with this sort but Ray Pulford and Don managed to achieve what were undoubtedly creditable performances.

Apart from the injuries referred to, Don had plenty of others, including eight broken collar-bones and several bouts of concussion. As if he had not had his share, he broke his skull when Civvy Street fell with him at Taunton in March 1946. This had a lasting effect which brought on headaches and spells of giddiness.

It was also responsible for a most unusual win at Fontwell. Don was badly shaken when Stormless was brought down but ran back to ride Funny in the next race. The horse made nearly all of the running and Don won by a short head without appearing to make much effort. This extraordinary riding mystified everyone present until it was discovered on his return to the unsaddling enclosure that all was not well. He recognised nobody and had to be led to the scales to weigh-in. Within minutes he was laid flat out in the ambulance room and to his dying day did not remember the race and did in fact ride throughout in a state of unconsciousness. Funny was another of those animals that got you tired. During a bad spell of weather I rode him on the seaside sand in a bit of slow work and was glad when we pulled up. His head felt as if it weighed a hundredweight. I also rode him in a school over fences at Folkestone racecourse before the start of a season and the silly old thing jumped the first so big that I was thankful to land back on the 'plate'.

Of any criticisms levelled at Don throughout his riding career there was only one that caused him any concern. This came after a win on The Diver at Windsor when Tom Nickalls of the *Sporting Life* described Don as 'all arms and legs compared with the French jockey, Bobby Bates'. What incensed Don was the fact that he rode a hard-pulling novice in his first race over fences whereas Bates was riding an experienced, foot-perfect chaser called Vol au Vent II.

Of the four runners, this pair dominated the race and Don wanted his horse, The Diver, to have company at the fences. To ensure this it meant a struggle with his free-running mount and this combined with some inexperienced fencing forced Don's usually immaculate style to clash with that of the crouching French jockey. Naturally, Bates was doing all he could to make Don's ride as uncomfortable as possible, and, what is more, succeeding. With totally different tasks to perform, Don considered that criticism unfair and unjustified but that is the only time he found his medicine hard to swallow.

For the sake of his health, Don finished with race-riding in the spring of 1948. His final winner was Coppards, trained by Harry Hannon, at Lingfield. This, like so many of his wins, was gained in spectacular fashion. He brought Coppards with a late run to catch, and pass, the leader half-way up the run-in. With a little more luck his career as a jockey could have been really outstanding but Don was always non-complaining and is satisfied that he carried out his tasks conscientiously and with a blemish-free record. I'm pleased I was at Lingfield to see his last winner, and not only because I had a few pounds on at 20/1.

The present-day style of jumping jockeys bears no resemblance to that of years gone by. They now sit up the neck of horses when crossing a fence and, not only that, do so with a much shorter stirrup leather and the ball of the foot in the iron. Compare this with the old style when jockeys rode much longer and used to slip the reins when crossing a fence, with the body in an upright position. I have no idea which style is the better, although I must say that I have not seen many unseated due to the present method.

When Andy Turnell rode as short as the flat race jockeys during the Seventies he came in for a lot of criticism. His father, Bob, was one of the old school but had to accept his son's style when faced with the question 'how many have I fallen off?'. Andy even finished third in the

The jockeys' old style of crossing a fence

1974 Grand National with his knees under his chin. This was on Charles Dickens.

It is all a matter of comfort and among the present crop, Andrew Thornton and Richard McGrath like riding longer which makes them easy to recognise.

My preference was to ride short, simply because I was more comfortable – and I never felt insecure. Don, with my best interest at heart, once asked Ron Smyth how he thought I was progressing and he said I rode too short. For me, handsome is as handsome does.

When going out on Kai Lung at Fontwell, Matt Feakes, the trainer, told me to let my leathers down a hole or two. I had to do so as I knew the fault would have been mine if any mishap had occurred.

The mention of Don retiring with a blemish-free record may be queried by those unfamiliar with the intricacies of racing. In brief, no horse can be at peak form for a long period and like humans has to ease up now and then. When returning to full work it is unwise to 'over-cook' them. Working at home can never be as effective as racing if the horse is thick-winded and to drive them hard would certainly do more harm than good. Constitutions vary enormously and the trainers have to know a thing or two to be successful. Call it what you like but there are tricks of the trade in all professions and some may not be readily acceptable. Believe me, there is not a jockey riding, now or in the past, who has not given a horse an easy race or ridden a non-trier as many like to call it.

The change in riding styles is of great interest to me. The long leather style of a century ago was modified before the first world war and has been changing throughout the period following the second conflict. In the distant past, the American Tod Sloan adopted the crouch position and it was not long before most of the other jockeys followed suit.

I am, of course, referring to flat race jockeys but the principle is the same for the jumping boys. Riding very short enables the rider to place most weight on the horse's withers which makes sense. It is the back-end of a horse that propels them so the less weight there the better. The most recent change has been riding with just the ball of the foot in the stirrup. It was ages before this innovation that I sat on a horse so cannot comment whether or not it is more comfortable or advantageous but there must be something in it to be so widely used.

When it comes to jump racing the case for removing as much weight as possible from the hindquarters would seem even more important as the hocks are what give the jumper a leap. Most of the jump jockeys start off with the ball of the foot in the stirrup but there must be a high percentage that finish with the feet right home. In comparatively recent times the 'monkey-up-a-stick' style over obstacles would have been ridiculed. Another change I have noticed is jockeys having four fingers inside the reins instead of having the little finger outside.

11

YOU WIN SOME, AND LOSE SOME

Soon after his wartime Army service, Don decided to set up as a trainer, which was fairly automatic as the war years were the only ones he had not been closely connected with horses. Even whilst in the army he had a reminder of racing. Don was a driver stationed at a secret destination in the New Forest and had to sign documents binding him to report to the Commanding Officer if he knew or recognised any of his passengers. Apparently this was 'cloak and dagger' stuff like dropping personnel behind enemy lines. When dispatched to pick up one officer both he and Don knew each other very well. It was the successful trainer Major John Goldsmith for whom Don had ridden many times, and a man who had a distinguished war record.

Prior to receiving his licence, Don trained some horses under the licence of Bob Maxwell whose Lewes yard was at Heath House. I must point out that Bob Maxwell was a larger than life personality – in fact he might well have leapt out of a Dickensian novel. Great sideburns, a shiny pate and dressed in a bold check suit, Bob was in the habit of pouring out the most enormous gin and tonics while mopping his brow with a coloured handkerchief the size of a tablecloth.

Back to the horses. The owner was 'Spitty' McClean, with whom I had stayed at Manchester and who handled the successful gamble on And How. He bought half a dozen yearlings fairly cheaply in Ireland with the idea that perhaps a couple of them would be worth persevering with. The animals actually ran in the name of his son and the object was to set them up for a gamble. The two that mattered did not do much as juveniles but plans were made for their season as three-years-olds. With this in view, it was arranged to borrow a recent winner from Vic Smyth's Epsom stable. The groundsman at the Lewes racecourse was Jack Cole and he would make the course available provided some appreciation, like money, was shown.

D. Dillon, S. Barnes, T. Redmond, P. Supple and R. Harrison keep fit while racing is snowed-off

The owner travelled down from Manchester to view the trial. It was made as realistic as possible with half a dozen in the line-up over a mile. The only one being tried was Valentine's Rose with Don riding. My mount was another filly named Cream Lace. The exact weights carried were fixed to ensure that Valentine's Rose had a stiff task and I know that my filly had top weight. The result of the trial was that Valentine's Rose finished upsides Vic Smyth's winner with Don not allowing her full ability to be exposed. Although Cream Lace was in the field to make up the number, she was the revelation. There was plenty of pace on so I had dropped her in the rear but when I pulled out she was galloping all over them. I managed to finish a neck behind the leading pair with the brakes hard on!

Valentine's Rose was a hyperactive filly who never stopped bouncing like a ball and on the gallops her only desire was to get to the finish in the quickest possible time. She was a tiring filly to ride out each morning so Don and I used to share this liver-shaking experience. All was now set for her to run in a selling race at Windsor. This was in 1948 and the late

Manny Mercer, brother of Joe and so sadly killed at Ascot, took the mount. He was a top apprentice and was unable to claim his full 5lb allowance so rode at a pound overweight, which meant that the filly carried 6st 12lb.

The trial suggested she was capable of winning with another 21 pounds on her back and the owner invested with confidence. Her opening price was 4/1 and she started favourite at 7/4. My trusty pub landlord friend, Guy, and I went in the Silver Ring at Windsor and decided to invest £100 between us. That was quite a hefty sum in those days. We agreed to put small amounts of money on with various bookmakers, and to our surprise, odds of 33/1 were available on many of the boards that started betting early.

Instead of asking for £100 to £3, called asking for the fractions, we made it £66 to £2 or £99 to £3, which is a real mug's bet. It wasn't too long before money started to come for the filly and we climbed the stand to watch the 'formality'. We had secured the average odds of £800 to £100. The hardest part would be going round the host of bookmakers and finding the right ticket to produce for our winnings. The only thing that went wrong was Valentine's Rose who did not play her part and finished fourth, beaten three and a quarter lengths. In setting up this gamble an obvious fact had been forgotten. Poor little Manny Mercer was slowly away but in front after a hundred yards. He was a passenger on this bubbly filly and she simply ran herself into the ground.

Fortunately that racecourse trial proved a blessing. I had told Don that Cream Lace could have won by many a length. Five weeks later she was sent from Lewes to Hamilton, near Glasgow, and was a springer in the market and won at even money. My advice to hold her up for a late run was ignored and jockey Ginger Dyson led from start to finish.

Don started with his licence at Neville Stables and had a mixed string of flat horses and jumpers. There were a fair number of winners, but the big change came when a young Gay Kindersley sent Tight Knight to be trained. As Gay tasted success he became more and more hooked on riding and became a fearless and accomplished amateur. The outcome was the purchase of Priam Lodge in Epsom and Don was installed as trainer not only for the Kindersley string but for other owners. However, there were good and bad days at Lewes. One of the worst was to get 'knocked' so soon after living on Army pay for five years and finding capital to set up a business. The man who failed to pay turned up to see his horse in a chauffeur driven Rolls-Royce. It turned out to be a scam.

It was while I was at a Newmarket meeting that I was introduced to a George Hatton who asked if I thought Don would take his horse to train. Don was now a bit wary of the unknown. Luckily I knew some of this man's associates and was assured on all counts. The horse was Rich Harvest who lived up to his name. He landed a few gambles both on the flat and over hurdles, and proved as good as his owner. Don was not a gambler and bet on very few of his horses but Rich Harvest was one of them.

I was riding out for Don every day and we always had chats about the well being and plans for the horses. It was well known among the regulars that most of his horses improved after their first race of the season. Rich Harvest was due to run at Wye with Alan Oughton riding and Don mentioned that the horse was very clean winded and took very little getting ready. This prompted me to say: 'Why not pull the trigger first time?' Don thought for a few seconds and then agreed it was a good idea. What is more it was a good result with Rich Harvest winning easily.

Evening Trial was another owned by George Hatton which was bought out of the Noel Murless stable. He proved unreliable but as he had won with Lester Piggott riding the previous season, Don thought it would be a good idea to see if he would ride him in a selling race. He agreed and, with Lester's forceful persuasion, was a very narrow winner.

Be Patient was another good servant and the renewal of an old partnership. Frank Hill, a master butcher in Tunbridge Wells, had horses with my father and grandfather and also rode point-to-point and National Hunt winners between the wars. He then lost interest and with the intervention of war did not give racing any thought. Out of the blue he rang Don and asked him to buy him a horse. Don responded by saying, 'You don't really want to start again.' When Frank makes up his mind that is final. 'Okay,' said Frank, 'I'll buy one myself.' With that threat, Don bought this horse called Be Patient for very little money.

When Frank first saw him, he said it looked like a teddy bear. 'Just you be patient,' said Don and that was how his name came about. The most memorable win was in a selling race at Newmarket in which he had bottom weight. As I was racing every day, Don asked me if there was a promising apprentice I thought capable of riding Be Patient. Without hesitation I said, 'Josh Gifford,' who was serving his time with Sam Armstrong. Who would believe that the future champion National Hunt jockey could ride at less than seven stones? Josh did the job like an old hand but there was a disappointing ending. There was a sizeable field and it was decided to back the horse at starting price rather than on the course. I was given the task of arranging for the £500 stable commission to be invested away from the course.

It had to be a man who regularly bet in those sort of figures – in those days a sizeable amount. The ideal man was Harrogate-based Harold Dixon who was a regular Newmarket racegoer, sometimes as a big stakes bookmaker or a well-informed punter. In this capacity he had three or four 'putters-on' – all of whom I knew.

I sat at the back of the stands so as not to be questioned by anyone about the chance of Be Patient. His opening price was around 5/1 which began to lengthen as no money had been placed at the course, or so I believed, and everything looked fine as his price drifted to 10/1 everywhere in the ring. What was in store sent a chill through my body as I saw three of the 'putters-on' dashing amongst the bookmakers and stacking money on Be Patient – that money being the £500 of our commission.

Be Patient won easily enough but instead of the winnings being £5,000, they were £2,000 as Be Patient was returned at 4/1 favourite. Imagine how I felt when I had to tell the owner. I wonder who pocketed the other £3,000? So much for supposed friendship.

Be Patient set a trend as Frank Hill named all his horses with the 'Be' prefix if they had not already been registered. The majority of them won but the best of them was undoubtedly Be Cautious. She landed a gamble at Lingfield Park at 8/1 before winning a major juvenile event at Newbury. Don bought this well-bred filly for 800 guineas and sold her to America for a sum more than ten times that price.

The star among the jumpers, owned by Frank Hill, was Bozetoff while in later years he landed a few touches with Marsh Harrier trained by the late and loved Charlie Moore. The trainer's daughter, Candy, won on him in a ladies race at Brighton at 33/1. The notes covered the floor when it was time for a share-out. How about the losers? There were, of course, a few but sorrows are easily drowned.

Frank Hill died at the age of ninety-four and did not bet at all in his latter years, but during his time with Don Butchers showed a betting profit when his racing was taken seriously.

With my wife Marian, we used to stay with Frank in his converted Oast House in Eridge on a regular basis. Eating out was a speciality and they were always enjoyable and usually somewhere a bit special.

It was at the George and Dragon at Speldhurst that the three of us went after returning from a good day at Folkestone. Marsh Harrier,

Frank and Candy Moore with Trophy hero North West

ridden by Paul Cook, won the last race at 9/2 so there were plenty of notes floating around that evening. Dinner was to be my treat, but Frank insisted that he bought a bottle of Bollinger while we studied the menu. I ordered another bottle of the same to be drunk at the table. We both paid our bills and on the way home Frank asked if I had a bottle of Bollinger on my bill. We ordered without looking at the wine list which made Frank think that he had paid for two bottles. That was not the case, and it was quite simply that the 'Bolly' was £48.50 a bottle, and very nice it was too.

There was a similar incident when the three of us went to the Honours Mill in Edenbridge. Frank was in the chair this night and he studied the lengthy wine list. For some years his favourite red wine was Chateau Gruaud Larose. This was not to be found on the wine list, so Frank ordered another red around £16 and slipped in the remark that they did not have his favourite Gruaud Larose. 'You will find it on the next page, sir,' said the wine waiter and find it he did – at £47 a bottle. There was no way out of that one, but these events and others merely made the occasions more lighthearted than they already were.

These reunions with Frank Hill were a source of pleasure and during our stays we also met up with his daughter Diana and husband Alan who lived nearby. Diana is a superb cook while Alan's specialities are his home-brewed beer and selection of wines. I am pleased to say we still meet them, but not as often as we would like owing to the miles we are apart.

The reunion with Frank came years after Don died of a heart attack at the age of fifty-six. His was in many ways a sad life. After moving to Epsom he had plenty of success, his best known horses being Saffron Tartan and Carrickbeg. Frank Hill still had horses with Don in Epsom and it was worth relating the origin of his racing colours. His old colours were green and black, but the registration had not been maintained and the set of colours had long disappeared. Most trainers have spare sets left by previous owners so Don produced the colours of Petunia, yellow sleeves and a green cap, and how lucky they proved to be. It was a little ironic as they were the colours of our Dr Sadler, mentioned elsewhere in this book, and one of the unluckiest owners.

This reminds me of Herbert 'Nat' Smyth. He was a robust, jovial character and, having a new owner visiting for dinner, the subject of choosing a set of colours arose. Nat produced an array of colours which prompted the rookie owner to ask why they were available. 'All of the owners went broke,' was the answer from the mischievous Nat.

Don Butchers was a man of principles but had the added bonus of living up to them. I am unashamed of singing his praises and anyone who may glimpse a shade of nepotism may change their view after reading the obituaries which I have no hesitation in reproducing. John Lawrence, now Lord Oaksey, wrote under his nom-de-plume 'Marlborough':

Don Butchers, who has died at Ashurst in Kent, at the age of fifty-six, was not only a fine jockey and trainer under both Rules but also one of the kindest, most modest men I ever knew.

A fearless rider before and just after the war, Don's greatest success as a trainer was with Saffron Tartan whom he took over from Vincent O'Brien in 1960 and with whom he won both the King George VI Chase and the Cheltenham Gold Cup.

Though a brilliant horse at his best, Saffron Tartan was far from easy to train, and it was a masterpiece of patient skill to bring him to Cheltenham on the one day that really mattered, fit to run for his life.

But if this was Don Butchers's finest hour my own clearest memory will always be of the supremely sporting way he bore Carrickbeg's narrow defeat in the 1961 Grand National.

No word of reproach or self-pity passed his lips that day and although he retired from training some years ago his death leaves both National Hunt racing and his many friends very much the poorer.

The late Len Thomas wrote in the *Sporting Life*:

> It was a fine gesture on the part of my good friend and colleague, Bob
> Butchers, to put up a trophy for the race in honour of Don Butchers.
> Of all the people I have met in my thirty years of racing there has been
> none nicer than Don Butchers.
> As a jockey, and later when he took up training nothing was too much
> trouble for him. I have yet to meet a more conscientious man and a greater
> horse-lover.

After many years of presenting the handsome silver horse I decided to
discontinue the race and have the trophy at home as a permanent
reminder of Don.

There were many more tributes on similar lines and I just regret not
having his company and advice for a longer period. Don retired from
training because of labour problems. He had been brought up to a
more disciplined routine. Lateness and unsatisfactory work were factors
he was not prepared to accept. His headman was Jack Morrissey, whose
son, Neil, rode several winners for the stable. Jack worked for my
grandfather and father and when Don started training he immediately
sought out Jack to become headman. During his absence from a racing
stable Jack had trained as a saddler which was very useful. Although
Jack ran a well disciplined staff, there were those who found reason to
complain. Don called a meeting in the tackroom and came straight to
the point. 'I have brought all of your cards so now you have the choice.
Complain now if you wish and your card is ready.' Nobody left but
Don had had enough.

I always arrived five minutes early to ride out but on just one occasion
I was two minutes late and the string had pulled out. Don had no option
but to look at his watch and say, 'I shan't need you this morning.' There
was no nepotism that day.

I know my mother's death had a profound effect on both Don and me
and it hastened his retirement. Her death in 1962 was a bitter blow.
Serious operations had weakened her over the years and caused her to
reshape her life to one of a very quiet existence. She adapted herself
bravely until overtaken by a stroke at the much too young age of
fifty-nine. Only after Mother's death did Don tell me the secret he had
kept. A specialist had warned him that ten years was her maximum
expectation of life. She died ten years later, almost to the day, and Don
had obviously found that burden of knowledge weighing heavily on him

towards the end. We were at her bedside in the Epsom Cottage Hospital when she died.

I have never been a churchgoer but have my own faith. After Mother's death on Saturday, I went to church on the Sunday to be alone with my thoughts. A lady behind me saw fit to lean forward and say that I was holding the wrong book. It left me speechless.

It is not until you become a parent that you realise the worries that come as permanent attachments. I now know the worries I caused my mother even though some were out of my control.

The announcement on 3 September 1939 by Neville Chamberlain made it a very grim day. The final words were, 'This country is now at war with Germany.' This followed the ultimatum given to Germany after they had invaded Poland. They were given until 11 a.m. to withdraw and the rest is history.

The immediate reaction was a mixture of fear, bewilderment, suspense and the unpredictable effects it would have on our lives. For me it was the start of another life and no doubt millions more had the same feeling. Looking back, I find it hard to believe how the mood and attitudes of the population changed immediately. As the days turned into weeks and then months and years, the people became more united. Quite often I sit and, with eyes closed, recapture the indescribable feeling of living through those long and dreary years. We got used to hearing, if not always seeing, the German planes passing overhead on their way to bomb London. Pubs and houses fell quiet during every news bulletin and not a word was missed when Churchill's speeches were broadcast. If just one man could uplift the nation, it was him.

Raids, shortages, the black-out and uncertainties ensured that every day was different in some way or other and for a long time the news became worse and worse.

It was not until after the war that I realised how close we were to being invaded and the unthinkable consequences. We escaped thanks to some brilliant kidology and throughout the campaign Britain earned the title of Great. I'm sorry to say that it no longer warrants such a superlative. I for one will never forget those six years when inner feelings were a one-off. Living in that era was a privilege and made me appreciate some of the better things but sadly it came at such a great cost for too many.

In hindsight, I am sure it was those left at home who suffered the greatest heartbreak as they saw members of their family depart. It is worth pointing out that eighteen-year-olds in those days had barely flown the nest and had neither the sophistication nor the independence of those today. Even now there are reminders of those war years. Music and, particularly, the words from *The Great American Songbook* collection are among my favourites and when I listen to several of them my thoughts immediately return to my time in uniform. I admit to being an old romantic and a sentimentalist and when 'Every time we say goodbye' is played the thought of parting at the railway station after a home visit springs back to send a shiver down my spine. Other titles with a similar effect include 'For all we know we may never meet again' and 'We'll be together again'. It would come as no surprise to learn that many more in my age bracket have their war memories stirred in the same way. When in some moods I make a decision not to play them. Perhaps I should adopt as my signature tune the Norman Wisdom hit 'Don't laugh at me 'cos I'm a fool'.

12

TWO OF THE BEST

Although Don Butchers had several of what I call 'middle of the road' horses he had never trained anything the calibre of Saffron Tartan. This fine horse was plagued with some sort of ailment all his life. He first raced for his joint-owners, Lady Cottenham and Colonel Westmacott, when trained by Vincent O'Brien in Ireland. He did not see a racecourse until he was six and made his debut in a amateur flat race at Naas. Starting at two to one on, he won by six lengths. Within three months Saffron Tartan had added two wins over hurdles and one over fences to end his first season unbeaten. From then on he had recurring problems but retained plenty of ability. He was a dual purpose performer, alternating between hurdling and steeplechases. The Gloucester Hurdle was one of the big events at the Cheltenham Festival and a race that Vincent O'Brien farmed for several years.

Saffron Tartan took that race in his stride and after winning or being placed in recognised trials for the Champion Hurdle went on to finish third to Amber Flash in that supreme event in 1960. By now he had crossed the Irish Sea to join Don as Vincent O'Brien was now concentrating on flat race horses and could not give the time to Saffron Tartan with his lameness troubles. Following his third in the Champion Hurdle, he turned out the next month to win the Gratwicke Blagrave Chase at Cheltenham by five lengths carrying top weight. That gave him a higher rating than his Gold Cup win which illustrates that handicap wins give a truer assessment of ability than weight-for-age events.

This strapping individual was sent to Don with the King George VI Chase at Kempton Park on Boxing Day and the Gold Cup as specific targets. It was reckoned he had the ability if he could be kept sound. It was the owner's wish that Fred Winter should ride and fortunately he was available and subsequently retained. Saffron Tartan was given just two outings before the Boxing Day race and in one of these was beaten

Saffron Tartan (Fred Winter) clears the last on his way to winning the Cheltenham Gold Cup

just three quarters of a length when trying to give a stone to the useful Mariner's Dance. He made little fuss about winning the King George VI Chase by three lengths, but the Gold Cup was a different matter.

Three miles around the sharp Kempton track was one thing, but three and a quarter miles over the stiff Cheltenham course raised a few questions. Keeping Saffron Tartan sound and fit between the two major events was a worry that was to become intensified. It was planned to give him just one race between events and that was in the Gainsborough Chase at Sandown. It was over two miles and he started at 9/2 on only to fall at the first of the three railway fences. That was a real surprise and absolutely the last thing one would expect of him.

Luckily he came to no harm but it was not the ideal preparation. Apart from handicaps, for which he always carried top weight, there was no other suitable event. He went to Cheltenham in great shape and it seemed that only two things stood between him and victory. The first was stamina and the second was the previous year's winner, Pas Seul. As one would expect, Fred Winter was in the right place at the right time and that included the winning post. It did, however, take Fred all his strength to keep the weakening Saffron Tartan in front up that gruelling hill. The gallant chaser took that race well and you can rest assured that Don would not have turned him out for another crack at the Gratwicke Blagrave Chase if not completely satisfied with his well-being. In going for back-to-back wins in this event, the horse carried 12st 11lb and gave 37lb and 39lb respectively to Moretons and Richard of Bordeaux. He was beaten a short head and three quarters of a length with the fourth horse six lengths away. That was a really tremendous performance. He raced twice the next season, including a gallant second when he failed to give a stone to Frenchmans Cove. He earned his retirement.

For all his size and bulk, it transpired that Saffron Tartan did best on a light preparation – a fact that Don discovered in quick time. As a comparison, in a different sphere I might add, the late Captain Boyd-Rochford had a classic horse called Black Tarquin and this bulky individual used to be exercised morning and afternoon. This shows that no two horses are alike in their requirements.

When Saffron Tartan arrived at the Epsom yard, he was put in the care of Tony 'Ginger' Green. Ginger was close to aggressive if anyone else

Grand National runner-up Carrickbeg (Bob)

got near to his idol. Usually he went off on his own for a good trot and a steady canter. I'm sure Ginger sulked all day when I was given the leg-up one morning. Don wanted me to have the chance of finding out how different he was. We cantered about six furlongs and he glided like a ballet dancer.

In all, Saffron Tartan ran twenty-six times and won eleven and was placed in another seven. When he won the Gold Cup I could not suppress tears of joy knowing what a worry the horse had been to Don. The only sad note was that the runner-up was trained by one of my closest friends, Bob Turnell, with whom Marian and I stayed for the Cheltenham meetings and other occasions on a regular basis. Bob and his dear wife Betty acted as you would suspect: delighted for us and making light of the fact that Pas Seul might have been 'got at' that morning.

Saffron Tartan had equine flu early in his career and also respiratory trouble, which needed the Hobday operation. Although well-deserved praise was heaped on Fred Winter for the ride he gave the horse in the Gold Cup, I'm sure Vincent O'Brien would be the first to give Don Butchers a huge amount of credit. In turn, Don praised Saffron Tartan for the courage and bravery he showed throughout his racing life.

Carrickbeg was a different kettle of fish and had Aintree written all over him. Strangely, like Saffron Tartan, he ran just twenty-six times, winning six and being placed ten times. From the very start he was going to be a chaser but was still able to win a hurdle race in his first season. This was when ridden by his owner Gay Kindersley at Wincanton. The following season, he started over fences and quickly showed that he was a natural. He won novice chases under three different jockeys, firstly Terry Redmond, then the owner, and finally Peter Supple.

Such was the improvement by Carrickbeg that he was runner-up to the smart Taxidermist at Kempton. It was ironic that the winner was ridden by the then John Lawrence, who later suffered that agonising defeat on Carrickbeg in the Grand National. The mark of his continued improvement was shown when he won the Kim Muir Chase at the Cheltenham Festival, and even more so when, as a comparative novice, he was beaten a length by Frenchman's Cove in the Whitbread Gold Cup.

As a seven-year-old, he started the new season by running second to Mill House who was the top chaser apart from Arkle. What is more, Carrickbeg was giving 6lb to Mill House and although beaten very easily, it was still a great performance. Before the turn of the year he had finished fourth in the Hennessey Gold Cup and a creditable third to Mill

House. The build-up to the Grand National was now reaching a critical stage and a spell of hard weather came at the wrong time.

Don was forced to take Carrickbeg to Ireland as part of his preparation and this went well enough with a respectable third place at Leopardstown. Another crack at the Kim Muir Chase at Cheltenham was the ideal event as it came seventeen days before the Grand National and was another chance for John Lawrence to get to know his mount. A second win in this race was expected, but Carrickbeg blundered badly and unseated his rider. No blame was attached to the jockey but, as with Saffron Tartan, a fall is not the best thing to happen in the final warm-up race.

As we know Saffron Tartan went on to win his target race, the Gold Cup, but history was not to be repeated in the case of Carrickbeg. It almost was but, with two horses giving their all, Ayala edged ahead in the last few strides to score by three-quarters of a length. Of course it was bitterly disappointing to have what seemed certain victory snatched away by so small a margin. I had ridden Carrickbeg in quite a lot of his work before the Grand National and felt a small cog in the wheel, but my heart bled for Don, Gay and John Lawrence.

Carrickbeg just fails to hold off Ayala in the Grand National

Giving Tiber Flight a pipe-opener at Aintree

John – we all know him now as Lord Oaksey – had bought a half-share in Carrickbeg in order to take the ride, and what a wonderful ride he gave him. At this juncture, I must pay tribute to a wonderfully gallant horse who at seven was the youngest in a field of forty-seven and was in only his second season as a chaser. The sportsmanship displayed by Don, Gay and John was magnificent as they accepted defeat like the real men they were on that unforgettable day. I read somewhere: 'No greater tribute can be paid to Don Butchers than that he never batted an eyelid. It was typical of the man.'

Carrickbeg ran twice the following season and in the second of them at Sandown gave John a winning ride as if to compensate him fractionally for that Aintree defeat. Sadly Carrickbeg broke down when winning that race and another shot at the ultimate prize was denied. We shall never know what was in store.

Other chasers that proved good servants were Bozetoff, Cluster and Tiber Flight. Frank Hill, from Eridge, owned Bozetoff and he landed some good touches when ridden by Alan Oughton. The other pair were owned by Kentish farmers. Cluster was owned by Ronnie Martin, and had he been a sound horse would probably have won a top race or two, instead of just decent events. He and Alan Oughton got on particularly well. The poor old horse finally went lame on all four legs and it was a sad day when he limped from his box to have his misery ended humanely by the vet.

Tiber Flight was the winner of several chases before Don moved from Lewes to Epsom. He was one of my regular rides at exercise. For some reason, Alan did not take to him. He was a bit wooden-headed and used to lay on you rather than pull. He was by Tiberius out of Slipaway and had two names. The first was Roman Fall before being renamed Tiber Flight – a couple of good choices. He ran forty-seven times, winning ten and being placed sixteen times – a record that included a good third to the Grand National winner Freebooter in the Becher Chase run over a circuit of the Grand National course. In his best season he won six which included four in succession. He was owned by the fruit farmer Walter Merricks, who on a stable visit, gave an apple to the lad in charge. Lucky him.

13

ALL CHANGE

Less than two years after my father died, war broke out and boys were turned into men almost overnight. I was fifteen and still at school but had been riding out for Tom Masson for nearly three years. We heard that Father had died around six o'clock in the morning and the news circulated fairly quickly. No doubt Masson was among the first to be told and he rang back a little later and asked to speak to me. He naturally commiserated and said it was my choice whether I rode out or not and that no horse would leave the yard until I had decided. Without hesitation I turned up on time but the whole yard was a sad place. The majority of the lads had previously worked for my father or grandfather, both of whom were proud to be good employers.

Tom Masson had taken me under his wing and was bringing me along as he did with successful apprentices Carol Orton, Bobby Elliot, Bunny Hicks and Jimmy Lindley. After I had ridden out that morning, probably twice or maybe three times, he suggested I should go and live with him and his family for a while. I must have been on school holiday, because he kept me occupied the whole of the time and I did not return home for a fortnight. He was kindness itself and I regret having a temporary fall-out with him through no fault of my own.

The period between leaving school and volunteering for the services was one of varying activities. Racing was curtailed, especially National Hunt, then there were a few scattered meetings, usually on a Saturday, and then they totally stopped. The blackout, reserved occupations, food and petrol rationing, clothes and furniture coupons, an exodus of friends and loved ones to the forces and a general fear of what was to come made for anything but a settled existence. It was not a happy time.

In my last year at school, I sat for a Bursary exam, which allowed me to attend a commercial college in Brighton at half-fees. Why I took the exam I do not know to this day because it was doing nothing but hampering my ambition to be a jockey. The object was to learn Gregg's shorthand, as opposed to Pitman's, touch-typing and elementary accounting. Sorry to say, I played truant on as many days as I attended and was embarrassed when I was asked to take a typewriting test on my own as I was absent on the appointed day. Add to this the fact that I was the only boy in a class of twenty-odd, and the hesitant taps on the keys clearly announced my incompetence!

When it came to shorthand I fared slightly better. There were two reasons for this: firstly it was a silent operation and secondly I scribbled the dictation in longhand. I had actually played truant to ride at Southwell on one occasion. I did manage to finish the term but it was all a waste of time and when I used a typewriter in later years it was a two-fingered job.

My formal education was near enough average with simple maths being my favourite, but only if algebra, geometry and logarithms were excluded. I once had ninety-nine out of a hundred in arithmetic. The master, Mr Pett, had never given full marks on principle! History and Shakespeare were non-existent as far as I was concerned, a fact not lost by my history master, Mr O'Brien. Somehow I found myself on a pub's dart team playing against the Green Man in the village of Ringmer, just outside Lewes. It was a bit of a shock to discover Mr O'Brien among the opposition. I found out he could sink a good few pints and he was to find out that I knew nothing about history.

It was not many days after the darts match that Mr O'Brien read out the end-of-term exam marks. There was no chance of my running into a place and when, as expected, he announced my last place mark of nine out of a hundred with the remark 'Sheer ignorance,' I did not look in his direction but I guess there was a twinkle in his Irish eyes.

Learning passages from Shakespeare was a definite no-go area. Sometimes I read the passage while eating breakfast and hopefully would be able to recite the first couple of lines. It was a matter of chance who would be called on to recite this piece of homework and I cannot recall that it was ever me. No doubt it was thought a waste of time to even ask me.

Apart from the horsey-set, my friends had always been older people among the masculine sex. This suited me but what I didn't like was the fact that I had to earn some pocket money. As stated earlier, this was a stop gap period. Three of my uncles were in local government and it needed only one of them to get me the job of an office boy in the Public

Assistance Department at a wage of twenty-five shillings a week. Needless to say the PA payments did not apply to healthy teenagers such as I. The support was given to institutions that catered for the under-privileged.

The law of the land required non-service personnel to contribute to the war effort with a worthwhile occupation. Boys were conscripted at the age of eighteen and this was something I did not relish mainly because it was certain to nip in the bud any chance of having a career as a jockey.

Situations were changing all the time and I had little option but to take the office job in the County Hall. As an office boy I had to collect the mail from the Post Office before signing in below the red line of our department's arrival book. This was one event in which I never failed to finish in the first three! Whatever one's job, I believe there is some enjoyment to be gained if you look for it, and while there were other things I wanted to do, my lowly post had its compensations.

A daily round of the various departments of the Local Government offices, delivering what is termed 'internal correspondence', made a bit of a break for there was no time limit attached to this task. At least I came into contact with different people and often had some amusing moments en route. The dispatching of the evening mail was my most important assignment, and being a particularly busy department, I often had to stay and work for unpaid overtime. It was my job to collect the signed letters from the various officers' 'out' trays, duplicate them, put them in envelopes, stamp and record them. There was also the loathsome job of parcelling huge ledgers but at least I had my own petty cash box to deal with such matters. This had its advantages, as my wage was only twenty-five shillings a week and the petty cash book had to be presented for checking and signing only on Monday mornings!

The boss of this department told me when I left that I was the best office boy he had ever had so when I applied to be taken on for a second spell I received promotion. This time they made me a proper clerk with my own desk to sit at and a wage of fifty shillings a week. The new office boy was now at my disposal but I would willingly have changed jobs with him. During my spell as office boy I was, not unnaturally, spending many evenings with a girlfriend. As so often happens, you are held late on the day your appointment is particularly pressing. On one such occasion I had to ring a friend and ask him to contact my boss with the urgent news that there was a special Home Guard gathering. There was no danger of

Tom Masson, F.B. Rees and Bob in the Mounted Home Guard Squadron

this little white lie being exposed as I belonged to one of the most exclusive units, the Home Guard Mounted Division.

As I was approaching call-up age I left the office job and joined the War Agriculture Department. This time it was manual work. I joined a four-man crew whose work was land drainage. With all the jobs being in rural situations I bought a bike, or more precisely was bought one by my mother, and set off early each morning with sandwiches and a flask of tea. Sometimes the work entailed cleaning out ditches to aid drainage or digging trenches of various lengths and laying clay pipes. It was a bit demoralising to see great stretches ahead that had to be excavated to a depth of around two feet. With today's machinery it is a simple task but our only tools were a pickaxe and shovel.

The work was paid by the hour and was well earned. We were given a portable shelter to which we retired if the weather was too bad for work. My contribution was not always as valuable as it might have been. On several days I chose not to work and the foreman used to call round with my money if I was absent on pay-day. This uncertain time was notable for two happenings in my life. The first was joyous as I met the girl who was to become my wife and the other was the unpleasant task of volunteering for the services.

Several of the racing fraternity had joined the Inniskilling Dragoon Guards, so after my eighteenth birthday I went with Don and my mother to the recruitment office in the Queen's Road close to Brighton Station.

The idea was for me to enlist and then stay in Brighton for lunch. To my surprise there were no vacancies in the 'Skins', as they were known. It was a disappointment, not because I was anxious to go to war with them, but because their dress uniform included very smart green trousers. No doubt I had a stroke of luck. The regiment was switched to tanks and suffered heavy losses in Italy.

Rather than being shunted into any arm of the services I decided to pay a visit to Mr Bradshaw, the headmaster at my last school and a very likeable man. Without hesitation he advised me to volunteer for Air Crew in the RAF. The very next day I returned to Brighton and signed on the dotted line. This was in September 1942 and then I was called before a selection board in Oxford and accepted even though I was shown a model of a Spitfire and was not able to tell them what it was. I received a button with the letters RAFVR that, surprise, surprise, went in a buttonhole. The identification was important, as most people did not take kindly to healthy individuals out of uniform. The VR, standing for Volunteer Reserve, denoted recruits awaiting call-up for training as pilots, navigators or gunners.

It saved me embarrassment, or worse, when a drunken Canadian soldier picked on me for not being in uniform. He was one of the First Division of Canadians who were under canvas on Lewes Downs. Many in this division were released prisoners who were awarded freedom if volunteering. Little did they know that prison would have been a better option. These brave men made up the company that took part in the ill-fated Dieppe raid. On the days following that raid the majority of the Canadians who visited local pubs were not to do so again. It was a very sad occasion, but so were most days during the six years of war.

Prior to volunteering, I had been a member of the Home Guard Mounted Squadron. Anyone who could ride was welcome to the squadron and it signified a return to the saddle of the brothers Fred and Bill Rees. It was like riding a bike – once you've learnt you never forget. The squadron's main exercise was to battle against the foot soldiers on the Lewes Downs. It turned out to be farcical, with the foot brigade refusing to play dead when we said 'Bang.' Likewise there were no loose horses. Was it this band of merry men that changed Hitler's mind about invading?

At around this time it was a girl walking up St Anne's Hill in Lewes during her lunch break that took my eye. I knew who she was and also knew her father, who had brought his family up from Devon to open a

Marian at 16

butcher's shop. Her father, Frank Richards, had been befriended by my father when first venturing into our local. A Home Guard Dance was due to take place, which seemed a good chance to make acquaintance.

My first move was to visit the local and ask if I might take his daughter to the dance. 'Which daughter?' asked father Frank. Marian was the second of four daughters, and he said it was fine by him and he would ask her. The following night he told me that she was already going to the dance with somebody else. That was good enough for me and the first job was to have my ill-fitting Home Guard tunic tailored. Marian was going with a boy I knew vaguely, so I made my move early with an immediate invitation to dance. We danced most of the evening, but I didn't chance my luck and she left with the boy who had taken her.

She knew who I was and had agreed to see me the following week. Our first date was on 19 December 1942 and we have been together ever since. We decided we would get engaged providing we both felt the same way when I was demobbed. My release from the RAF came in early December 1946 and I had written to her on almost every day of my service. Within a very short time of becoming a civilian again, I went

Richards-Butchers, a true prediction!

with Don and my mother to buy a ring and the deed was done with both families sealing the occasion over a drink. Huge letters, reading downwards on the corner stones of the shop, spelled out RICHARDS – BUTCHERS so presumably it was meant to be. I tipped plenty of winners in the *Daily Mirror* but Marian was, without a doubt, the best winner of all.

In early spring I received the call-up letter and I shall never forget leaving our house with just the bare essentials, they being a toothbrush and washing items. My spongebag did not include a razor because I was not yet having to shave – a luxury that was to be ended pretty quickly.

Another local lad, Geoff Baird, was called up at the same time so we travelled together and reported for duty at Lord's Cricket Ground. With formalities completed we were marched to the Blue Star Garage in St John's Wood to be kitted out. The garage had, of course, been requisitioned for that purpose. The next step was a march to a huge block of flats at Abbey Wood, a venue made famous years later by the Beatles. There were hundreds of recruits and we were given cards and had to clock in and out. It was very uncomfortable and our mediocre meals were

The unhappy one. (Extreme left)

served in the underground garage belonging to the flats. With a huge crowd of virile teenagers it was necessary to lower their natural desires and this was done by putting copious amounts of bromide in the tea urns. With inoculations, medicals and other details complete, we were sent to various units to begin our training. It was goodbye to life's little luxuries, even though there were few available at that time.

It has occurred to me that I never had a normal childhood. From around 11 or 12 years of age it was school and horses, with the latter a priority, and then the RAF. On leaving the Service I started work with the *Mirror* after just a couple weeks' breathing space.

14

HAPPY, HAPPY DAYS

I am now going back to the time before joining the RAF. My ambition to be a jockey was not shared by my family; in fact they tried hard to dissuade me. I was anxious to start when I was fifteen, and there was no minimum age then, but I knew that would be unacceptable. Soon after my sixteenth birthday, I made real efforts to get approval from my mother and Don. Many will think it should have been my decision but I had respect for my family and would have been unhappy without their blessing. Although I was very light there was no question of me riding on the flat as I intended to start as a amateur. There was talk of me being made a Member of Lingfield Park which would have allowed me to ride in a forthcoming flat race for amateurs but I heard no more of that.

Mother was uneasy about the whole matter and suggested I write to Don who, by then, was in the Army. He knew very well that I had the ability but it was the uncertainty that they were against and 'I don't want my little boy to get hurt' was no doubt Mother's reason, although she didn't actually say that. The letter to Don set out all the positive reasons why I should ride in public and he had no negatives that carried any weight. I eagerly awaited his reply, which came sooner than expected. He rang home the day he received my letter, and my mother answered and said Don wanted to speak to me.

I honestly did not know what the answer would be, but Don played the game and came straight to the point. The answer was 'Yes', with a couple of conditions – start as an amateur and ride only over hurdles. I abided by his conditions as I intended to start as an amateur and would probably not have had much to ride in steeplechases as several in the yard were owned by amateur riders for their own pleasure.

Most of my time was spent in Tom Masson's stable; he had been keen for me to start for some time and I only had to say the word and he would give me my first ride in public. He was true to his word, but more

Guy takes a turn at handing over the Trophy

about that later. It is my happy time with Masson that I want to recall. He left his wife and two daughters soon after moving to Lewes and treated me as if I was a son. It was years later that he really had a son, Michael, who also trained, but sadly died before reaching middle age. Each day was something to look forward to and as an octogenarian it has even more significance now. I would ride out the two lots either side of breakfast and probably engage in other activities after that.

A horse named Loch Royal arrived in the yard with the tag that he would refuse to go near the gallops or simply plant himself anywhere. This is what Masson relished. Before setting up as a trainer, he had schooled and ridden the show jumpers belonging to the famous circus owner Bertram Mills. Masson walked beside me as I rode Loch Royal onto the Downs that first morning. It was less than a hundred yards before the horse planted himself. I was armed with a thin whip and was told to 'give him just a couple on each side'. The horse spun round in circles and then lay down. On remounting, Loch Royal walked on straight away and on reaching the beginning of the gallop we hacked off and there was never any more trouble. The whip did hurt him and it was a treatment that I would not have undertaken in later years.

Frank Hill has the Trophy he was so keen to win

We had plenty of fun breaking in youngsters and one day he decided to do it in what he described as 'the quick way'. It was a chestnut colt by King Salmon named Good Turn. It needed a call to my dear friend Michael Rees to discover the name of the animal and he remembered because he witnessed the rodeo show that was to follow. Good Turn had been having a 'key bit' in his mouth for some time. The 'key bit' had three pieces of metal hanging from the bit and horses played with these as a means of softening their mouths. The colt had not had any other pieces of equipment on apart from a roller which was a pad held on by a girth and had rings through which the driving rein could be threaded. There was no fuss when a saddle was put on him, so we went on to the Downs where Masson gave him a few turns on the lunging rein. Soon the fun was to start. I was given a leg up and he gave an almighty fly-leap followed by a dart in a different direction, which was enough to sever the partnership. Me on the ground was nothing to worry about, but the colt had got one leg over the lunge. What is more he got his head straight which means his head, tail and the holder of the lunge were in a straight line. This combination means that the horse is in control and Masson had to let go.

Alan Aylett wins the Plumpton Trophy

It was some hours before Good Turn was captured and he was frightened by the experience. The following day he did not want a lot to do with humans. After a few days' rest, Masson took the colt to the barn in which there was a good covering of straw. The next step was to employ one of Masson's gadgets. There were special boots on each of the colt's legs and they also had rings attached. Through these was threaded a rope in such a way that Masson was able to collapse his victim's four legs and get him in a prone position. Eventually it was my job to sit on him while he was collapsed. He was allowed partially up a few times before the session ended.

The next day, the double gates to the yard were closed as a precaution. The colt was saddled in his box and before I got on him, Masson used a twitch – a looped cord on a pole put on his upper lip and tightened by twisting. Once the colt was in the doorway, the twitch was removed and he shot out at some pace. His antics made 'Bucking Broncos' look an easy ride. He really went through his repertoire and I never budged or looked like falling off. The reason was simple. I was literally fixed on. Masson had a contraption that was made up of a straight wooden pole about eighteen inches long with a girth attached. The pole was placed across my knees and tightened by the girth. It certainly worked, but I'm not sure what would happen if a horse fell over! The most uncomfortable moment was when he rubbed me against a wall. The colt did eventually reach the racecourse but did not enjoy any success.

Cuban Cabby was another inmate that needed further education. He showed no respect for his fences and fell a few times. Frenchie Nicholson experienced one of his falls and, not surprisingly, did not want to ride him again. This opened the way for Masson to employ another of his 'tricks of the trade' which was used and probably still is, by the show jumping profession. He struck a bet of a 'tenner' with Nicholson that Cuban Cabby would complete the course in his next race at Folkestone.

With immediate effect, Masson gathered the materials for the special fence he was to build on a quiet part of the Downs. Two sturdy poles fixed firmly in the ground was the main structure and in between them was a fence consisting of piles of gorse about two or three feet high. This small obstacle was of no consequence, but what lurked behind certainly was. A sturdy length of pole was controlled by the pulley attached to the two outside poles. Fred Ensten, now departed, was a tough, no nonsense horseman who was to ride Cuban Cabby in his forthcoming race. Naturally he was to ride Cuban Cabby over the pulley obstacle. No doubt most readers will have guessed the next stage by now. Yes, the pole was raised behind the gorse fence as the horse took off. It needed an experienced handler to raise the pole at the right moment and Masson was just that man. Cuban Cabby crossed the fence many times and was made to land on his nose or worse. The outcome was a clear round at Folkestone and Masson's winnings of a 'tenner' were handed straight to Fred Ensten, and that amounted to twice his riding fee at that time.

Mrs Lambton, wife of the legendary Hon. George, and mother of the one-time trainer Teddy, seemed to be a lady with connecting links to the Masson yard in the early days. I think this must have been due to John Hislop and his friendship with the Lambtons. Big Ben, an appropriately tall chaser owned by Mrs Lambton, won a series of low class races ridden by John Hislop and was notorious for making a jumping mistake nearly every time he ran. He would hit a fence halfway up but was strong enough to remain on his feet.

At home he was ridden by 'Slim Jim' Gatrell, who was challenging Methuselah for age. Big Ben was equipped with a chain bit and went off

Gina Elliott receives the Don Butchers Trophy

trotting and hacking on his own. One day he turned up at the schooling ground just as a couple had been dispatched to school over five fences. Completely out of the blue, Tom Masson told me to 'jump on Big Ben and follow the other two'. I was probably aged fifteen and a featherweight. It crossed my mind that if the horse hit a fence really hard I would fly between his ears and land a long way ahead of him. When we set off the old horse didn't pull as he could and crossed the five fences without touching a twig. I never once changed my hands and simply enjoyed flying through the air with the greatest of ease just like the man on the flying trapeze. For any younger readers, 'The Man on the Flying Trapeze' was the title of a popular song, probably before I started school or even before I was born. It was possible to school two miles over fences without going over the same ground but this facility was seldom used mainly because it included a 'water-jump' but instead of water there were three lengths of corrugated iron sheets. You can imagine the clatter and potential danger.

The next animal from Mrs Lambton was an unnamed filly known as Angelus, the name of her dam. In those days they were allowed to race as such. I knew nothing about her, why she came or for what reason. After two lots had been out, I was told to get on this filly and trot up to the stands on the racecourse and walk her back home. My suspicions were aroused because she was tacked up with drawing reins. These went through the rings of the bit and back to the girth. The main purpose of drawing reins was to keep an animal's head in the right position, but they could be dangerous if used clumsily. An animal wanting to resist them had only one choice and that was to rear. Rearing often leads to falling over backwards, a danger to man and beast. There was no trouble for two or three furlongs as we trotted towards the stands. Then, without any warning, she stopped dead and that was me on the deck in a flash. The filly set off back to the yard while I was cursing at having to walk back. Before I had gone very far, the governor, as I called Tom Masson, pulled up in his car. 'I expected that to happen,' said he, with a grin.

The third time that Mrs Lambton came into the equation was by far the most exciting for me. The *Racing Calendar* was eagerly awaited by every trainer. It arrived by post from Weatherbys on Friday morning, but Tom Masson had one of the sorting staff take it to him on Thursday evenings. Well done, Charlie Cox!

I was in the yard on one of those evening when the governor called me up to his flat. He showed me an advert in the *Calendar* offering for sale two horses belonging to Mrs Lambton and the price was £400, not too bad even in 1940. He must have had his card marked because he said, 'I want the grey one', which was Milk Bar. They duly arrived and my whole attention focused on Milk Bar to the extent that I can't even remember the name of the other one. The grey was by Miracle out of Take a Glass, which made him a half-brother to Boozer's Gloom who is mentioned elsewhere in this book.

Milk Bar was a really good sort and I was to be his regular partner at exercise. It was immediately evident that he was a bit of a playboy. We were walking up the chalk road onto the Downs on the very first morning when he skipped aside and put in the most powerful jump and a kick. Being unprepared, I slid down his shoulder and landed on my feet. His powerful jump and a kick became a daily occurrence. As most of the lads were getting on in years – the younger ones were in the forces – they did not relish the idea of riding Milk Bar and that suited me. He was a lovely horse to sit on and a pleasure to ride in his work. His daily antic could be performed at any time, on the way out or on the way back or even

On Milk Bar after a trial on Lewes racecourse

approaching the work ground. It was a relief if he did it early on but he never got rid of me again, although he had me hanging off him a few times.

Two unplaced efforts on the flat was his record when he joined the Masson string, but he worked so well that it was decided to stage a trial on Lewes racecourse over a mile. He was always going better than his three rivals and I let him coast home many lengths ahead of the rest. With a couple of warm-up races under his belt he was sent to Worcester and, ridden by Michael Beary, was a comfortable winner. His opening price was 5/2 but was backed down to 11/10. He later finished second to Monsieur Pons at Nottingham and the pair of them were due to clash in a hurdle race over the course in the not too distant future.

I schooled and rode Milk Bar in his first two races over hurdles and I don't think anyone else even sat on him while I was there. Tom Masson sold a half-share to the gambler Gil Bennet, and later the grey was sold to John Hislop. When National Hunt racing ceased in this country, Milk Bar was sent to Ireland and had wins there before returning here for more success. Milk Bar won on the flat and over hurdles and fences. He was also ante-post favourite for a wartime Champion Hurdle that was subsequently abandoned.

I was reminded of Milk Bar's playfulness by an eightieth birthday card that pictured a horse behaving in the same manner. Inside was a verse by Mary Lascelles, which I take the liberty of reproducing.

WHOA now my beauty, the sun has dried the tan,
The Guv might keep us waiting, but we're all within his plan.
We'll work out in a moment, now don't you take a hold,
There's no need to give a buck, we know you're strong and bold.
You'll stretch your legs, feel the wind brush your side,
So just settle down and give me a quieter ride.

15

AT LAST

Tom Masson is in the frame again and I make no apologies because he played a major part in my teens and also provided some of the happiest years of my life. I trusted him implicitly and that was reciprocated. One day he led the string along the Ditchling road, not far from Plumpton. High above us was Black Cap – a plantation of trees perched at the top of a hill. The ascent was not only long and steep, but the last few yards looked suicidal. To ride to the top was not everyone's idea of fun and Masson told all of the lads it was optional. Their refusal was a sensible choice which left 'muggins' to join the Governor on this mountaineering expedition. It showed either our bonding or my stupidity, but I prefer it to be the former.

We made the climb with the horses straining every muscle. It was scary and I dared not look back. Just one slipped step would have seen horse and rider rolling forever. The final few yards looked impossible, but we made it even if it was bravado. I am not exaggerating when I say it would be almost impossible to walk down without sliding most of the way. Undoubtedly the worst part was knowing that once you had started there was no turning back.

The two best horses that Tom Masson had were Cloncarrig and Persian War. Cloncarrig's target was the 1950 Grand National won by Freebooter, and jockey Bob Turnell was emphatic that Cloncarrig would have won easily but for falling at the penultimate fence. That we will never know. Persian War was a shrewd buy. He won good races, both on the flat and over hurdles, before being sold to Mr Alper for a handsome sum. Persian War went on to win the Champion Hurdle in 1968, 1969 and 1970 before finishing second to Bula the following year. These horses, of course, were running while I was working for the *Daily Mirror*.

Going back to the war years, there were many incidents involving the Governor. He moved into a small farm just outside Lewes, which

At Tom Masson's Barn Stables in Lewes

prevented a call-up and quickly found ways of getting round restrictions. A Canadian soldier became an acquaintance, and it was not long before a transport vehicle backed into the stable yard and emptied a huge amount of canned food into a loose box. I had some of them and they mostly contained a whole meal in one tin. It was while I was with him that he pulled off another stroke of skulduggery. There was a handsome antique corner cupboard on viewing day before an auction to which he had taken a liking. A cupboard without a key is a bit of a nuisance, a fact that was made clear at the auction. The cupboard looked well in his flat and it came as no surprise that Masson found the key in his pocket! It must have saved the old rascal a few quid.

The opposite sex was another of his enjoyments. Masson's tall, upright figure, streaks of grey in his well-groomed hair and a bow tie certainly gave him a distinguished presence as he stood at the entrance of his yard. He had a smile and a wink for all of the young ladies on their way to work. They were in no danger, but not so the pretty nurse who tended him in hospital after a car accident. He showed his appreciation by inviting her to stay for the weekend to see the horses. The only thing the poor girl saw was the solitary bedroom in his flat. It was a hasty exit with no thanks necessary!

All who knew Tom Masson were aware of his liking for the girls and other dubious antics, but it was hard not to be taken in by his charm. In those early war years we used to gather in the Pelham Arms, where regular visitors were the masters of the Tooting Bec school, which was evacuated to the school I attended. A couple of the masters liked the town so much that they never returned to London. The art master, Jack Elvin, painted objects that were in short supply, and he did one for each year of the war and they were hung in our 'local'. Stockings, onions and toilet rolls are three that I recall and I would like to know where they are now. Jack also did portraits in oils of Don and me in racing silks.

Darts were the main pastime in the pub, and Masson and I were partners. I wish I could have been as successful as a jockey as our partnership was at darts. Although a lot of my time was spent in the pub, I was not a drinker. Peppermint and water was my tipple and a couple of those lasted a long time. They were lovely days for me, despite the war: good company in the evening and a sound night's sleep before

Marian ready for school

running to the stables for more enjoyment. Masson also taught me to drive a car when I was sixteen, and in those days eligible for a Provisional Licence. There was no driving test then, and as a holder of that licence I did not have to be tested when testing was eventually introduced.

When racing was stopped, my life changed. My girlfriend, Marian, was on the scene and I had volunteered for the RAF. We did, however, have enough time together to think it was for keeps. Looking back and realising that I was eighteen and Marian not yet seventeen, it is something of a miracle we are still together.

Prior to these events, Tom Masson was true to his word and quickly arranged for me to have my first ride in public. I had just turned sixteen, and my first ride was to be Lutin III at Nottingham, and a few days later the same horse at Manchester. There were a few hairy moments before my dream became reality. In those days, horses travelled long distances by rail and the horseboxes were dirty and far from comfortable. We took three horses on this trek, the other pair being Tribune and Makina. I was accompanied by Mick Barry, a jovial Irishman who had ridden himself and was well versed in everything equine. We loaded up in the goods yard at Lewes Station and hooked onto a steam engine that made a round-the-world trip to London, and then hooked onto another train going north.

Having reached Peterborough by a roundabout route, we were informed that the horse-box would be coupled on to a later train. We had ample time to make the horses comfortable and have a high tea in the town. On returning to the station our horse-box and horses had disappeared. We discovered that the box had been coupled to an earlier train, forcing us to follow on the next passenger train. Slowly we crept into Grantham Station and there we remained for some little while. It transpired that a porter, complete with oil-lamp, in the black-out was questioning each compartment as to whether anyone had lost three horses. We were relieved to hear that they had arrived safely at the racecourse siding in Nottingham. After a discussion with the guard, it was decided that we should travel in his compartment and he would halt the train in the racecourse siding. His help was appreciated but when detrained we still had the task of getting three horses and all the luggage across to the racecourse stables, and that after we had actually found them in the pitch dark.

Not only was it late and dark, but there were only two of us to cope with three horses. Mick rightly decided that it was important to get the horses settled down in comfort as quickly as possible. With this in mind, we saddled two of the horses and threw some of the loose luggage over the back of the third horse, Tribune. As Makina was liable to kick anything within reach she was ridden on her own while I jumped on Lutin III and led the 'pack' horse. We rode them the few hundred yards to the stables and after putting them to bed returned with a hand-cart to collect our hamper, fodder and various oddments in the way of luggage for our several days away. That was the first and last time I rode a horse in the black of night!

This journey certainly provided an adventurous start to my eagerly awaited trip, but the accommodation provided on the course was not in the slightest way 'Ritzy'. It was, in fact, a bit of a shock when I went to my room to find it crowded with beds and bodies. This particular building has long since been modernised, I'm pleased to say, but on the occasion of my first visit it was a case of climbing into bed with three complete strangers. Luckily, there was a free day before our horses were due to run. This was November 1940, and not only did Mother worry about me riding, but she was not at all relaxed about me going to major cities, Nottingham and Manchester, with bombing raids taking place.

When we moved on from Nottingham to Manchester, there was another first-time experience. The three horses had to be got from the station to the racecourse at Castle Irwell. Mick grabbed a body at the station to lead one of the horses and we set off on a march through the streets of the city. The walk seemed to go on forever and it was certainly a good few miles. People must have thought a circus was in town. I think Mick found someone with transport to convey the luggage.

For Mother's peace of mind, it was arranged that I would stay in a Manchester suburb with Harry 'Spitty' McLean. He was the man who had worked the commissions on And How and Cream Lace but who came unstuck on Valentine's Rose.

I can't remember a thing about the return trip to Lewes, but going back to Nottingham, I had an anxious time, which may well have prevented me riding at all. Charlie Stalker had been Don's valet and it was he who attended to my needs. All valets have an ample supply of breeches and boots for those who have yet to buy their own. No trouble with the breeches, even if they were a little big for my small frame. The boots, however, posed a different problem. I tried pair after pair and none would pull over my high insteps. There were no zipped boots in those days. Dear old Charlie was puffing and blowing, and then a beam came over his face. He delved into his large hamper, throwing contents to the side, and produced an enormous pair of boots. They belonged to the tall ex-jockey Bruce Hobbs, who at the age of seventeen won the Grand National on Battleship. For all I know he may have worn those boots then, but my main concern was being able to get them on. They passed over my instep but were several sizes too big. They became my 'property', but like breeches and colours were hardly elegant.

Tom Masson did not attend the meetings but told me Lutin III would not be fit and to have a quiet run round and enjoy myself. There was a big field of twenty-seven as was usual with few meetings over which to spread the load, and the race was uneventful. It was a thrill at sixteen to be in the line-up with jockeys like Nicholson, Rimell and Ron Smyth. Incidentally, the race that gave me my first ride provided the first winner for my friend Tony Smyth, a brother to Ron, and sons of Herbert 'Nat' Smyth, who owned and trained the winner, Steel Blade. I must also mention that Piggott rode in the race: not Lester, but his father Keith who later trained Ayala to pip Carrickbeg in the Grand National.

In the Manchester race there were only fifteen runners and after making the running for a mile Lutin III faded. I have two memories of that day. As I walked from the weighing room to the parade ring, I was joined by Wing Commander Peter Vaux, of the brewery family, one of the top amateurs of his day. He chatted away and was kindness itself to a little lad amongst men. The other memory was of seeing George Owen, riding Horatio, fall when he was upsides of me. I'm sure I'm right in saying his injury that day proved serious enough to end his riding career. He became a top trainer and the highlight was winning the Grand National with Russian Hero.

The mention of the 1949 winner reminds me that I was staying in the same hotel as his jockey, Leo McMorrow. On the morning of the big race, he sat in the lounge reading a book and looking as contented as a man enjoying a well-earned holiday.

I conclude this chapter by disclosing Tom Masson's crowning moment. He was a Royalist and after entertaining the Queen in his small but charming abode, he was fussy who sat in the chair she had occupied. I trust the Governor did not allow Her Majesty to leave in the condition that was par for the course in my later association!

16

DODGY CUSTOMERS

With my couple of rides on Lutin III, seemingly a psychological victory gained, I had no intention of asking permission again. At this time, Tony Grantham was attached to the Masson stable and like me was an amateur.

There was a horse in the yard called Irish Stew who had won the Great Metropolitan Handicap at Epsom, when trained by George Beeby and ridden by Peter Maher. That was when the race was run over two and a quarter miles. It started at the winning post with the runners racing towards Tattenham Corner and zigzagging across the Downs. In those days the 'Great Met' was part of a popular double with the City and Suburban Handicap being run over one and a quarter miles. They were notable events at the time, but now they have faded into insignificance with the 'Great Met' reduced to one and a half miles in distance and run over the Derby course. A pity because the old race was a spectacle but such happenings have been overtaken by safety regulations.

Back to Irish Stew. When he arrived to be trained by Tom Masson we discovered a peculiar trait. It was not possible to mount or dismount Irish Stew without somebody holding his head. If you tried to jump on him unaided he would run round in circles or scoot away in a panic. Once aboard he would still scoot away, as if chased by the devil, if you as much as turned your head. There was nothing vicious about the animal but the job of exercising him each day was shared by Tony Grantham and me. When the time came for Irish Stew to race both Tony and I were hoping for the mount. The luck was mine, and I partnered him in all his races. He showed promise in his earlier races, but I knew him to be totally unpredictable and any backers he had were certainly courageous.

There was always a selling race on the card, which meant the winner was auctioned after the race. It was in these low class events that Irish Stew ran. I rode him a few times before he won, and on one of the occasions there were specific instructions from the trainer. I was to finish second or third, but on no account was I to win. It transpired that the owner, Barbara Jameson of the Irish whisky firm, had given Tom Masson the cash to have £100 each way on the horse. Ready money must have been short, so instead of £100 each way, the £200 was put on the Tote for a place. This meant the trainer had the £100 win money plus the Tote return for a place, which paid two shillings and ninepence to a two shillings stake. The trainer won £139 and ten shillings and the owner lost £60 and ten shillings.

I have said earlier that Tom Masson and I trusted each other, so I was flattered at the task given to a teenager with only a few rides under his belt. It was a tight finish to the Pyecombe Selling Hurdle on 15 February 1941. Bright Boy beat Overseas by a length with Irish Stew a head further away and only a length away was the fourth horse, with the rest close behind.

Chaseform gave Irish Stew a squiggle, signifying he was unreliable, with the comment: 'improved halfway, ran well.' The trainer was pleased with my performance and sent me to a country tailor to have a pair of jodhpurs made. I found it quite exciting even though I probably missed the chance of riding my first winner. One of the stewards, Commander Courage of the brewery firm, said they did not call me in because of my inexperience. A week later Irish Stew ran in an even lower class selling race at Plumpton and started 3/1 on. There were only six runners and going down the hill on the second circuit a horse called Landed had opened a lead of some twenty lengths. Irish Stew liked to do things his way, so it was with the most gentle persuasion that I closed the gap. Slowly but surely the ground was made up and we jumped the last hurdle alongside Landed and won by four lengths.

The same steward remarked: 'A bit better this time, Butchers,' but it was not as easy as it looked. Three teenagers rode winners that day. The others were John Grantham, who was killed in the war, and Lionel Vick who broke his back and spent the rest of his days in a wheelchair. John was the brother of my pal Tony.

The mention of being sent to have jodhpurs made reminds me of an old tailor in Lewes by the name of Mr Warner. His shop went under the title of A Breeches Maker and the family, including me, had used his services on numerous occasions. Even though there were war-time restrictions I came in possession of a length of real cavalry twill, how, I know not; but I went to Mr. Warner and asked him to make me a pair of trousers as I had jodhpurs. He was very reluctant to make such a

Riding Irish Stew, on left, at Plumpton when just turned 16

garment and it needed a lot of persuasion before he agreed. When I collected the trousers and tried them on I discovered that it was a compromised situation with the tailor making them with a 'riding seat', that being with a baggy bottom. That was not the style a teenager needed to create an impression.

Being an amateur I was not allowed to receive any money presents, but a few days later Miss Jameson rang from Ireland to ask if I would like a suitably inscribed cigarette case, even though I was only sixteen and didn't smoke, or £10 with which to buy a memento. I elected to take the cash but it never reached me. Perhaps it got lost in the post! The trainer introduced me as 'your unpaid jockey' when the lady came over to see her horse run in a later race at Cheltenham. Some months later, but only through my uncle, Reg, who was racing secretary to Tom Masson, I got the tenner. No doubt it went on Miss Jameson's account in a disguised form.

There are lots of things that, in hindsight, I should have done differently. No doubt Irish Stew was having me on. I rode him in a pretty decent 'seller' at Cheltenham and was in contention approaching the last hurdle. I had it on my mind that he would not respond to any pressure and as none was forthcoming he was only too ready to call it a day. It is quite likely that he would have done a bit more if I had got after him.

A horse named Cornet Jumbo was the opposite. I used to see him on the Downs in a chain bit and taking charge of things with boundless enthusiasm. I was asked to ride him at Plumpton and he was well named, big as an elephant and as it turned out just as slow. It was when the first hurdle was halfway down the hill and approached at breakneck speed. Even though there was the usual large field of mostly moderate animals Cornet Jumbo was almost tailed off when we reached the first flight. I pulled him up before half-way, which didn't take much doing, for fear of being lapped!

George Todd was a great man for giving youngsters a chance and while still with Masson, he gave me the ride on Peace Disturber at Cheltenham. He ran well enough and I got the ride on him later over the same course. The old horse was well fancied in a race with a stack of runners. He couldn't do anything quickly which meant you needed a clear run. I found myself on the inside and needing to get a bit nearer the leaders. A gap appeared and as I tried to take it I received a warning. It came from the many times champion jockey Gerry Wilson, 'Stay where you are,' was enough for me to obey and it probably cost me the race. When we managed to get a run it was a bit too late; even though

Peace Disturber ran on up the hill to be third, he was beaten by a head and half a length. I told George Todd that I should have won. A few days later he wrote to me saying not to blame myself as he took a cupful of pus from the horse's foot that evening. Very nice of the trainer, but I still think I should have won.

Lutin III, the bonny little horse who gave me my first ride, was to give me several more. He ran at Taunton on Boxing Day and with the horse and Mick Barry we travelled down on Christmas Day. Mick had found us lodgings for the night and when we arrived the landlady said we probably needed a hot meal after our journey. Her very nice thought was better than the meal, which was beans on toast. We ate them and then went to the Castle Hotel for the proper Christmas fare.

It was the tough and experienced champion, Gerry Wilson, who probably cost me another win at Worcester. Again, I was stuck on the inside following Gerry on Accept. He gave me enough room to see each hurdle and then moved back hard on the rails. The wily old bird slipped me approaching the final bend and finished up beating me by six lengths. I had been offered the mount on Peace Disturber in this race. He fell and no doubt stood off too far as he so often did. Don't let anyone tell you that experience is not an almighty asset. Gerry Wilson knew all the tricks and I was beginning to learn them the hard way. When not riding, Gerry was a lovely man. On his retirement, he became landlord of the Blue Boar at Wantage. In later years, I wrote an article about the brilliant jumping jockey, Bryan Marshall. During our conversation I mentioned how he used to hug the rails and never seemed to get into trouble. 'If you wait long enough a gap always appears,' was his answer but it needs a champion with confidence and patience to execute such tactics.

Previously Lutin III had given me an exciting ride when third to Interlaken in a good three miles hurdle race at Cheltenham, followed by an easy win at Plumpton. These runs entitled him to win at Worcester, so it was a huge disappointment for me to be second. When Lutin III won the last race of the day at Plumpton in March 1941, it signalled the end of racing at the course for the duration of the war. That was a bitter blow to me. The race over three miles was a strange affair with just four runners. The Chaseform comment said, 'All four runners raced level for over two miles.' This formation continued until the penultimate hurdle when I went on for a comfortable win.

Prior to the race whilst waiting to be called out I was sitting between Ron Smyth and Danny Morgan as the three of us had Charlie Stalker as our valet. They were riding in the same race and it was Ron who said, 'You'll win, won't you?' followed by, 'What do you know about the other fellow?' The other fellow was Mr Alec Hunter, riding Blue Pencil. I didn't know much about him but was empathetic that my horse would win. So empathetic was I that I met Mother on the way to the paddock and asked her to put ten shillings on the Tote for me, a good bet for a teenager who was not earning a penny! At the start, which for three-mile races at Plumpton an elastic rope was used, there was little competition for the inside position so I made sure it was mine. It must have saved me lengths during the race, but I never did ask Ron Smyth if he and Danny had won a few quid on Lutin III.

On that day I had three rides but Mother thought I had two, and so did I, until about ten o'clock the evening before. As I was leaving the local pub, Tom Masson said, 'Get to Plumpton early because you ride in the first race.' I knew the first race was a steeplechase and it was to be my first ride over the bigger obstacles. Arriving at the course early was the problem as my mother would be driving and she would be mental if she knew I was riding a horse named Birnam in a steeplechase. Once again our local landlord, Guy, came to the rescue. He didn't drive and would have been coming in our car anyway so he asked my mother if she would join him and other friends for lunch at the course which meant getting there early. Problem solved until just before the first race when she got a shock to see my name in the frame. She was in a state as I came out of the weighing room but at least she had only a few minutes to worry about it, instead of all night.

The first race was an Optional Selling Chase which meant horses carried weights according to the price they could be auctioned for after the event. The prices ranged from fifty guineas, or if the horse was not to be auctioned it carried twelve stone. Birnam was in the lowest category and had ten stone minus my five-pound claim. Two of the other runners were classy animals. Sable Marten had carried 12st 7lb in a handicap and finished second while prior to that he had won an Optional Selling Chase at Cheltenham with two Gold Cup winners behind him. They were Red Rower and Roman Hackle. In this re-match, Sable Marten was the 2/5 favourite with Roman Hackle at 11/4. It was less than a year earlier that Roman Hackle had won the Gold Cup so he was a big attraction for the Plumpton crowd. Could you imagine Best Mate having been risked at Plumpton? Just twelve days later he failed to follow up his 1940 win.

Birnam gave me a lovely ride as we bowled along in front and jumping beautifully. As we ran down the hill on the second circuit with that notorious fence facing us, Frenchie Nicholson on Sable Marten and Evan Williams on Roman Hackle came either side of me and the three of us flew the fence together. It is a deceptive fence on the take-off side and there is a drop on the landing side. Birnam pecked on landing and I had gone almost to the buckle-end of the reins only for him to recover in a flash. Nearly every jockey will know the feeling as you exit 'out of the back door'.

Sable Marten met Roman Hackle on the same terms as at Cheltenham. The bookmakers must have had a good win with an odds-on chance of being beaten. Birnam started at 100/8, whereas his chances of winning were nearer 1000/1. As I made my way back across the course my dear old Uncle Jo wanted to fuss over me, but all I wanted to do was to get back as quickly as possible to ride in the next race. There were no vehicles running around to give fallen jockeys a lift back in those days.

Talking of vehicles reminds me of the taxi that left the centre of the Plumpton course and was driven across the track at the station exit. That exit had not been closed, with a simple rope in those days before plastic rails, and the taxi was on the track as the runners rounded the bend. Luckily, there were only five runners and four of them swerved either in front or behind the car but Sean Magee, on Roman Chief, had no choice and attempted to jump the obstacle. Roman Chief was badly injured and had to be destroyed. I remember seeing a very shocked taxi-driver sitting on a chair outside the Stewards' room. The enquiry found that nobody was to blame. How about the person who should have closed that exit?

17

KISS AND MAKE UP

Clos du Roi was a useful selling plater owned by Mr Warwick Thompson, of the then powerful bookmaking business. There was a time when he was being aimed at a selling race at Nottingham. It was always a good excuse to say a change of jockey was the reason for any improvement and the stewards were not so vigilant in those days. They were frequently depicted as retired Army Officers who officiated mainly for the free lunch and copious amounts of port.

Among the so-called preparatory races was one at Southwell. I played truant from the Commercial College, having travelled up to Newark by train the previous evening. I stayed in the Lamb Hotel and was up early the next morning as Clos du Roi needed a pipe-opener. Having been told that the racecourse was near Newark, it came as a shock to learn that near meant a few miles. It must have been my lucky day as a milkman offered to take me to the course. The race was uneventful, and we finished sixth or seventh as requested but what stuck in my in my mind were the hurdles. I walked the course as it was my first visit and discovered that the hurdles were practically upright, and as if knocked in with a pile driver. Perhaps the groundsman was a sadist!

The day for the big gamble at Nottingham arrived. I had travelled up with two horses the previous day armed with an Authority to Act letter signed by Tom Masson. I duly declared Clos du Roi with Matt Feakes riding and my own mount, John Peel, who was in the same race. It was the first race and as I sat waiting, having already weighed out, there was no sign of Tom Masson or Matt Feakes. I had already informed a steward of the situation and had Edgar Taylor changed and ready to be substituted. About twenty minutes before the race in rushed Matt. The owner, trainer and Matt had been involved in a minor accident and the jockey somehow got a lift to the course.

There were twenty-nine runners in the race and I had been told to finish eighth on John Peel. The result was as expected with Clos du Roi winning by four lengths and being returned second favourite at 7/1. How, when and where the money was invested I don't know, but there were happy faces when the trainer and owner arrived. As instructed, I finished eighth on John Peel but then the one thing I can do is count! When asked what I would have done if Matt Feakes had not arrived, facetiously, I replied that Edgar Taylor was standing by and I would have told him to finish ninth! I well remember having a quiet ride round when John Peel made a mistake and me going to the buckle end causing Cyril Mitchell, who was alongside me, to ask if I needed some hay strings! Cyril, the father of trainer Phillip and grandfather of apprentice Jack, had his greatest success when training Attivo to win the Triumph Hurdle at Cheltenham and the Chester Cup for owner Sir Peter O'Sullivan and, of course, the same owner's top-class sprinter, Be Friendly. Sadly, he died before seeing his grandson riding with such promise.

John Peel was to have his turn next in a race at Ludlow. Again there was a big field of twenty-two and he had been backed each-way by his owner, Jack Dennis, an Army officer who enjoyed some fun on a mare called Ergo. My main recollection of that event was not racing over the many roads that crossed the course, but the height of the ferns as we turned into the back straight. I swear they were two feet high on the inside but they did not present a hazard. No doubt I was always a little too easy on horses and with third place seemingly assured I dropped my hands on John Peel and the same Cyril Mitchell, on Carnival Girl, came with a wet sail to pip me for third place. At 10/1 he would have shown a profit but luckily neither trainer nor owner was present. It seems I made a habit of costing people money! These days it would have earned me a long suspension.

That Ludlow meeting was the venue for a sharp and unpleasant experience. The meeting was a long way from Lewes and it meant a stay before and after race day. The army was stationed in the middle of the course and our accommodation, by military invitation, was also there. The evening after my race, I was invited to the Sergeants' Mess and with nothing else to do I duly arrived. At that time I was a teetotaller and knew nothing about drinks so when asked what I would like I said whisky, for some unknown reason. One led to another and another until I felt strange and a little later violently sick. The night seemed never ending and I still had to face the long journey back to Lewes in the horsebox.

On arrival home, I went straight to bed and remained there for two whole days. My mother was at a loss to know the reason and I wasn't going to tell her. It was one evening that I heard my sister Fay telling Mother that she knew the cause. She had met Tony Grantham somewhere and he told her it was whisky, and he knew because he had been with me. That one bad experience turned me off drink; in fact it wasn't until I joined the *Daily Mirror* that I took up the habit. My first drink on visiting Fetter Lane, and inevitably the pub, was a tomato juice, which met with disbelief and the prediction that it would not last. I'm sorry to say they were right but I was able to keep it under control and for the most part enjoyed drinking and still do, albeit less regularly.

By far the most exciting ride for the Masson stable was Milk Bar. This fetching grey was the best horse in the yard at that time. He was 'mine' from the first day he arrived. It was I who survived his antics at exercise, rode him in that important trial for the winning run on the flat at Worcester, and I who schooled him over hurdles. I had not been promised anything and rather suspected that an experienced jockey would ride Milk Bar in his first race over hurdles. It was a moment of joy when the Governor told me I was to ride him at Plumpton. I was also to ride Irish Stew in an earlier race and he was to be my first winner.

A field of twenty-two turned out for the maiden hurdle and there was an early incident. No fewer than five fell at the second hurdle and it was like a battlefield with fallen horses and jockeys strewn all over the place. We were behind this bunch of fallers and I vividly remember Milk Bar threading his way through with absolutely no help from me. I was always travelling well on Milk Bar who was foot perfect throughout. We moved close to the leaders rounding the final bend and without applying any sort of pressure finished seventh. My post race comment to the Governor was 'I think I could have won.'

Before Milk Bar ran again a share had been sold to the former trainer Gil Bennett who was a heavy gambler. It was at Bennett's stable that Don broke his leg schooling. The next outing for Milk Bar was again at Plumpton. This time there were sixteen runners, which included stablemate Orchill. Having just weighed out and given the saddle to the Governor, I was grabbed by Gil Bennett who asked if I was sure I could again drop out Milk Bar followed by the promise to give me a 'tenner' to make sure. I did the job, but am still waiting for the 'tenner'.

It was almost a repeat of his first outing. He was always going well and I was hard against the rails amid a tight group when Matt Feakes, on the

A John Skeaping sketch of my favourite, Milk Bar

fancied Orchill, owned by Gil Bennett, called, 'Let me through.' It was difficult to move out and how Matt squeezed through I don't know. It was all in vain and at the winning post Orchill was behind Milk Bar who finished sixth. My post race comment was similar to the previous one except this time it was 'I'm sure I could have won.' There was, of course, no sign of Gil Bennett. Perhaps he couldn't find a 'tenner' after doing his dough on Orchill. It was at another Plumpton meeting that Milk Bar ran again but this time it was Don Butchers in the saddle. The thinking behind the change was that Don could, hopefully, confirm the positive comments I had made. There was another good field of eighteen and plenty of chances to get cover. Don made it a really good test and took the lead round the last bend and was still in front going towards the last flight. Milk Bar was the sort of horse you could put anywhere. He settled well and would only respond if you picked him up and got serious. Not having been asked a question he dropped himself out but had shown Don enough for him to confirm what I had told connections.

Milk Bar won plenty of races, over both hurdles and fences, and when there was no racing in England he went to be trained in Ireland, but well before this had been bought by John Hislop. This reminds me that John married Barbara Jameson who owned my first winner, Irish Stew, but later had a second marriage. The third run of Milk Bar more or less marked the end of the season and sadly a split between Tom Masson and me. Much later he disliked it when I wrote in the *Daily Mirror* that I thought Freebooter would still have won the Grand National even if Cloncarrig, trained by him, had not fallen at the second to last fence. Everyone makes mistakes and that may have been one of the many I have made in my long existence. His jockey, Bob Turnell, was certain he would have won but there is a very long distance between the penultimate fence and the winning post.

These were very uncertain times and you kind of lived day by day. The time for call-up to the Forces was getting nearer but I volunteered ahead of that. Even so riding was still number one in my life. Don Butchers caused the split with Tom Masson, but in my interest, so he thought. He really didn't want me to be a jockey, but also wanted to let me down lightly. At no time did Don and I fall out. The fact of the matter was that Masson wanted me to turn professional and be the stable jockey the next season. I discussed this with Don who said he had got me a place at Mr J.V. Rank's private yard at Druid's Lodge. Don had ridden a lot of the Rank horses and thought I would get more opportunities there. I think the true reason was that at Masson's yard I would be on too many unfancied horses. A lot of people go on about non-triers, but a lot of those so-called couldn't win in any case.

Despite the split and conflicting views over Cloncarrig, Tom Masson and I were again firm friends for the many years after these incidents, until his tragic death in a car accident. I don't think Don knew how very close was the relationship between Masson and me. He lost his protégé at a crucial stage and neither of us was able to find out if I could have fulfilled the promise he anticipated.

It was coincidence that I was going from the Barn Stables to Druid's Lodge on Salisbury Plain. Way before the war, Mr Rank had his horses at Barn Stables trained by Gwyn Evans who was a bachelor and came to our house for lunch every Sunday. He would always say, 'That was grand,' and my sister and I waited to hear him say it and had to suppress giggles. However, Gwyn was a lovely fellow and moved to Druid's Lodge to train the jumpers while Noel Cannon had the flat horses in another yard. Sadly Gwyn was killed when his car hit a telegraph pole while returning from a race meeting.

Frank Horris, who had been head lad, was the trainer when I arrived at the yard. I had never actually 'done my two' before, but had seen enough to perform these duties automatically. The two horses given to my care were Skoiter and Competition. There was a passage in front of the cage boxes, and Competition stumbled as I led him out into the yard and after I had been given a leg-up he fell over his own feet and trampled all over me as he got up. Not the best start to my first morning at the yard especially as it happened on the road.

Jimmy Doyle, a lightweight jockey on the flat, was somehow getting the rides on the jumpers while the amateur, Harry Applin, was also getting rides. One evening as I laid my rubber down for Frank to put a feed on, I plucked up the courage and asked when I was going to get a ride. The following day he said I could ride Monsieur Pons at Nottingham, but more of that later.

Druid's Lodge was certainly a fabulous training establishment planted on the wide open plain nine miles from Salisbury, and only a few miles by road from Stonehenge. As the crow flies, Stonehenge is no distance at all but the novelty of riding past this pile of stones quickly wore off. At the beginning of the century, John Fallon trained at Druid's Lodge and several horses emerged from this yard to land big gambles. The most notable of these was Hackler's Pride who won the Cambridgeshire in 1903 and again the following year. I feel sure, though, that the flow of winners was at its greatest in the days of Mr Rank. An attractive archway from under which was the staircase to the stable lads' dormitories separated the two well laid out yards, one for the flat horses and the other for the jumpers. My quarters were up those stairs but the dining and recreation rooms were situated away from the stable yards. Unfortunately, mice were unwelcome guests in the dormitories.

Mr Rank's big house, complete with gardens and swimming pool, was within a hundred yards of the stables while the trainer's house and various other cottages were conveniently sited. One of the cottages was occupied by 'old' Sam who drove the private bus. His duties were various. He did the shopping for the dining room, ran a shopping expedition to Salisbury in the afternoons and several times a week drove the lads into town for an evening out. I seldom used this service and was quite content in the recreation room. This helped me to save some of the twenty-five shillings a week I received. My nominated savings were deducted at source by the secretary, for Mr Rank had introduced the admirable scheme by which the lads' savings were subsidised by him and paid out at Christmas. For every shilling saved, Mr Rank added another.

The stable routine was strict, with smartness and cleanliness most essential. The doors of the cage boxes inside the long passages were fitted with brass catches and the rings to which the horses were tied in the boxes, as well as the nameplates on each wall. Brass, it seems, was invented to clean, at least that was the view of the men in charge of this establishment. Additional 'bull' included the washing of all window panes and the cleaning of fork and broom handles with silver sand once a week. Army discipline had little on Druid's Lodge and when Mr Rank inspected the premises he would use his walking stick to clear the dormitory walls of 'pin-ups', unless they happened to be of the equine variety. I got properly caught on my first Sunday when just I and one other were left to sweep the huge yard at the end of morning stables. Those who wished to attend Church were allowed to do so and I was surprised by the number of religious employees!

The stable routine was also regimented. At inspection time in the evening the order was: litters stacked, tools laid out, a light covering of straw on the floor with a 'twist-in' of straw at the entrance and a soldier-like appearance from the lad standing at his horse's head. This may seem unnecessary but all the stable lads years ago were taught this method. Unfortunately, few stables today have such a routine, and while it may not assist in the success enjoyed, it certainly provided that little extra something in which to take pride. If I were a wealthy owner with a private training establishment, I would find delight in a stable run on such efficient lines. I believe it to be good for all concerned and not least the horses whose minds are given some distraction during this active evening session. After all, racehorses spend most of their time looking at the walls of their boxes.

The most plentiful commodity on the training grounds was hares. On my arrival, I was immediately warned to try to avoid letting my horse tread on these precious creatures. They were to be found crouching in the tufts of grass, but just before the greyhound coursing meeting took place at Druid's Lodge, the 'beaters' drove them to a field, enclosed by wire netting, adjacent to the coursing ground. Some of the famous horses had retired when I was there but it was still a pleasure to ride work on such horses as Beachway, Waylaid, Timber Wolf, Brian Boru, Lost Property and Le Maestro.

Riding at exercise on Salisbury Plain was a pleasant experience. There was a big choice of gallops and a variety of ways to approach them. I rode my fair share of schooling over hurdles and fences while there, but unfortunately, the majority of the horses in the yard were now getting old. There were not many opportunities of having a mount in public for this stable; in fact, my only ride was on Monsieur Pons at Nottingham. I was extremely proud of the chance to sport the famous blue and primrose colours of Mr James V. Rank, and even though Monsieur Pons finished fourth in a field of twenty-nine, I had my knuckles rapped by the trainer after the race.

He had given me orders to jump the first hurdle in front and be with the leaders all the way. I have little doubt that many other jockeys in the race had similar instructions. With such orders a quick start was vital and to ensure this I had to push my way into the crowded line which was just a little too wide for the course. When horses are packed tightly at the start a quick beginning becomes impossible if you have your horse's shoulders behind those of the horses on either side. In my anxiety, Monsieur Pons was kicked inside the hock by John Hislop's mount, Frivolous Friar. I withdrew from the line and trotted round in order that the starter could judge his soundness. Despite a trickle of blood, it was considered that the horse was fit to race. Somehow I got in and got a good start and jumped the first in the lead, then dropped him in behind a couple. I took up the lead entering the straight and waited for the inevitable. It was not long before it occurred and as Matt Feakes came upsides he grinned and said, 'How are you going?' He knew my answer, which was 'Not as well as you.' Matt went on to win with Monsieur Pons finishing fourth. Oh, by the way, and just to rub it in, Matt was riding Milk Bar.

It was a bit of a blow as I had done all the donkey work and missed the ride on what to me was a certainty. To add to the agony, I got a rollicking from Frank Horris for not withdrawing Monsieur Pons as by now the hock was beginning to swell. In a way it was a revenge for Milk Bar as he had been beaten by Monsieur Pons in a flat race. Thinking back to the start, it and all others were in contrast to those taking place at the present time. We had to line up with the horse's head nosing the tape and there was seldom any delay. Nowadays the walk-in start for jumping races quite often leads to delays as jockeys try to steal a march and the field has to be called back.

Soon after that race I received a telegram from George Todd saying, 'Be at Cheltenham to ride The Shaver and Peace Disturber.' I was not happy at Druid's Lodge, so decided to contact George Todd and ask if

I could go to work for him. The move was agreed and I packed my bags and took them to Cheltenham intending to join him after that day's racing. Unfortunately, things did not work out as planned. The Shaver was one of a field of nineteen, and was owned by the shrewd gambler Mr Tom Westhead who hit the bookmakers when his horse Punch won the 1937 Cesarewitch.

Dudley Williams who rode the 1933 Grand National winner, Kellsboro' Jack, was the trainer. Although he was at the meeting, he did not come into the parade ring, which was strange. The only person in the ring was the travelling head lad, and he did not know what was going on. All the other horses had left the paddock and were cantering to the start. I was getting in a state as I had never seen The Shaver before and would have liked some idea of how he should be ridden. At the last minute, the portly Tom Westhead entered the parade ring puffing and blowing. I asked him what I should do and the only two words he uttered were, 'Bloody win.'

George Todd had recommended me for the ride as they wanted someone who claimed a five pound allowance. That was the only claim in those days and was lost after riding fifteen winners. Knowing the set-up, I thought they might be giving the horse a quiet run round. It transpired that The Shaver had been backed at all prices from 33/1 to 8/1. In my eagerness to get to the start as quickly as possible, I started cantering immediately after leaving the paddock. The runners had to go past the stands before cantering back to the start and making the turn The Shaver's hind legs slipped and he almost fell. As a result, neither horse nor jockey had time to be composed. We set off almost as soon as we had arrived at the start and at the very first hurdle he stood off so far that he was lucky to survive. I covered him up at the next flight and all was OK. That seemed to be the answer, so approaching the third hurdle I stuffed him behind a couple of horses. To my cost, I didn't let him see anything of the hurdle and he picked up with those in front and was on his descent when the hurdle arrived.

It really was a somersault, and when I sat up it was a relief, although a bit dazed. I knew immediately that my collar-bone was broken and was also worried about an ankle which had probably been wrenched by the stirrup-iron. My main thought was that I would not be able to ride Peace Disturber in a later race. The ambulance took me to the first aid room where the doctor asked me to raise my arm above my head. This I did, and he passed me fit to ride. I changed into another set of colours and weighed out and gave the saddle to George Todd. Back in the changing room, I was still worried about my collar-bone and was simulating the action of pushing out a horse in a finish. My colours were unbuttoned when Tom Masson came in and asked what I was up to and pointing to my collar-bone said, 'With that?' He could see it was broken and I went back to the first aid room. The doctor was a bit embarrassed and said he would send details to be included in *The Lancet*, a medical publication. It seems I may have been a bit concussed, as I was told to lie on a bed and didn't remember anything until just before the last race when I hobbled back to the weighing room to get dressed. The doctor's suggestion that it might be better to stay in hospital overnight was not adhered to for another reason.

The intended ride on Peace Disturber was taken by Frank Wren, and he was beaten by three quarters of a length by my favourite horse, Milk Bar. Tom Masson's words to me in the weighing room signalled the renewal of our friendship. Although I was knocked about a little, I don't recollect anyone asking after me.

The reason I would not be hospitalised was my mother. She had come by train from Lewes to see me and I had no intention of letting her make the return journey on her own. Remember, this was wartime with the black-outs, disruption, shortages and possibility of bombs. What a horrendous journey it was. By now my ankle had swollen and was made worse by the very tight binding which was more uncomfortable than the collar-bone. The ambulance took us to the station and a member of the Tote staff kindly carried me to a carriage and found us seats. It was a stop-go journey to London and we managed to get a taxi across town to Victoria Station, only to find the last train to Lewes had departed. Luckily there was still a train to Brighton, but on arrival there were no taxis. Now it was past midnight and still eight miles to go. How? was the next problem.

After a while of mind searching, Mother came up with Hettie Thompson who lived in Brighton and was likely to have some influence. Sure enough she was able to be our saviour. We rang back a little later and she had managed to locate a taxi to take us to her home, and then after refreshments, non-alcoholic, another taxi to take us to Lewes. It is nice to know who your friends are. It was only a fortnight before I was able to take up lodgings at George Todd's stables at West Ilsley.

Before leaving the subject of Druid's Lodge and Salisbury Plain, I must say my favourite place for riding is still on the Lewes Downs. Riding through Honeysuckle Valley on a summer morning is my idea of heaven. The early morning dew glistening on the grass and the scent of the honeysuckle is the perfect start to the day. I was a teenager with the world at my feet, but it didn't work out as I had planned except for my marriage which has been blessed with happiness, due, in no little way, to Marian.

18

A CALL TO ARMS

With my collarbone mended, it was off to join George Todd. He asked how much I wanted and I said the same as at Druids Lodge which was twenty-five shillings a week and my keep, but I always found three pounds in my pay packet even though the boss had paid for my keep. The West Ilsley yard, named Hodcott House, was shared by George Todd and the ex-Lewes trainer Eric Stedall. Charlie McKinnon was head lad to Stedall at Lewes and moved with him. He had a house in the yard and it was there that I lodged. The bath was in an outhouse, but to use it we had to fill the copper with water, light the fire underneath and then ladle the hot water into the bath. I went through this performance even though George and Audrey Todd had invited me to use their bathroom.

When I arrived the weather had turned very cold and the ground had frozen, so we had to lay a straw bed in the yard and walk and trot the horses in endless circles. We never expected the freezing conditions to last so long and George Todd regularly told me what rides he had for me. On and on the bad weather went and after six weeks not only had I missed a fair number of rides, but not even once did I get to ride on the gallops.

That cold spell made life in the stable yard repetitive and boring and I made that an excuse to go to a pub in East Ilsley. I went with another lad named Nick Sparkes to a pub whose landlord was Harry Graves, an ex-jockey. I think we tried a beer and as we left to make the trek back to West Ilsley we must have been spotted by the local policeman. It was while I was mucking out the following morning that the 'Bobby' appeared in the doorway. In a calm and kindly way he told me I would not be served in the future and that Mr Graves had been informed as we were under-aged. No doubt he had a similar chat to Nick.

Again this showed the decency and understanding of George Todd. The policeman would not have entered the yard without permission and

Not as happy as he seems

must have been told which boxes to go to. I did, however, go to the same pub a few days later wearing a trilby hat and was served a soft drink. I'm not sure whether the landlord was fooled by my attempt at disguise.

I returned home and awaited my call-up to the RAF. There was now no racing until 1945 and my dreams of being a jockey diminished as each day passed. I had ridden only two winners and dear Don may have prevented me having more as he confessed to having turned down rides without my knowledge. When I was called up early in 1943 at the age of eighteen and a half, it was like entering another world. I really knew nothing about life even if I thought I did, as in the forties the young were not so precocious or sophisticated as the modern teenagers.

Recruits were given a rail voucher with the call-up papers and had to report to Lord's Cricket Ground. There we went through administrative matters and were issued with a pay book and identity disc. You were now a number, and as with every serviceman, it is never forgotten. Mine was an easy one to remember. It was 160 62 64, but when you were called upon to identify yourself the last three were used, in my case: '264 Butchers, Sir.' We were paid twenty-eight shillings a fortnight and that

123

A photo carried in RAF days

was the amount given when I joined and exactly the same when I was demobbed nearly four years later. With no savings, I had to be subsidised from home on numerous occasions.

I had a professional jockey's licence in the hope that racing would be resumed and that I might pick up a few crumbs. As a pointer to the scarcity of jump meetings, the leading jockey in the 1940/41 season was Gerry Wilson with twenty-two wins. Ron Smyth was the champ in 1941/42 with twelve wins and then jumping did not take place in the next two seasons. It resumed in the 1944/45 season when Frenchie Nicholson and Fred Rimell tied with fifteen winners apiece.

Marian was now my steady girlfriend and that did nothing to ease the much-feared call-up. The worst thing about joining up, apart from death or wounding, was not knowing for how long it would last. National Service was probably a bind, but at least you knew you would be free in a couple of years.

When racing was resumed in 1945, there were only occasional fixtures but Windsor staged a two-day meeting with eleven races on each day. Tommy Isaac rode four winners one day and three the next. Several jockeys rode in nine of the eleven races but it was Isaac who topped them with ten mounts. During this time, the changing rooms looked more like barrack rooms with all types of military uniforms hung up. I don't think the officers expected any formalities, such as the saluting of their uniforms by the other ranks – they were equals at the starting gate and during the race there were definitely no calls of 'After you, Sir.'

After my call-up, much of the time was spent waiting to go on various training courses and while I joined as a 'white flash' boy, denoting Air Crew Cadet, I managed to be demobilised with the lowest possible rank of AC2. An educational course at Putney, ITW at Downing College, Cambridge and elementary flying at Marshall's airfield, just outside Cambridge, completed the training in this country and then came the big wait for a posting to an advanced flying school. During those courses I enjoyed playing football for our flight team and, curiously enough, found satisfaction in doing Continuity Drill in the market square in Cambridge. This consisted of the flight carrying rifles, performing every move in the drill book with only the order to commence. It was evidently a spectacular sight judging by the crowd of spectators we attracted. There was always plenty of 'spit and polish' on these courses, such as having your boots shining, to the extent of cracking, for morning inspection. It was during my very first course that I started to shave, only because an officer ordered: 'You start shaving in the morning.'

The Initial Training Wing was where would-be aircrew received training in Theory of Flight, navigation, weaponry, meteorology and other appropriate skills. Square-bashing and guard duties were other activities. Life at Downing College may sound cushy but it was far from that. There was an ablutions block some distance away but to use any facilities you needed to get there in the middle of the night or queue outside. I, and many others, used the outdoor cold tap and waited till evening for a more detailed cleaning.

Before moving to the next course for elementary flying at Marshall's Airport, I was told to report to the Commanding Officer. This was a mystery as I was unaware of any wrongdoing. It turned out to be a cosy chat. He wanted to know if I had any connection to the racing family of Butchers. It turned out that he was a member of the Watson family of whom Geoff Watson was a high-profile trainer in France, while Donald was a successful trainer in this country. Both had the Rothschilds as their chief patron.

We marched with our full kit to Marshall's Airfield. It is a journey I frequently make now and even in a car it is a fair way. Our elementary flying training was done in Tiger Moths and was quite enjoyable, even though I had no real interest in planes and wondered why I volunteered for aircrew. Among our duties was guarding the perimeter fence which none of us took too seriously until an officer burst into our room in the middle of the night. Carrying some sort of weapon, he announced, 'You are all dead.' It transpired that nobody had been on guard; surprisingly no action was taken. On our first trip, the instructor gave us a display of aerobatics which could only have been for entertainment purposes. After that we had normal training and Tiger Moths were easy to handle. No solo flights took place there and very few failed this initial flying course. It was now a case of waiting to be posted to another airfield for advanced training.

There had been a mass of volunteers for aircrew and we were queuing up for the advanced flying course. We did general duties at various airfields. An example was an attachment to the recycling squad that entailed baling up waste paper and cardboard and delivering the bales to a central point near Huntingdon. One day, a flying boot had somehow found its way into our skip instead of the incinerator. Luckily for me, it was another who found that the boot contained a leg.

This posting was at Graveley, where I was taken ill and asked a hutmate to report it to the medical officer. The return message was that I should report in person. Our hut was far enough away to warrant the issue of bicycles, so with difficulty I reported. Within minutes I was in the camp hospital and wrapped in a thermogene jacket with pneumonia. During recovery, life was more as I liked it, nobody shouting and the care of sympathetic nurses.

It was at this airfield that there was a system known as 'Fido'. This involved the lighting of small flares on either side of the runway to enable the planes to land at night. It all seems very primitive now. The world was a small place even in those days and quite by chance I met a boy named Fischer, who had been billeted with my grandmother when the Tooting Bec School moved to Lewes. He was an officer but I made a calculated decision not to salute as he had acted like a spoilt brat in Lewes. No doubt it was childish of me not to respect the uniform as it was that and not the man that required respect.

19

OFF TO COWBOY COUNTRY

While awaiting the call to an advanced flying school, I was posted to Leconfield where my duties were on the bomb dump. This was undoubtedly the most useful contribution I made to the war. On arrival we were taken for a long and boring flight in one of the planes. There were no seats and we sat on the floor staring at each other. I never could see the point. This was a Lancaster station from where the bomber planes made regular raids with 2000lb bombs. I was at this Leconfield Airfield during D-Day, although this vital event was not known to us beforehand. It was not long before the change of activities gave us a clue. Our gang loaded the bombs onto trolleys which were towed to the detonation shed. The whole station worked around the clock and as soon as the planes returned they were reloaded and off on another sortie. The sad thing, of course, was that some didn't come back. On the eve of D-Day, I met a boy named Ron Farley who had been in the same class as me at school. He was a rear-gunner and that was considered the worst job on the plane. I asked Ron what the bombing raids were like and he said it was very, very scary. I never saw him again and could only assume that he was one of the many to make the supreme sacrifice. On a lighter note, the bombs that were in stacks were lifted off by a pulley with a hook, which went into the eye on the bomb. It was a regular occurrence for one to slip off. Luckily they were harmless until detonated unless, of course, you happened to be in the way.

Eventually I was posted to Heaton Park in Manchester. This meant only one thing. From there the cadets were kitted out, given the necessary jabs and sent to flying schools outside England. I was taken off a draft for Southern Rhodesia, now Zimbabwe, and sent instead to Arizona in the USA. This meant that topee (sunhat) and light clothing were handed back and we had to have another load of injections. We went across the Atlantic to New York in the *Queen Mary*, which was returning American wounded. Our job from the time we went aboard was to mount guard over the sick quarters. This meant ten days of duty, as the ship could not sail for four days because of a German submarine lying in wait at the mouth of the Clyde. No doubt this was the closest I came to danger during the war as the *Queen Mary* was too fast for anything once she got under way. The train journey from Manchester to Glasgow was terrible with the men or, more precisely, boys stacked in carriages plus kitbags. The journey took ages but there was a better train journey awaiting us.

We docked in New York and a train took us to Moncton in Canada with a meal of buffalo meat on the way. We were in a 'prohibition' State but that was no hardship as I was teetotal all the time I was in uniform. There was thick snow on the ground but that is as much as I can remember about this New Brunswick town. I know we had a day in Montreal and have only recently fathomed out how that came about as it is some 430 miles from Moncton. Evidently our troop train to Arizona started from there. Our week-long journey from Canada to Arizona was memorable and also enjoyable We detrained at Mesa and were transported to the airfield. In a matter of days we had experienced both snow in Canada and soaring temperatures in Arizona.

It was no ordinary troop train as each coach was set out with tables and separate sleeping bunks, which were luxurious compared with the hammocks over the engine room on the *Queen Mary*. The luxury for troop travelling did not end with this, however. To each coach was assigned an attendant who looked after our every need and even cleaned our shoes. All we had to do was to amuse ourselves for a week. This was not difficult, as it was interesting to see the many changes of scenery as we passed through the various States. Unfortunately, we crossed the America-Canada border at Niagara Falls by night. We did, however, make several interesting stops, including one for twelve hours in Chicago. I had an interesting tour around the main part of the city and accepted an invitation to what I thought was a burlesque show but which turned out to be a religious meeting. Just for the experience I looked in at the burlesque show a few doors away when my mind had been partially purified! I also went to one of the Great Lakes which was overlooked by the Wrigley's skyscraper.

It was Easter when the train stopped at Kalamazoo, and there the local girls presented us with painted hard boiled eggs on which was printed the title of the then well-known song 'I've Got A Girl In Kalamazoo'.

Our holiday came to an abrupt end when we arrived at the airfield, about nine miles from Mesa. The heat was intense, sometimes reaching as high as 120 degrees, but we soon changed into the thin American khaki twill uniforms with which we had been issued. The field was in a most picturesque setting. On three sides was desert, complete with cacti, and a range of mountains that seemed close but which, in actual fact, were some seven miles distant. There were also orange groves close by but they were out of bounds to us.

The heat meant that we started our day early, reveille was at five in the morning, and we worked through to about two o'clock. Part of the time was spent at lectures and the rest, flying. The only trouble with lectures was that you had to pay enough attention to score at least fifty per cent in each subject at the weekly exam. The penalty for failure was confinement to camp at the weekend. This, however, was bearable as we had our own swimming pool, and I should know as I had only two weekends out of camp! The first of them I spent in the local town of Mesa during their Carnival time. Cowboys, fully equipped with guns, were sitting on the steps of shacks; in fact the setting was just as it is portrayed in Western films. My other weekend was much more interesting. I hitched to the much larger capital town of Phoenix, some thirty or forty miles away, and visited the World Championship Rodeo. This provided a spectacle that I'm sure could not fail to thrill any sports minded person. To say there was a thrill and a spill a second would be underestimating the scene.

The flying in Arizona was peaceful and serene. Although we had an English Commanding Officer, the flying instructors were American. My technical knowledge of planes was never good, and it is even rustier now, but I'm pretty sure the type we used were P16s. In any case they were single engine planes that were once used as the American fighters. It is a common belief that people who have ridden can adapt themselves quite easily to flying. The reason for this is that the light touch of the hand is usually a common factor. In my case it was not so; in fact it was the landings that caused me trouble. The take-off, flying and approach can be carried out to perfection but the dropping of the plane on to the runway is often tricky. Firstly, the height you are from the ground can be deceptive and then there is the matter of pulling the stick right back at exactly the right time. Once these two points have been mastered there is nothing difficult, but I could manage a perfect landing only every now and again. Wheel landings were not allowed and they had to be three-point ones. Neither were we allowed to 'slip off height' in order to lose altitude quickly on the approach to land. It was a matter of over-banking which qualified pilots used regularly but this was not good enough to reach the extremely high standard set by the RAF. Because of my erratic landings and facetious remarks to my instructor, I was sent on a test flight with the Commanding Officer. My remarks had been made more seriously than the instructor ever realised. Having taken off, and commenced climbing away from the airfield, my instructor cut the throttle and blared over the intercom, 'Your engine has failed, what are you going to do?' To me the obvious answer was, 'Hand over to you, Sir,' but this form of remedy was not appreciated, although I don't mind telling you that this American guy did not waste time arguing with me in the next few seconds. There was a similar incident when I was flying straight and level. This time the order was to bale out. I'm sure my polite retort of 'After you, Sir' earned me another black mark.

The most frightening part of the flying was putting the plane into a spin. It was nose down and full pressure on one rudder. We were allowed to do only one and a half turns and at my first attempt I froze and my instructor took over. With flying boots on, your feet fit snugly on the two rudders, and to get out of a spin it was nose up and opposite rudder. Small planes are really quite easy to fly with a bit of practice, but you did have to possess the right attitude.

There were some lighter moments with the instructors. I was taken for a 'hedge hopping ride' but in Arizona the hedges were huge cacti. It was a wonderful experience.

Flying did not make any great appeal to me, particularly as the war with Germany seemed likely to end before too long, and a friend of mine had already failed and was waiting to be sent home. Thus, when the day for my flight with the Commanding Officer arrived I did not care much what happened to me. I did not set out with the intention of purposely failing this test but anyone could be forgiven for thinking so, judging by my errors. The test was just routine. All I had to do was taxi to the end of the appropriate runway, perform the cockpit drill, take off, fly a circuit at a thousand feet and land. Simple enough, except perhaps the landing, but this time I gave my passenger a real example of stupidity. With my concentration on straight and level flight, I forgot my altimeter and climbed to 2000 feet and then committed the unpardonable sin of neglecting to check with the wind sock which would change direction with the slightest breeze. It was not until I was making my approach to land that the Commanding Officer said that he would take over and complete the trip. Sure enough, the windsock had changed direction and I was coming in to land with the wind, such as it was, instead of against it. The CO apologised for failing me and did so in the most sincere fashion. Inwardly I was delighted and was looking forward to seeing my family and, not least, Marian. That stupid windsock was always hanging limply and would have benefited from a course of Viagra! With hardly a breeze it would have been perfectly safe to land in the direction I was aiming but all things had to be done by the book. The lads who did pass were sent out East as the war against Japan had not ended.

Before leaving Arizona, a first for me, and no doubt several others, was playing football under floodlights, and that was in the early forties. Because of the heat, we had to take salt tablets with our meals but I fancy that would be scorned on today. Another thing to get used to was the scorpions. You made sure the bedding was free of them, but my worst experience was to find one in the lavatory pan. Even though there was a pool on the complex I was a non-swimmer and seldom used it until Harry Beeby, a member of the racing Beebys, told me to jump in and he would look after me. I jumped in the deep end to where Harry was and then panicked. Using his head as a launching pad, I got myself to the rail without drowning my would-be saviour. I had an earlier poor experience at the Seymour Baths when stationed in the London area. A group of newly recruited lads were taken there and we lined up along the pool. Then the fun, or fear, began. Each recruit had to jump off the six feet high diving board, swim to an upturned inflatable dinghy and put it in its correct position. When it was almost time for me to jump, I whispered to the PE Sergeant that I could not swim. It was a relief when he handed me a Mae West, an inflated lifebelt, but it was only the shame of refusing that made me jump.

A few days later, my pal and I were given rail tickets to make the four day trip by passenger train back to the transit camp in New Jersey. It was on this journey that I bought a paper that had only three words on the front page, which were 'German War Ends'. We arrived in New York on VE Day and joined in the hilarious celebrations. There were several weeks to pass away in the transit camp without any duties but, towards the end, without money either. Prior to sailing back to England, we had a couple of days in New York, courtesy of a family who gave us a bed and meals. Although not a drinker during my service, I visited Jack Dempsey's bar. The manager took pity on us Brits and asked for my address. After returning home I received a food parcel as the American people thought us near starvation. Although we had VE Day in New York, I would much prefer it to have been with my family and Marian.

Eventually we left our camp in New Jersey and returned home on the *Ile de France*. I spent the entire trip peeling potatoes. Not only did I peel them, but I had to carry a sackful from the store on the top deck. Carting a load down iron steps that suddenly became perpendicular is something that needs more practice than I had the time, or the inclination, to acquire.

That was a particularly rough crossing with large numbers going to their bunks for the rest of the voyage. A seasoned old chef in the galley told me to keep my head up and work or otherwise I too would be a victim. I managed to last out the voyage.

Some 35 years after leaving the RAF, I had a phone call asking if I knew a man named Derek Bates during my time in the service. A negative reply was followed by the caller saying that we shared a bunk bed when stationed at Heaton Park and regularly went out together. I was then asked if I remembered Harry Beeby.

It was only then that I asked who was ringing me. The caller was a researcher for the television programme *This Is Your Life*. They were planning to feature the man who in latter years was known as 'Blaster' Bates, a larger-than-life demolition expert who had several, in those days, fairly outrageous series on TV. Derek was also a 'Wall of Death' stunt rider and in later life an after dinner speaker, unsurprisingly better suited to an adult audience. After our paths took a different direction, Derek went on to become a bomber pilot.

They gave me the phone number of Harry Beeby who confirmed that the three of us were good pals. My memory still lets me down, especially with anything to do with my service days. When Derek's picture appeared with his Obituary I began to visualise the cheery face that greeted those, for me, miserable mornings at Heaton Park.

20

DECISION TIME

After a rough crossing from America I had to report to West Kirby in Lancashire. This seemed to be a gathering place for airmen that the RAF did not know what to do with. I was pushed off to a Maintenance Unit (MU) in Stafford where they had even less idea about our use. My mother was in poor health so I put in for a compassionate posting backed up by a doctor's certificate. This appeared to be a bit too complicated for the powers that be and after refusing me a forty-eight hour pass they solved their problem by packing me off to Eastchurch on the Isle of Sheppey. It was good to get away from the MU which was used as a holding camp, and being awakened late at night by a drunk who had urinated in my boots. It was not my idea of fun. To have complained would only have worsened the situation so it was simply a case of grin and bear it. At the far from luxurious Eastchurch camp in Kent I was asked if I would re-muster to be a navigator or an air-gunner. They could not get rid of me that easily so they had to think of something else. As a last resort I was presented with a bucket and brush and set out on my new career as Dan, Dan the lavatory man. The only other aid I had was a packet of Woodbines to act as fumigation during my visit to every lavatory in the camp. It was certainly an eye-opener although it was better to keep them closed. I was beginning to lose faith in the human race when, to my relief, the compassionate posting came through and I was sent to a radar station at Wortling, near Pevensey in Sussex.

This move enabled me to live at home, and during these last few months the question of my future cropped up again. I was still set on trying to carve out a career as a jockey but Don was equally keen that I should find another occupation. This time he had an additional lever with which to emphasise his point of view. I would be four years older than when I joined the services, and those were the years during which a jockey should have become established if he was to make it a success.

Even more important was the fact that had I continued riding for a few years and then discovered that I was not going to make it, the problem of finding an alternative occupation would have been more difficult than ever.

It was during those last few months of service that Don was speaking to an old friend who used to stay in Lewes as often as possible. In conversation, he asked what I intended doing when my release came. On hearing the position he was pleased, as a new man was needed for racing on the *Daily Mirror* and he thought I might fill the bill. This friend was Bill Jennings, who, for many years until his retirement, held the esteemed position of Company Secretary to the *Daily Mirror*. Don put this proposition to me and I showed not the slightest enthusiasm. Then Don put life for me in its proper perspective and thank goodness I had just enough sense to realise the wisdom of his words. I'm sure he must have been relieved at my decision to have an interview for this job but it was with great reluctance that I gave up the long cherished hope of becoming a jockey.

My interview was satisfactory and it was arranged that I should join the *Daily Mirror* on 1 January 1947 – less than three weeks after my demobilisation from a dreary, boring, unhappy and far from distinguished spell in the RAF. Unknown to me then was the fact that I had had my last ride in a race. Now I was cursing my change of status from amateur to professional jockey. There was no reverting then, which meant I could not do my journalistic job and enjoy myself riding in flat races for amateurs, or even a few hurdle races. For me this was the end of the line and a bitter disappointment.

On looking back, the decision to give up riding was the right one. Having been called up at eighteen, and without any qualifications, it made sense to accept the journalist job. Obviously, the four years in the RAF could not have come at a worse time for me and others of my age. The main disappointment was not being able to find out what might have been and not having time to choose any other career.

During my service, I managed to have a few rides but getting to some of the meetings was not easy. While stationed at Quedgeley, near Gloucester, I was asked to go to Wye, in Kent, to ride two for Harry Lawrence. Neither of them had any chance, but after one had been pulled up because loose horses had prevented me jumping a hurdle, there was an accusation. The race was won by Don Butchers, and the trainer accused me of pulling up to enable Don to win. Not surprisingly, he refused to pay my travel costs. I had several rides for Harry including Loch Royal, the horse that refused to go anywhere when trained by Tom Masson. Perhaps he remembered me because he ran a super race to be second at 33/1 to the smart Tabora in a big field at Cheltenham. That form was never repeated and I never rode him after that second place.

It was Cheltenham where I had an unusual fall. Riding Stormless for Ray Pulford, my one instruction was to make sure I had a horse on my inside as Stormless might try to run out. He had actually gone through the wing and fallen at an earlier meeting here. Stormless, the favourite, had only four rivals but when the tape went up nobody moved. We were almost down to a trot as we passed the stands amid jeers from the crowd. Worse still I was on the inside and had to go even slower to get out of that position. After the last hurdle down the far side there was a rail all the way to the finish. I had no option but to make the best of my way home from that point as Stormless had plenty of stamina and I knew one of the runners was a speedy horse and the race had been run to suit him. Sure enough Salver, ridden by Jack Moloney, swept past us between the last two hurdles. The worst was still to come, however.

We were still second and inside the wings of the last hurdle when my stirrup leather broke. I landed in the hurdle on the take-off side and one of those following completed the double by giving me a bit of a kicking. I must have been concussed because the next thing I knew there were several people looking down at me. The trainer had made his way from the stands and among others were ambulance men. Stormless was owned by the late Bill Wadey, a Sussex farmer, who had managed to get hold of some nylon and had his green and white colours made up. This was their first and last outing. Not only had the colours been badly torn, but my breeches as well. So ripped were the breeches that I had to use a blanket tied round my waist like a skirt. On seeing that I was alive, Ray Pulford said, 'What a mess you've made of those colours.' When my head had cleared, my main thought was how to get back to Staverton airfield where I was stationed at the time. I had slipped away without a pass, but it seems nobody had missed me!

I had also gone to that Wye meeting without a pass and a hutmate sent a telegram to say there had been a hut inspection and we were confined to barracks. Again I wasn't missed and I got our local MP to try and get my release as I seemed to be unhelpful to the war. I actually received a personal reply signed by Sir John Strachey, the Under-Secretary of State for Air. Although it was a very nice letter, the answer was in the negative and he even explained why. He said that if I were given my release he would have to release footballers, ballet dancers, jugglers and anyone who relied on their youth for a livelihood. While still in uniform I rode some very moderate animals but was able to draw my riding fee from the Weatherby's staff in the weighing room. I regret not keeping the American paper that said 'German war ends' and also the letter from Sir John. At the time I wanted nothing connected with the war.

Before the Stormless affair, Ray Pulford would phone someone at my station to get me to ring him back. Usually it was to ride something schooling, but I was able to do that only once. A more urgent call was for me to go to Worcester to ride Lower Red. The object was for me to get to know the horse and have a 'feeler' in a novice event. Don rode in the same race and after the last hurdle on the far side he told me to join the leaders and see how I was going. After racing, Ray, Don and I had a hush-hush meeting and my report was most encouraging. It was then that Ray told me it was imperative that I got a pass for 30 March. The objective was a selling race at Hereford in which I would ride Lower Red while Paddy Murray, father of the flat race jockey Tony, was to ride stablemate Hook On in a race at Bangor. It was some days after the race that I was told that apart from single bets there had been big bets on the double.

On the day, Lower Red was really hotted up and ran very freely as soon as the tape went up. So freely was he running that I knew his chance would be ruined if I couldn't settle him. Luckily, a horse ridden by Mick Prendergast drifted away from the rails and I was able to slip upsides him in the lead and Lower Red settled immediately. The horse won by a couple of lengths at 7/4. I rushed to weigh in and then literally threw on my RAF uniform and got a taxi to the railway station. I had ridden the winner of the two o'clock race and caught the two-thirty train to London and then home.

None of the family were very good at handing out praise but you knew things were OK if they had not pointed out any fault. Don and the family were pleased for me, and I was in good fettle as I was also able to have some time with Marian. When Don was not around, my mother told me that Ray Pulford had rung Don to say, 'Bob is the best claimer I have seen for some time.' A little praise is good for morale as there was not much else to celebrate in those gloomy days. Even though I was flattered to learn of Ray Pulford's praise, I'm afraid I disagree. I was very happy with my performance that day but I had made lots of mistakes on other rides. You may be a natural on a horse but race-riding needs experience and that is what the allowance is for. The present day system makes sense. The three stage allowances provide young jockeys a longer learning period.

I had left the course without seeing Ray Pulford who had a cash present for me. A few days later there was a cheque for £25 in the post, and an apology that it was not more as Hook On had failed to win. That one started as 3/1 joint favourite only to fall at the last fence, while the rest had only just jumped the second last fence. What a beautiful 10/1 double to go astray, but that's racing.

21

GOODBYE TO UNIFORM AND RACING SILKS

I almost picked up a winning spare ride at Plumpton. This was M and B who eventually became a course specialist with eight wins. His intended rider, George Turner, had been injured in a fall in the previous race so owner-trainer Mr. R. Tomsett looked into the changing room and asked if Butchers would ride. I was already changed as I had ridden in the first race and was due to ride in the last. Incidentally, my last race win on Lutin III was the last race at Plumpton for the duration of the war.

I quickly put on the Tompsett colours and went to weigh out. With my 5lb allowance, M and B was set to carry 9st 9lb. My dear old valet, Charlie Stalker, always gave me his heaviest saddle as I was so light and when I sat on the trial scales he added an empty leadcloth which, by chance, took my weight to the required 9st 9lb. However, when I got on the official scales they registered 9st 10lb. With no slabs of lead in the cloth there was nothing to remove and, with time short owing to circumstances, I asked if a pound overweight was OK. It was then that Mr Tompsett, who was at hand to take the saddle, realised that it was Bob and not Don sitting on the scales. He had already declared Don Butchers whose name was on the number board. He said I could ride if he couldn't get Bill Heavey. As I sat in the changing room, Bill came in and asked me for the colours. It was a case of nearly, but not quite. M and B started the Plumpton ball rolling with a short head win. Mr Tompsett was fined £5 and warned to be more careful in the future. My remark about the overweight cost me the ride but the outcome might have had complications. Firstly I might not have won on him and if I had there was the fact that he had been ridden by a jockey who had not been declared It was D. and not R. Butchers that had been declared and whose name appeared on the number board.

Whilst being shunted between Stafford, Eastchurch and Wortling I had been asked if I could ride Kai Lung at Fontwell where there was a race for jockeys who had not ridden fifteen winners. Luckily my compassionate posting came through and it was a cushy one with just three officers and a small number of men. I was able to live at home and go direct by train to Pevensey. The train stopped at Piddinghoe where the station sergeant joined me and arranged transport from Pevensey to Wortling.

The job given to me was that of batman to the officers who lived in a small house on the site. My main task was to collect three meals from the cookhouse and lay the table. I also had my lunch in comfort and the three officers were nice and friendly. On the second day at this luxurious posting, I asked if they would allow me to go to Fontwell in a few days' time. They were more than happy to oblige and I was able to let Matt Feakes know that I could ride Kai Lung in the Pegasus Chase. This was to be just my second ride in a chase and the restriction events, of which there were few, were open to amateurs at that time and among the riders was Tony Grantham, who happened to be the only amateur in the race.

Kai Lung was one of several horses bought in Ireland for Mr A.B. Askew. This nephew of the late Mr James V. Rank had had a long spell as a prisoner of war and on his release intended to enjoy himself by riding his string of horses. Unfortunately, Mr Tony Askew's riding career was cut short when Kai Lung gave him a nasty fall at Plumpton, resulting in several broken ribs and a punctured lung. The owner never lost interest in racing, however, and paid a small fortune for the brood mare Festoon at the Dewar dispersal sale. It was indeed a pleasure to see Festoon's offspring, Pindaric, winning Mr Askew his most important race, the 1962 Lingfield Derby Trial Stakes.

Kai Lung was a fairly useful chaser around the smaller courses but the absolute limit of his stamina was two and a half miles and he was even more effective at a distance below that. He undoubtedly ran his best races when allowed to stride along with the leaders as these tactics fitted in with his usually brilliant fencing. Although a 5/1 chance for this race, four of the other runners were better backed and I looked forward to an enjoyable ride rather than a winning one. Tony Grantham, with whom I have always been friendly, was riding Fleet III and this was another confirmed front runner who could set a scorching pace. He was not, however, anything like so safe a fencer as Kai Lung. Tony and I agreed before the race that we would try to avoid cutting each other's throats, that is both insisting on the lead and thus setting a ridiculously fast pace.

Approaching the first fence, Fleet III and Kai Lung were disputing the lead. Racing downhill, the pace began to quicken appreciably and I sensed the situation might be getting out of hand. A slight mistake at that first fence would have steadied Fleet III and perhaps enabled me to set my own pace. It would no doubt have given Tony an easier feeling as well, but as it was we both raced for the next fence, gathering momentum with every stride. Again we picked up and landed stride for stride and then I realised the pursuit of these tearaway tactics had gone on long enough. Perhaps the brilliant jumping of Kai Lung would have caused Fleet III to make a mistake eventually but the pace was too strong to be maintained. I let Tony go on but at the next fence Fleet III made a right mess of it and I landed upsides him. Tony was hanging round his horse's neck and fighting the laws of gravity.

It must have brought some relief to the jockey when he felt my hand grabbing his colours for I figured that only a helping hand would enable him to restore his equilibrium. It was not so much an act of kindness on my part, but something done instinctively. Fleet III continued on his merry way without making any more outrageous jumping mistakes but after crossing the water jump for a second time he showed signs of weakening. The fast pace and that atrocious mistake at the third fence were beginning to take its toll. The leeway of several lengths was closed effortlessly round the final bend and Kai Lung cleared the last open ditch, three from home, in a slight lead. It was plain sailing after that.

It was a great thrill for me and I think the happiest person on the course was Don Butchers plus my very relieved mother. The present I received for winning on Kai Lung was £15 which Mr Askew dispatched on the eve of his wedding with a jocular note saying he had better settle all his old debts before taking on his new responsibilities. The money was acceptable enough but the act of winning had been just as pleasurable. It is impossible for me to say which of the four wins I enjoyed most because each was a special moment for me. My presents for those victories would not keep me for long. The first £10 was secured only by fiddling the books, followed by a ten-page letter and a fiver, which I wish had been reversed, a straightforward £25, and finally £15 which was sent nearly a year after the race.

Fontwell staged the Victory Hurdle to mark a year of peace in 1946. Harry Hannon engaged me to ride Carrabawn in this race with £500 added money which was a big prize then. Quite a good field turned out and included M and B and Shining Penny, but the one to beat was the top-weight Your Fancy. I don't like thinking about the race because my effort was far from good. I had him settled in the rear, but it was me who went to sleep. When the pace quickened I was left with a lot of ground to make up and then panicked. I gave Carrabawn a couple of cracks to which he responded immediately. I kept at him all the way up the straight and he was really running as we jumped the last barely a length behind Your Fancy. The horse entrance and exit from the paddock to the course is a chute half-way up the run-in and it was here that Carrabawn attempted to go instead of in a straight line to the winning post. He swerved violently across the course. I was hanging on with just my ankle but managed to stay on and finish fourth. In hindsight, I should have had my whip in the right hand. I honestly believe that Carrabawn would have won but to make it worse the each-way backers lost their money on this 100/8 chance. The whole episode was upsetting and I vividly remember saying as I threw down my saddle in the weighing room: 'I'll never make a bloody jockey.'

It was over this course that I had my final ride. Trained by Matt Feakes and owned by Gerald Askew, an older brother of Tony, the horse was Scotch Sauce. It was a three-year-old race and was run over one and three quarter miles, although most of these events were over one and a half miles in those days. There was no fairytale ending and Scotch Sauce never looked like winning or being placed.

That final ride was on 16 October 1946, the date my son Guy was born fourteen years later, but another important date was 2 December 1946. That marked the end of my time in the RAF. I had to go to Tangmere in West Sussex for a reason I cannot recall, but from there I went to Blackpool to collect my demob clothing and complete formalities. My Service and Release Book is still in my possession and one of the officers at Wortling filled in the reference section. It reads:

This airman has only been on the unit for a short time but he has left me with a most favourable impression of his character. The willingness and ardour he has put into all duties assigned to him have been most marked. Bright, alert, intelligent and smart in his bearing. I feel he should do very well in his future employment.

My flying log book assessment said: 'Not up to RAF standard but would make a good civil pilot.'

On the train from Blackpool to London I had to keep reminding myself that I was once again a civilian. I marked the occasion by leaving my de-mob suit, hat and other garments on the train and kept only my raincoat. Oh, what a glorious day.

22

A NEW BEGINNING

When Don retired from training he helped Gay Kindersley in the new yard he had built in East Garston. After a short while he decided to break away from racing and asked Frank Hill, the master butcher from Eridge, near Tunbridge Wells, to find him a job. You may remember that Frank had horses trained by three of the Butchers family. He thought Don was joking, but on being told he was serious, a job was found for him where sausages, pies and delicacies were made in rooms above the shop.

Matt Feakes and Don had been lifelong friends and with Matt living in Ashurst, his wife Mary insisted on Don living with them. It was in this house that Don died. He came home from work, sat in an armchair and simply slumped. It happened when I was staying in Bury St Edmunds for Newmarket races. The sports editor of the *Daily Mirror*, Jack Hutchinson, told me to take time off and resume when I felt inclined. Jack and his wife, Wyn, had met Don on several occasions and liked to look round the horses.

It was Matt Feakes who put Jimmy Lindley back on course. At one stage he was so low that he got a job in the kitchens at Glyndebourne Opera House. Jimmy had gained a lot of weight and was letting himself go until Matt suggested he should ride over hurdles, which he did successfully. Jimmy then married Matt and Mary's daughter Pat. Sadly their other daughter, Jill, was killed in a car crash in Ireland.

The mention of Ireland reminds me that, prior to the war, Don brought off the big Galway 'double' as I briefly mentioned earlier. It consisted of a chase and a hurdle race and Symaethis and Serpolette were both mares. Symaethis was bought shortly after by a member of the Sainsbury family to be trained by our old friend Jock Langlands. The objective was the 1940 Grand National. Ridden by Matt Feakes; she scored at Windsor and went on to finish a gallant fourth to Bogskar at Aintree. This was the last Grand National until after the war and sadly the last for the winning jockey, Mervyn Jones, who was killed in action.

The time between leaving the RAF and joining the *Daily Mirror* was about three weeks, so my holidays were few and far between, but probably the most exciting was VJ Day. I was stationed somewhere in Gloucestershire and most of the camp were given a pass to leave for forty-eight hours. It is all a bit hazy but I remember dancing with Marian at the Saturday night 'hop' in the Lewes Corn Exchange. Everything seemed glorious and we all hoped normality was around the corner. When I'd come down to earth I returned to camp. I was expecting the worst as I had overstayed my forty-eight hours by a few days. The men in the guardroom, where you had to present yourself, could be very strict and one of them was a real bastard. If he was on duty when I returned I couldn't care less. He was on duty, and all he said was: 'You're back early, there's hardly anyone here yet.'

The war was over but for many of us the handcuffs were still on. My release number was fifty-two, and when you heard or read that number thirty was the next group to be freed it was depressing. My release came just over sixteen months after the Japanese war ended. I was aged twenty-two and a half when I was free and had not the job on the *Daily Mirror* appeared on the horizon I would have been in a quandary. If I carried on riding it would be precarious and might find me unsuccessful after a few years and then what? My head ruled my heart and following the interview with the Chairman, Guy Bartholomew, the job on the *Mirror* was mine. For some reason my appointment was kept secret from all departments. The Company Secretary, Bill Jennings, gave me a choice of nom-de-plumes. I told Bill it was his choice, and he settled on Newsboy.

This selection had no connection with the paper industry. It was the name of a horse owned by Sir Blundell Maple on which Bill had won a few pounds.

Being secret reminds me of an occasion when Marian and I, while I was still in uniform, stayed at the Sun in Windsor as I was riding Counselette at the meeting there the following day. I had not even told her I was riding. When on the course, I said I had to go and would meet her in a little while. After the race, I met Marian who said she was watching the jockeys going into the parade ring and that one of them was my double. When I told her it was me, she was really puzzled. That's what I call a secret but on reflection we must both have been a bit simple or blinded by love! In case anyone wonders about the sleeping arrangements at the Sun for a couple of young lovers, I can tell you that we had separate rooms and I showed Mother the letter confirming the booking, but Marian's parents obviously trusted me with their daughter! Whether their trust was justified is our secret but chastity was the order of the day. When we booked in the understanding receptionist said our rooms could be changed to a double if we wished. I can't remember when my halo slipped off but it wasn't then!

It was after riding Counselette that my mind started to concentrate on which direction I should take. My time in the RAF had ruined any chance I might have had of being a jockey, let alone a successful one. Having an occasional ride in a race without having sat on a horse for weeks was not the ideal situation. I had no idea when I would be demobbed but it was clear that Marian and I were going to get married. My mind was going round in circles. I had no money, not even a shilling, my longing to be a jockey was slipping, or more precisely had slipped. I was in love, hating my life in the RAF and seemed to be facing a dead-end. I remember distinctly that ride on Counselette started to make me think, 'What am I doing this for?' It was not a job, it was no longer exciting and the fee would not have bought us a high tea. It now became obvious that I had been fighting an uphill battle even before my first ride as a featherweight sixteen-year-old.

A topsy-turvy few years ended with a wonderful ride on Kai Lung who did not make one mistake when winning a chase at Fontwell; my release from the RAF; my marriage to Marian; and, at last, earning a living wage. Incidentally I told the trainer that Counselette would certainly win a small race. She somehow finished up at Peter Cazelet's smart establishment and won several races over fences.

The arrangement at the *Mirror* was that I should send in my reports by telegram rather than using the phone. In those days each course had a telegraph office and the forms to use for the messages. After a few weeks my reports appeared in print and continued to do so for almost thirty-nine years. There was speculation as to the identity of the mystery reporter. For some reason it was kept secret for close on three years. This was responsible for a great deal of curiosity among members of the racing press, who, I discovered, were naturally more nosey than any other community.

Undoubtedly this secrecy was maintained only because I did not hold a Press Pass, which meant I paid my entrance fees to meetings as an ordinary racegoer and did not, of course, have the Pressroom at my disposal. Inevitably, my identity leaked out and the man who unearthed me became a good friend of mine for many years. He was Cyril Fairchilds, one of the best known pressmen on the course who compiled the list of runners and jockeys for the Press Association. 'Fairy', as he was affectionately known, often told me of his delight when he discovered the identity of the mysterious 'Newsboy'. There had been a certain amount of speculation amongst the racing press and Norman Pegg, 'Gimcrack' of the *Daily Sketch*, then chairman of the Racecourse Press Committee, jokingly boasted that he would find out. It was because of this that 'Fairy' was filled with glee, as he was able to go to Norman Pegg and dangle the news under his nose. These two have always pulled one another's leg, so after keeping Norman in suspense for a while he said, 'It's Bob Butchers.' Completely baffled, Norman asked, 'Who's he?' but 'Fairy' solved the mystery once and for all by explaining, 'You know, that geezer who used to have a few rides over the sticks.'

I was more than pleased to receive my first official Press Pass in 1950 for it meant that I no longer had to try and keep a secret and also that I could avail myself of the facilities offered by the Pressrooms. It was also good to become acquainted with my colleagues who I found accepted me willingly and helped me in many ways. Now it was no longer necessary for me to do my work in odd corners, in fact my whole job was transformed. At this time, George Kreiner had retired from the position of 'Bouverie' and Joe Sarl temporarily took over the post, but a big change was taking place and before long 'Newsboy' superseded 'Bouverie' as the chief racing correspondent and tipster on the *Daily Mirror* and the position has remained as such ever since.

Although I joined the *Daily Mirror* on 1 January 1947, I did not start tipping until 24 October 1949 which meant I had to try and find winners in the last few weeks of the Flat season. This, as all punters know, is just about the trickiest period and I know my start was inauspicious even though I did manage to break the ice on my first day with a 5/4 winner in the last at Alexandra Park. That was a horse named Damnos, but in the remaining twenty-two days of the season I tipped only seventeen more winners; but I was hoping for more success in the National Hunt season.

23

SECRET WEDDING

It was a relief to go travelling without a RAF uniform. If stopped by a 'Red Cap', the military police, and asked to show your pass it meant some sort of punishment if you didn't have one. The London mainline stations were the danger points. When coming from the north I often got off at Finsbury Park and went by bus to Clapham Junction and continued my journey by train to Lewes. From the Isle of Sheppey I did the whole trip to Lewes by bus, and it was worth the time it took. Journeys back to camp could be uncomfortable if you chose to catch the latest train. The last train to Gloucester was packed with troops and a seat was not guaranteed. It was a tedious stop and go journey and the arrival was around about four o'clock in the morning. There was just one truck to meet the train but you had to sprint to ensure a lift. Not once did I succeed and it was several miles back to camp. An hour's rest on the bed and then the task of being respectable for 7.30 parade. Once again it was worth the trouble to gain just a few extra hours at home.

In 1947 very few young men or women had cars as soon as they reached the age at which they were allowed to drive and it was three years or more before I had a car. Ken Oughton, elder brother of the jockey Alan Oughton, had a garage in Eastbourne and also the Lone Star Horse Transport business. He also had a horse trained by Harry Hannon. However, I asked him to look out for a second-hand car and shortly afterwards he rang to say he had just the one for me. The one owner was well known to us and the car had very low mileage on the clock. It was a Vauxhall Velox which cost £400 and made life much easier. When I got it home to my house in De Montfort Road, it was the only car to be seen. There was one other car owner, a Mr Harris, who had hired a garage somewhere else. I have been back to Lewes several times in recent years and both sides of the road are lined with cars, as are all adjoining streets. Even with a car I travelled by train to some faraway places. Now

With my best man, Matt Feakes

that motorways are available I expect most of the meetings are reached by car. When the M1 was opened I was on it minutes after on the way to Birmingham. It was not crowded and a real time-saver. The fogs were worse in those early days and on one journey home Bob Watson, a press colleague, had to walk in front of the car waving a white handkerchief.

Before possessing a car, I had married Marian. It was six years, almost to the day, that we had been together, in spirit but not physically, that's what I call patience. With Marian's father being a butcher, we married on a Wednesday, which was half-day closing, at St Anne's Church on 22 September 1948. It was an experience which, I am pleased to say, has been the only one. Tony Grantham and Dave Dick were among the few racing folk who attended and I believe there were high-jinx after the occasion. My best man was Matt Feakes, who has weaved through my life during his riding and training careers. The best horse he trained was King's Bench, who was second in the 1952 Two Thousand Guineas. We had a small reception at the Crown in Lewes but the bride and groom didn't hang around too long. Things are different these days with a party going on for hours and the happy couple still around. A honeymoon after

September 1948

September 1998 – Golden Wedding

modern weddings seems a little pointless as they have probably had several of the equivalent before. For Marian and me it was off as soon as possible in a little Morris car that seemed to be vintage even then. No Greece, Caribbean, Maldives or other luxurious retreats for us. Once settled into our old banger, which was hired, it was off to the Berystede Hotel at Ascot. The three-day September meeting started the following day.

Our marriage took place without a soul at the *Daily Mirror* being aware. I had filed my copy to the paper shortly before setting off for the church. As I left, Towser Gosden came from the house next door to wish me luck. The reason he emerged from that house was because he lived there with his first wife.

We indulged in the luxuries at our hotel and it was Champagne all the way. To make things even more enjoyable I fancied Peace Envoy to win one of the sprints and with the small, but forceful, Percy Evans aboard, scored at 100/8. Marian and I tried to hide the fact that we were newly married, but I don't think we succeeded. Perhaps I should have worn a notice saying, 'Our room is twin-bedded.' We did not allow that fact to

Les and Don with their parents

spoil our happiness. Any innuendoes should be taken with a pinch of salt. I am no prude but control and mutual respect was very much the way most lives were conducted in those days. Unfortunately standards of behaviour seem to drop lower and lower as the years go by. The only hiccup came a few days before the wedding. They were austere days and morning suits did not come into the equation and I had a dark suit made by a Brighton tailor. When I went to collect it and try it on it was discovered that the trousers were a couple of inches too short. Luckily trousers had turn-ups in those day so they were taken down and a false turn-up added. I was disappointed and gave the suit away without wearing it again. I learned later that the tailor had a serious drink problem.

My mother still owned the house in De Montfort Road, where I had been born, and I bought it for a pittance. It had tenants so I had to go to court to get them out. Judge Archer heard the case and he was known to be keen for people to buy their own property if possible. They were told to vacate the house within a fixed period after saying they had been there for twelve years at a rent of £2 a week. While waiting for the house to be vacated we stayed at the Black Horse, the pub near our old stables. I have two memories of that stay. Our bedroom was directly above the

Most of the family at the Golden Wedding of George and Isobel Butchers

public bar and one evening the bed completely collapsed causing a clatter loud enough for the landlady to knock on our door to see if we were all right. On another evening she asked if we would like steak for dinner and few would turn down this rarity with food still in short supply. We thought it looked a bit overdone but were soon to find out that it was not beef steak but whale steak.

Still on the subject of Lewes, around about this time, Gosden was training here with Andy Jarvis as the stable jockey. Andy had been with Gosden since leaving school at fourteen, while Harry Hannon was about to set up as a trainer after working for Tom Masson. Harry had previously worked for George Poole and ridden winners for the stable.

I am still a Lewesian at heart and feel proud of the achievements of these sons of Lewes. What a trio to fly the flag – John Gosden, Michael Jarvis and Richard Hannon. Between them they have won almost everything there is to win. John Gosden's mother, Peggie, was one of the Geering girls on whose farm I enjoyed many happy times while I was also well acquainted with the other two mums.

24

RETURN TO AMERICA

Quite a lot happened in the first few years as 'Newsboy'. While still not identified, except by a few, I had a scoop. I was still going into the weighing room and one of my friends, Glen Kelly, knew about my new job and pulled me aside. He told me that Jack Moloney had been sacked from the position as stable jockey to the powerful James V. Rank stable at Druids Lodge and that he had been appointed. The story appeared in the next day's paper with the headline which could not be missed. Jack Moloney, a veteran, had seen it and naturally had a word with Glen. He had not been told about the new arrangement and wanted to speak to whoever was 'Newsboy'. It was a bit of a miracle that he never found me despite being close on several occasions. The mighty Prince Regent was to be Glen's first ride for the stable at Lingfield in a few days' time but before then there was a letter from Mr Rank's solicitor requesting a disclaimer be published. This was done and Jack Moloney retained the ride on Prince Regent but Glen took over after that. I was much happier when my by-line appeared as 'Newsboy (Bob Butchers)'.

There were no race commentaries until Bob Haynes was chosen to perform that task at Goodwood. Bob worked for *Raceform* and *Chaseform*, and was asked if he would like a colleague in case of emergency. He was confident, but said he would like somebody standing by and he chose me. All went well and I didn't have to open my mouth. Bob was paid £360 and I got £90 for doing nothing. There have been commentaries ever since. Shortly after I was asked to do a test commentary at Kempton. When it was played back I was informed that the accuracy was good but could I acquire a 'Charterhouse accent'. My reply was blunt. How did he know my tape was accurate and what the hell is a Charterhouse accent? I know several people who went to Charterhouse and they all speak differently. In the early days one of the course commentators confessed that he did not worry about accuracy because 'who will know?'.

153

The Glen Kelly and Jack Moloney incident was later followed by a similar happening with Willie Stephenson wishing to speak to me. Charlie Spares, with whom I worked at George Todd's, was riding for Stephenson and told me there was going to be a change of jockeys in the Two Thousand Guineas. I found Willie, who asked me where I had got this news, but I was not prepared to tell him and we parted amicably, but it was not the best way to be introduced. Later that year, I was staying in the Mayflower Hotel in Washington for America's International race at Laurel Park. One of my companions was Ken Gethin who was due to ride King of the Tudors for Stephenson in the big race. We were invited for drinks in a private room, which turned out to be Willie Stephenson's bedroom, so my second meeting with this trainer came under abnormal circumstances. We enjoyed our drinks, our differences were soon forgotten and he and I got on well and in later years became good friends.

Ken Gethen and I flew to America together in what I believe was a Stratocruiser, but whatever it was you went down the stairs to a bar. Planes took a long time in those days, and from Heathrow we landed at Prestwick in Scotland and Reykjavik in Iceland before crossing the Atlantic. There was a stop at Gander in Newfoundland for refuelling and then New York. Because of the hours it took, the plane had sleeping berths, one of which I had reserved. It was while Ken and I were enjoying a few drinks that a female passenger remarked that she had not booked a berth. As I was enjoying the experience I offered the lady mine. In another hour or so I was tired and, with still a long way to go, I regretted my chivalry.

Ken Gethin was a laid-back character. We were both going to a dinner in London and I arranged to pick him up at a certain time when both of us were living in Epsom. At the appointed hour I rang on his door but there was no sign of Ken. It was in the garden that his wife found him adding lumber to a huge and smoky bonfire. He was stripped to the waist and wearing the trousers of his dress suit! He was obviously a quick-change artist.

I stayed on in the USA and based myself in Lexington to visit the many famous studs in the Blue Grass State. Everyone was made welcome and received a memento of some sort. I still possess a steel shaped jockey's cap designed to remove the crown tops off bottles. It was here that I bought some scarlet blinkers with Don's initials emblazoned in white on the front. Gaudy in those days and certainly not the thing Don would have bought himself.

Earlier while staying in Baltimore I went to Churchill Downs where the Kentucky Derby is run. I had a lift home from a friend who dropped me somewhere near my hotel. It was dusk and I took the wrong turning and walked along a street with all the houses having a couple of marble steps up to the front door. Later in the evening I was speaking to a local who told me that I had walked through the black area. He added that I would be ill advised to go that way again as there was still a deal of tension between black and white. Even on the railway platform the facilities were marked for white and coloured.

One of the many parties on this trip started at six o'clock so I asked for a sherry as an aperitif prior to dinner. The waiter was ages before returning with my drink and only then did I realise that he had gone to find a sherry at what turned out to be a Bourbon-on-the-Rocks party. No regrets for my faux-pas as any sort of whisky was very much on my barred list! I also went to the estate at Richmond owned by Mrs Marion Scott. She had won the Grand National with Battleship. I had been told of a meeting there and was looking forward to seeing races over fixed timber fences. Unfortunately I was given the wrong date. Although that was another slip-up it was enjoyable as I made the journey by train and was able to see a variety of landscapes. Luckily, I had a pass that allowed me to make internal flights so was able to return by plane. It was strange to get on a plane that was more like a bus with a conductor aboard. It was also pretty scruffy.

When I returned to New York and went to the *Daily Mirror* office, Desmond Wilcox said he would show me the New York sights in one night. With Desmond and his wife Patsy, we had a happy time that included many jazz bands. Desmond, who was later a prominent figure at the BBC and married Esther Rantzen, certainly did me proud. It was round about five o'clock in the morning when I walked back to my hotel and was accosted by a man wanting to sell me a diamond ring. To prove it was a real diamond he pulled it down a shop window that no doubt left a scratch but I did not hang around to find out.

A visit to the first running of the Washington International in 1952 was an experience. The only two British racing correspondents that made the trip were Clive Graham of the *Daily Express* and me. I remember the stop at Reykjavik where three of us had breakfast and one of them was the Maharanee of Jaipur, reputedly the most beautiful woman in the world. I did not know her but was invited to join them by one of the More O'Ferralls. John Shapiro was in charge of the Laurel operation and

Des and first wife, Patsy, Wilcox took me for a night out in New York.
Des later married Esther Rantzen

the British contingent, including Clive and me, were given the red carpet treatment. Instead of having a cardboard tag to allow you into certain parts, they stamped the back of your hand with a design visible by ultra-violet light.

Charlie Smirke was there to ride Zucchero but did not arrive until late and is reputed to have ridden at something like a stone overweight. The real British hope though was Wilwyn, owned by Bob Boucher from Kent, trained by George Colling and ridden by Manny Mercer, one of the leading jockeys retained by Jack Jarvis and therefore rider of the large Lord Rosebery string.

It was an open secret that John Shapiro needed a foreign runner, and preferably British, to win in order that the race received maximum publicity. This it did for several years, but has faded into obscurity. My part as a journalist was made comfortable as a Western Union man was at hand to take my copy page by page and send it by telegraph to London. Owing to the time difference it was a rush job to make the later editions of the paper.

The trip was made memorable by Manny Mercer. He, together with Bob Boucher and Sir Leslie Doubleday, were returning home on a British plane while I had a ticket on Pan-Air. At the airport, Manny asked why I wasn't flying with them. With that, he went off with my Pan-Air ticket and returned and said, 'You're flying with us.' Before boarding the plane, Bob Boucher handed me the winner's trophy and it was for me to look after during the flight. Manny and I were invited to the flight deck to see how everything worked and it was while there that Manny told the pilot to have £5 on something he was riding the next day. He also took the pilot's address and said he would send him the fiver if it lost. I know it won but can't remember the horse's name but do remember that I forgot to have a bet! Before we landed I was told to hold on to the trophy and go with them to the Customs room where they would be greeted and duly celebrate. It was as they said, and a fine way to round off the trip. How it was all arranged I have no idea, but Sir Leslie Doubleday, a real English gentleman, was, or had been, Lord Lieutenant of Kent.

Manny Mercer was a lovely little chap who rode instinctively and loved life. I remember walking down Newmarket High Street when he called me and said, 'Come for a ride.' He had just got a new car and was going to find out how fast it could go down the 'murder mile' which is the straight length of road that runs between the entrances to the Rowley Mile and July Course. It went fast enough for my liking.

Manny was killed at Ascot when unseated as the runners walked past the stands before turning to canter to the start. A kick on the head proved fatal and no other race took place that day. I still remember the sadness that chilled the air. It was a terrible day.

25

THE AINTREE FIASCO

The Grand National of 1952 will be remembered for the row between Aintree supremo Mrs Mirabel Topham and the BBC. As no agreement was likely, she decided to gather her own team to broadcast the race. This, may I remind you, was radio and not television. My sports editor at the time was Tom Phillips and without consulting me he suggested to Mrs Topham that I should be one of the team. This was two days before the race and the first and only gathering of the team was on the eve of the big event. Jack Topham, no relation, worked for *Raceform* and *Chaseform*, Mrs Marie Draper had broadcast at Hawthorn Hill pony racing, John Kirkpatrick, who was on the Aintree staff, plus myself and one other made up the team of five. I say one other because the original member, Mr Archie Stock, was found to be a disqualified person and not allowed on any racecourse. A replacement on the day was a man named Steel and I had no knowledge of him.

It is rare for me to blow my own trumpet but when anything connected with the 1952 Grand National crops up, I certainly will. What's more, it was my part in the broadcast that prevented it becoming a complete farce. At our early meeting it was decided that I would do the build-up to the start and the run to the first fence and then pick up the field at the second last fence on the first circuit and round to the first fence on the second circuit. First in the saga was the weather. Norman Pegg, the *Daily Sketch* correspondent, said in his book *Focus on Racing*:

> The fog at Aintree on Teal's National day was the worst I've seen there when racing has not been actually fogged off. A coal black curtain hung around and blotted out completely everything between the first fence and the far end of the course.

That description of the weather was in no way exaggerated but worse was to come. I was shown into the room from where I was to commentate but the cable on the hand-held mike would not reach to any power point. Panic was in abundance! I moved to another room and when the mike was plugged in, it allowed me to kneel on a table and peer through a window six inches high and eighteen wide. The next thing to ponder on was the ability to operate with a mike held in one hand which left the other hand to hold binoculars and a race-card. The first to be discarded was the race-card. The only way to describe the discomfort is for readers to kneel on a hard table with binoculars and any object resembling a mike for a long time. Having moved to a fresh position, there was the question of vision, and I don't mean the weather. It had started to rain and the people outside the window had put up their umbrellas so a man was sent to ask politely that they should be lowered.

The scene was now set, and as the forty-seven runners emerged from the paddock my duties began. I could not use my race-card, but I was professional enough to know all of the field as if they were members of my family.

It seemed that there were more obstacles to this broadcast than in the National itself. When it was time for the 47 runners to make a line, some horses rushed at the tape which was broken. For a reason unknown to me, instead of knotting it someone was sent to get a new tape which meant a search in the storeroom. Now you have to remember that this was radio and not television, so I had to keep talking. From the time the horses left the paddock to the time the race started was at least twenty minutes and so well did I know my subject that I didn't draw breath and as I said earlier, 'I'll blow my own trumpet' on this occasion.

The broadcast was disastrous. Marie Draper was hesitant and called numbers as well as some names. Jack Topham was at Becher's Brook and in a bit of a state and Legal Joy was called as Legal Paget – probably worth giving him the benefit of the doubt as the animal was owned by Miss Dorothy Paget! The race was now taken up by Mr Steel who gabbled the names of a few horses before saying, 'I'll hand you over to Don Butchers in the grandstand.' Thanks a bundle, and incidentally my name is Bob. Listeners were now able to learn if their fancies were still in the race as I announced clearly every horse in order as they crossed the water jump and set out on their final circuit.

More incoherent voices until it was handed over to me for the last two fences and the finish. I could not see them until they were approaching the final fence where I was able to pick up Teal ahead of Legal Joy, but my one error was to call Wat No Sun as a faller at the last fence. This I corrected immediately as it was a horse in similar colours that fell. I was told to leave the placings and let the Judge's announcement take place. Mr Kirkpatrick's role was to announce the race and little else.

Norman Pegg wrote that I did a very good job in the impossible conditions. Mrs Topham showed her appreciation by sending me a double fee, that being £20 instead of £10. The formidable Mirabel wrote:

> Dear Mr Butcher   7th April 1952
> I would like to thank you for your kind help on Saturday and especially I appreciated your valiant impromptu commentary rendered necessary by the delayed start.
>
> We seem to have incurred the displeasure of quite a number of the public who entirely missed the point, that the BBC were asked to do the Broadcast for us and refused.
>
> Please thank Mr Tom Phillips for proposing that you should do it.
> You were a blessing.
> With the best of good wishes.
> Yours sincerely
> Mirabel Topham.

There are two things wrong about that letter. The first is that my name is Butchers and not Butcher. The second is that it says 'we incurred etc etc.' It was they who incurred the displeasure not me as the press cuttings show:

> Only one of the five commentators reached anywhere near the standard set by the BBC: He is a London sporting journalist. (*Sunday Times*)

> Mrs Marie Draper was obviously nervous. So were her colleagues except racing journalist Bob Butchers who gave listeners a smooth sound picture of his section. (*Sunday Express*)

Another cutting says:

> At no time except when they came to the Grandstand did listeners get an exciting picture of what was really happening.

There is a sting in the tail. Mrs Topham stressed on me her thanks and said that if there was anything she or Aintree could do for me I only had to ask. The whole recording of the race took up five double-sided records. I asked Aintree for them and they duly arrived with a bill for £2.50. Perhaps I look like a mug because I had a similar surprise when I went to the house of Eph Smith who won the Derby on Blue Peter. In conversation he was telling me how many apples he had in his garden and invited me to go and collect some. We went into his greenhouse where they were kept and he duly put some on his scales and charged me!

A lot of water has passed under the bridge since that murky Saturday. It was thirty-four years later that I had a call from the BBC to say they were gathering material for a new television series called *Sporting Archives*. They wanted Harry Carpenter to do the interview about that infamous Grand National broadcast. It was an informal affair and luckily there was a record player in the house so they could play certain sections of the broadcast. I received a small payment which goes under the heading of 'disturbance'. The interview went smoothly, but it was something entirely divorced that I remember most. The interview took place in our sitting room so my wife thought she must have everything presentable and gave the silver a polish. The first thing the lighting man asked was for the silver to be moved as it was causing reflections. You can't win them all!

With television able to do so many things these days, you needn't move from your armchair. The Grand National has always been a major attraction and in the days before television we had to wait for it to be shown in the cinema on the Pathé News. In Lewes we had the Cinema du Lux, whose manager, Reg (Fatty) Briggs, was an obliging individual who gave my father a pass for two to get in free to any performance. Unfortunately, it was long before I was seeing Marian. More important is that Fatty invited the racing fraternity to a special viewing of the Pathé News and would run through the Grand National two or three times. It attracted quite a crowd and no doubt the next step was the White Hart, which was fairly adjacent.

The BBC has never been known for its generosity even if that has been exaggerated over the years. There was a case, however, that not only yielded a paltry sum but was most inconvenient. Derby day is a very busy one for journalists and not only the reporting side, but also the travel worries. Normally I would get to Epsom no later than ten o'clock and start work on the following day's tips, but I was rung the evening before to ask if I could go to the BBC in London to give my idea of the winner on the *World at One* programme. In those days, the Derby was on a Wednesday and I needed to completely reorganise my day, which involved car and train. The programme went well and I gave a confident prediction that Charlottetown would win the 1966 Derby, and he duly obliged at 5/1. A few days later, I received a cheque for £5 which I

The Lewes racing fraternity watch a private showing of the Grand National

returned with a note saying give it to charity. With train fares, petrol and taxis, I was well out of pocket.

Some years before Roger Mortimer and I were on the *Dateline-London* television programme that went out at 10 p.m. There was no mention of a fee on that occasion. There were several other appearances but I cannot remember the name of the programmes. An amusing event was the *Down your Way* radio programme, not the national one but a similar programme aired by the Guildford radio station. I knew one person who was to be questioned, who would choose a complicated piece of music with several movements and other musical terms as his taste in most things was opposite to mine. It gave me immense pleasure to choose 'anything by Max Bygraves' to be my musical contribution.

Roger Mortimer, who wrote for several publications, was a wit and delightful company. He lived a few miles from Newbury and retirement did not really suit him. I had to pass nearby when racing was at Newbury and Roger had smoked salmon and Champagne ready when I called on him. The other personality in his village was Cliff Richards, younger brother of Gordon who kept the local pub.

26

A SOCIAL CHAUFFEUR

Most journalists seem to have a fairly hectic social life and most of them are associated with the job. The lunches were a nuisance as they took up valuable hours that could have been devoted to the formbook. The dinners did not interfere with the job, but the changing into a dinner jacket and travelling to London was always a bit of a rush. Getting home could be more stressful as that 'one for the road' frequently saw me wondering what to do when the last train had departed. No doubt the most prestigious was the Derby Dinner over which Lord Derby presided. The event was held at the Savoy and after the speeches there was the famous auction sweep of the Derby runners or, to be more precise, the names of the runners.

Members of the Derby Club invited their guests, and there would probably be between two and three hundred present. Tickets were bought, for £1 in my day, and the first stage was to draw a horse. Each lucky drawer of a horse then had it auctioned, usually by a member of the Tattersalls Sales Company. The bidding was fast and furious, and often reached four figures. Half of the auction price went to the lucky ticket holder and the other half went into the prize pool.

For twenty-one years I was the guest of Lord Derby and sat at the top table next to his retained jockeys Doug Smith and, in later years, Willie Carson. There was always an interesting and diverse guest or two at this table. Gordon Richards, Bud Flanagan and Lord Mancroft are just three of the excellent speakers I can remember. At one of these gatherings Lord Derby asked what I had tipped for the Derby. I had napped Parthia and Lord Derby bought it at the auction and invited some of us to buy a share in this 10/1 winner. Unfortunately, the odds worked out at a paltry 4/1. Parthia was a repetitive name for me that summer. A few weeks after his win, we moved to Epsom to live and named our house Parthia, but not after the Derby winner as most of my acquaintances

Receiving the Naps Cup from Lord Derby

believed. Parthia was an old Persian village from whence the Nomads came and being a bit of a wanderer myself I considered the name appropriate.

Bud Flanagan never missed the chance of a laugh and one year as he approached the top table, he inquired of Lord Derby, 'How are the Farmer Giles, John?' This reference to haemorrhoids was heard by the guests on surrounding tables and Bud got his first laugh of the evening. This amusing character told me the reason why he left Brighton and returned to live in London. He said: 'After our show at the Victoria Palace I would catch the last Pullman train and be half cut before we got to East Croydon so I thought it best to return.'

I only ever bought one horse at these auctions and paid something over £300 for Pentland Firth. I sold a share to his trainer Geoff Barling and was relieved when the colt finished third to Roberto at 50/1. I'm afraid I've forgotten how much we won but it can't have been much if I can't remember.

I used to take my car into the embankment entrance of the Savoy where one of the doormen would get it parked. With a queue for taxis after the dinner, I was nabbed by Sir Randle Feilden who asked where I was going. In a flash he was seated in the front with three others in the back of the car. Richard Stanley was one of them, but the names of the others escape me. They directed me to White's Club and one of the rear passengers was trying to make me park on the pavement until Sir Randle Feilden, being a real gentleman, put him in his place. I was asked in but all I remember is Lord Vestey buying me a brandy after which I departed before a real session started. It is very easy for people to say you need not miss the last train or carry on after a dinner, but with drink inside you as well as the party spirit I'm afraid rational thinking is seldom present. If the naming of titled people seems a bit over the top it is not so because regular racegoers mix with very few formalities.

Anyone with a car in London after these dinners was a very popular fellow. On one such occasion, Sir Gordon Richards knew I was going back to Marlborough where he lived. He intended catching the last train to Reading where he had left his car but that was not an option and Gordon asked for a lift and would I mind going to the Stork Club. He had gathered up Fulke Walwyn and Tom Egerton, so it was four of us who pulled up outside the club where Gordon was greeted like Royalty. He ordered a bottle of Champagne and scrambled eggs on toast for four. Gordon was another gentleman and declined the services of the 'hostesses', but being naturally generous told the manager to give them £2 each and put it on his bill. Fulke Walwyn and Tom Egerton went their various ways and Gordon and I set off for Marlborough. After going round in circles trying to find the road that went West, Gordon suggested I stop and ask a policeman who was on his beat. I countered by suggesting that he asked the policeman but it was a joint decision to carry on.

Eventually we were nearing Marlborough and there was a transport café on the main road. 'Just right for a cup of tea,' says Gordon. It's now daylight as we entered the café in our dinner jackets. The only words I heard were, 'There's a queer lot in here this morning.' I dropped Gordon at his house and drove back to my hotel in Marlborough. I imagine Gordon changed in London as I found his suitcase in the boot. When I took it back, Lady Richards answered the door with the greeting: 'What on earth have you done to Gordon? He is still in bed and very unwell.' So much for doing good turns. When another London dinner was on the horizon, Gordon asked Don 'whether that Bob is going and if so tell him to keep out of my bloody way.' He was, of course, joking and making out it was me who got him in trouble the last time Towards the end of his riding career, Gordon moved from Marlborough to a smaller house in Kintbury and held a sale of his large collection of wines and other household items. He invited Marian and me to tea before the start of the early evening sale and I bought a brass chestnut roaster and brass toasting fork as a permanent reminder of this racing legend.

For a similar reason I bought a quantity of carpet from an area in the house that did not have much traffic. After a short time it showed signs of wear which explained why, on a couple of occasions, Gordon asked, with a grin, 'How's that carpet?' Quite often Gordon would request wine instead of a money present after a win for outside stables and this accounted for his sizeable cellar. It contained a lot of Taylor's port which was sold by the case but at the auction was bid for by the bottle. It was an embarrassed young lady who thought she had bought a bottle only to find her expected outlay was multiplied by twelve. A large quantity of the stock was bought by a local hotelier.

When the valuable hurdle race at Newbury in February was sponsored by Schweppes, they gave an eve-of-race dinner at Boodles. The gathering was usually around twenty strong with the chief racing writers forming the majority. One regular was Sir Martin Gilliat, the Queen Mother's racing secretary and manager. He was a delight and was told by the Queen Mum to remember any saucy jokes that were told. After one of these dinners, I walked with Martin Gilliat to the bottom of St James' Street where my car was parked. I offered Martin a lift to wherever he was going, only for him to remark that he had some comfortable digs across the road. Stupid me!

The pre-dinner speciality was a carved ice image with oysters at the base. I was not even tempted to have one, as I have been ill on two occasions. The first time was in Brighton, and luckily not far from home. A long time after, there were three oysters among the starter of the dinner given by the Mayor of Doncaster. It was a toss-up as whether to leave them or eat them. Unfortunately, I made the wrong choice and was once again sick, but not quite as ill as on the previous occasion and was well enough to attend the St Leger.

The oyster story I like best took place in the Queen's Hotel in Manchester. It was when the November Handicap was run there and marked the final day of the flat race season. Before going to the races it was a tradition for Captain Charles Elsey and Harry Peacock to have an oyster feast with Black Velvet, that being Guinness and Champagne. I, together with my good friend Lionel Cureton, who was 'Templegate' on the then *Daily Herald*, had not stayed at the Queen's before. Those two delightful trainers, Charlie and Harry, invited us to join them at a table that was attractively laid out with this good English fare. When I declined the oysters but accepted the Black Velvet, Harry jokingly called me a soft southerner, or words to that effect. There was no tempting me, however, but I enjoyed the ribbing. When the new flat season opened at Lincoln, one of the first I bumped into was Barbara Fenningworth, the daughter of Harry Peacock. She knew all about the oyster feast and said her father had been very sick afterwards and vowed never to eat an oyster again. I think the North-South ribbing ended in a draw.

The many occasions on which I missed the last train still haunt me. Nights in the Mayfair and Savoy Hotels were not so bad while the Cavendish Hotel in Duke Street did an all night breakfast. I availed myself of this on one occasion but it was still a long night followed by a leisurely stroll to Waterloo to catch the milk train home while still in a dinner jacket. That was better than trying to hitch a lift along the M4 in a snowstorm. Eventually I stopped at a service station and asked if they would order me a taxi. What arrived was a chauffeur-driven limousine which made it an expensive night. There were, however, a couple of lucky breaks. Firstly it was Peter Walwyn who had a car and a driver and kindly offered me a lift and a bed at his, then, Seven Barrows Stables near Lambourn. The second stroke of luck came as I was wandering along the Strand wondering what to do when the trainer Bill Wightman walked past. We had been to the same affair and I knew he had to go through my home at Odiham. Naturally Bill was kind enough to transport me on one condition, that being that I did not mind travelling at 130 m.p.h. on the M3. He had the latest Jaguar and I have never got home from London so quickly.

27

SICKENING OCCASIONS

There is seldom a dull day in racing and Jeffrey Bernard has to figure in some incidents, one of which it is hoped will not be repeated by anyone. Jeffrey was the character portrayed by Peter O'Toole in the London play *Jeffrey Bernard is Unwell*. He was well known as a heavy drinker and must have brought up a small fortune when sick in the flowerbed in front of the Queen's Box at Ascot. He was escorted from the Members' Enclosure and was, I believe, temporarily barred from Ascot. He used to have a weekly column in the *Sporting Life* and had written something that caused irritation to an owner/trainer named Mr H. Handel who was a wholesale butcher in the West Country. His best horse was Royal Toss who was second to Glencaraig Lady in the 1972 Cheltenham Gold Cup.

Whatever the differences, the pair had not met. It was after the last race at Fontwell that my then local butcher and friend Bob Mayes and I adjourned to the bar, soon to be joined by Jeffrey. I introduced Bob Mayes as 'Your friendly butcher, Tim Handel'. They were getting on well until we went our different ways. It came as a bit of a shock when I read Jeffrey's column saying how he had now met Tim Handel and what a pleasant man he was. When I next met Jeffrey I told him it was meant as a joke and was sorry he thought otherwise. That was the end of the matter, or so I thought. The next big occasion was the Royal Ascot meeting and that week's column by Jeffrey in the *Sporting Life* included the following:

> The Gold Cup was a great race with some fine stayers on view but the best stayer of the day was Bob Butchers who stayed in the Trainer's bar from the first race to the last.

Touché!

It was Jeffrey who also wrote under the nom-de-plume of Colonel Mad in *Private Eye* and had a little dig at me in a column entitled 'Sporting

Life'. The contents make me laugh every time I read them or picture them. I attended the dinner hosted at the Jockey Club Rooms by Lord Howard de Walden. Among the guests was Jim Stanford of the *Daily Mail* who arrived late and drunk, and managed to be sick several times during and after the dinner. It was certainly a substantial affair with a continuation of drinking in the lounge. Hopefully you can now get an idea of the sort of evening it was: drink, drink, drink. Jeffrey wrote hilariously about the occasion and the article warrants reproduction.

'Sporting Life'.

The incredible Jim Stanford, alias Captain Heath of the *Daily Mail*, ex racing manager to the House of Holland and self-styled English representative of Daniel Wildenstein, close friend of Her Majesty Queen Elizabeth II has surpassed himself yet again.

On his first outing for many months he put in a splendid display at Kempton Park on Boxing Day when he was sick, without flinching, at the William Hill table as a result of a Bill Marshall success. On that occasion, Spanish Armada was solely to blame. Like a Pavlov dog, Stanford reacts utterly predictably to a Marshall winner.

After the Kempton chunder, most of us thought that the patrician of puke would be put out to grass for a few months, but, so fit was he seen to be two weeks ago, it was decided to invite him to a Press dinner given by some of the Jockey Club stewards in the belief that he could stay the extra few hours until midnight.

Picture if you can, the incredible scene. Hosts Lord Howard de Walden and Jocelyn Hambro eagerly await the giants of the press. Stanford arrives at 9 p.m. when it's 8 for 8.30 wearing a Liberace-type shirt covering a body that looks like a beetroot that's just heard bad news. He is tired, unsteady and confused. Seated next to Simon Weatherby, he sleeps throughout dinner and it's a dinner at which even hardened and experienced imbibers like Bob Butchers and Monty Court behave impeccably throughout.

The dinner over, there's a question and answer session in which the Stewards invite the Press to chat about mutual problems. Suddenly it's seen that Stanford is being slowly, relentlessly and colourfully sick down his shirt front. The apple crumble ejected, Stanford falls asleep again only to wake up and interrupt Jonathan Powell's speech to say, 'We've all got a job to do'. He then passes out again while the assembled company leaves for the withdrawing room for further cocktails.

It was during the cocktails that Stanford showed he can get a trip by an amazing revival which lurched him into the after dinner session, custard now dribbling from his mouth, and up to de Walden to ask a pertinent question. Still issuing forth like a meat and two veg Vesuvius, Stanford then popped his question to de Walden who wisely and wittily answered, 'I'm glad you brought that up, Stanford'. Later, reeling out of the Rooms, Jim threw up another three times in the hall.

Local cleaners had to be appeased by a tenner from Tony Fairburn and I'm told that the Rooms still smell of Stanford and disinfectant. The girl who wiped it up with the *Daily Mail* has now switched to the *Daily Mirror* and they now call three carpets and one shirt 'Jim's Yankee.'

You have to understand that the mention of the House of Holland, Wildenstein and Marshall in the early part of his article is real micky-taking. Jim used to think he had inside information about horses owned by the trio but was not taken seriously by his colleagues. To get maximum impact from this great piece of writing you really had to know Jim Stanford.

An incident in another Newmarket racing club, the Craven, pales into insignificance compared with the Stanford affair, but was nevertheless something that irritated me. I had just bought a round of drinks and looking back saw that a set of false teeth had been put in my gin and tonic. The culprit was the former steeplechase jockey and later trainer, George Archibald. It was a half-hearted apology that I received at the races the following day.

One of my very early social affairs was a dinner given by the racehorse owner Claude Harper. There were no more than a dozen of us and the host called on individuals to stand and talk about a racing topic. I was very much the new boy and dreading the occasion, so not only was I drinking the plentiful red wine available but I was writing notes on the starched cuffs of my dress shirt. It was all in vain. I was not asked to speak and have never been keen to do so.

A more enjoyable occasion, or so I thought, was when I took my daughter, Lesley, to Longchamps for the Arc de Triomphe. Ernie Sparrowhawk had a betting shop in Epsom but had never been racing in France. He asked if he could go to the track with me but I was taking my daughter to lunch at Fouquets so told him to have a look round and meet at the restaurant at a given time. The weather was not too good so we had mackintoshes and I had a hold-all in which were my binoculars, car keys, English money and a few other items. I got a cab to the races and asked Ernie to bring my things while I paid the driver. He brought my mac but not my hold-all. It was not until the cab had departed that I became aware of the situation. Luckily, tickets and passport were on my person. I was taken to somebody who phoned appropriate places where lost items might have been left but they were not recovered.

Peter Scott, 'Hotspur' of the *Daily Telegraph*, was on my flight home and able to lend me the English money that I might need. The big issue was the car keys. My wife was a non-driver so my neighbour kindly volunteered to meet me at Heathrow. There was a drawer in my bureau with keys to all manner of things so my saviour brought the lot. All ended well, but my daughter remembers the occasion for a different reason. The racecourse was packed and I had to send my copy to London. Using a phone in France used to be a nightmare, that is if you could find one, so I told Lesley to stand by a particular oak tree and not move as I was afraid of losing her. After about an hour, I returned to find the poor girl standing by that tree and not wishing to go racing in France again. It was all a bit of a nightmare and on other visits I would go to our Paris office which was the other side of town. To complicate matters the taxi would take you no further than the Arc de Triomphe and trying to get another usually involved a long wait.

Greyhound racing has never appealed to me but my friendly landlord, Guy, said he had been asked to put £200 on one at Portsmouth. There was a racing link as one of the major shareholders in the track was Joe Childs, the King's jockey and winner of several Classics. We went early as the greyhound was in the second race. The £200 was invested together with our few pounds and the creature finished last. That was enough for us and we returned to the car that was parked in a quiet cul-de-sac, or so we thought. The road was now full of cars and we had to wander about until well after the last race before we could get out.

A far better experience was an investment at the long gone Alexandra Palace, more commonly known as Ally Pally. The course was shaped like a frying pan and in sprints the field did not come into view until about two furlongs from the finish. The same amount, £200, but not from the same person, was duly placed for a friend of mine, who was close to the animal's connections, plus my few quid, at 2/1. When the runners appeared in view the juvenile that carried our money was in the lead. Not only was she in the lead but it was some while before the next one appeared. Trained by the diminutive ex-jockey, Johnny Dines, the filly was eased a long way from the finish but still won by ten lengths. Her name was Careless Nora who won York's Nunthorpe Stakes among other top sprints. No wonder she annihilated a sub-standard field.

28

FOGGY DAYS

The four days at Royal Ascot were hectic, both work-wise and socially. Any chance of a lie-in on the Saturday was not possible as I and David Phillips, the racing editor, had to be at Gatwick Airport by seven thirty to catch a private plane to Redcar. It was the Andy Capp Handicap, a good class race, sponsored by the *Daily Mirror*. A competition was run by the paper and the winner could take a guest to enjoy a Champagne lunch, private box and other incidentals. David Phillips and I had to host the occasion, which caused no hassle but it would have been better on some other day. One of the winners was Bill Cooper and a friend introduced as Mrs Nickerson, which caused a ripple of laughter. They were great fun and had come from the Isle of Wight. Bill Cooper had his own business but when he retired took a job as porter at the Farringford Hotel, which had been the home of Lord Tennyson at Freshwater. As a hobby, Bill Cooper produced lovely watercolours. He enjoyed his Redcar trip so much that he painted the Farringford Hotel and it has been hanging on a wall ever since his daughter personally delivered it in the seventies.

We had been doing this Redcar trip for years and on one occasion we were more than halfway home when the pilot announced that he was unable to contact Gatwick on his radio and was forced to return to the airfield at Stockton. If you add that to a flat tyre on my car and a missed dinner date on different occasions it made the race a bit of a Jonah.

While living in Lewes, our social gatherings were getting a bit too big for our house. We were the only married pair among our friends at that time and it was usually 'Back to Bob and Marian's' after we had left the pub or dance or whatever. As we all wanted to be together I booked the function room at the stately Southover Grange. Beer, wines and spirit plus a buffet had all been arranged by myself but on the chosen day I was forced to dedicate some of the jobs as I had to go to Ireland for the

Thyestes Chase, a recognised trial for the Grand National. The returning plane was heading for Heathrow when the crew was told that the fog was too bad to land. The nearest airport in the clear was Barry, near Cardiff. Just the delay I didn't want. We were issued with rail tickets for London and after that it was down to us to get home or take a bus to Heathrow that was waiting at Paddington. I chose to go direct to Lewes by train or else I would have missed all of the party. With the Southover Grange being so close to the station, I was there by half past eight and the troubled journey was soon forgotten. There were around forty people at the party and, believe it or not, each of us paid just £1. It cost a lot more to retrieve my car from the Heathrow car park!

Fog, the enemy of racing, again caused delays when most of the racing correspondents were heading to France for one of their important races. I was sitting with Clive Graham at the airport when he was approached by someone he knew with authority and he asked both of us to go with him to the VIP lounge. He said he would ensure that we were on the very first plane available. The only other person in the lounge was Lesley Caron, whom I did not recognise but was told she was a famous French actress. After not too long a wait, we were driven to the plane and congratulating ourselves on a flying start, and no pun intended. When we arrived in France, we discovered that the flight on which we were originally booked had landed some twenty minutes before us. It did not prevent Clive and me calling at the George Cinq for some refreshment. It never needed much of an excuse to reward ourselves.

I was not too keen on working in France and in the spring of 1951, I was sent there to assess the chance of a French colt winning the Derby in June. After Airborne had won the first post-war Derby, three of the next four went to the French. The raiders were also winning other top races in England and a complex had developed. Every French horse sent here was looked upon as a world-beater. The assignment was for as long as it took, but in my case it was all decided in a few days. The language barrier, transport and the reluctance of many trainers to provide information was not the sort of task I relished.

At that time, the Royal British Legion Club in Paris was managed by Alf Gordon, who, I mentioned earlier, was the champion flat jockey in Denmark prior to the war. The only reason I knew he was there was because his daughter, Jacqueline, married my brother-in-law. He was a big help and arranged the transport problem. A friend of his was employed by the Godfrey Davis hire-car company to run-in their new

173

Danish champions Don Butchers and Alf Gordon

cars. For a small remuneration he would drive the car in any direction I wished. I did visit the Geoffrey Watson stable, but that was all.

On a lovely spring morning, I sat outside a café and watched the world go by and at the same time wrote a powerful piece telling millions of readers my verdict. It told how I had visited all the principal stables in France and was emphatic that there was no colt good enough to win the Derby. An equally strong headline went over my article and much to my relief the Derby was won by Arctic Prince, trained by Willie Stephenson. To make it even better, I received congratulations from my Sports Editor.

It turned out to be a lot better than talking to a lot of French people who, through patriotism, may well have convinced me that one of theirs was unbeatable.

29

A BIT OF BANTER

Considering journalism was not my chosen profession, I suppose I was lucky to stick it for almost thirty-nine years. I enjoyed the tipping part of it and was happy writing factual pieces, but jazzing it up or writing controversial articles gave me not the slightest pleasure. When bad weather was responsible for a lengthy period of no racing, it was a nightmare trying to fill the space. I would sit for hours trying to think of something different or interesting to write. The tipping side of the business was tackled with gusto and I'm not boasting when I say I delved into the formbook for hours and probably worked as hard as anyone and more likely harder than most. My tipping was not confined to the principal meeting. When there were fourteen and, at times, sixteen meetings on a Bank Holiday I would tip for all of them and devote as much time as was humanely possible before the deadline.

On several occasions I put genuine friendships before the newspaper and never had the slightest conscience. The most glaring example appeared in the *Sporting Life*'s 'Jack Logan' column written by Sir David Llewellyn. It followed a dinner at which Fred Winter won an award after he retired as a jockey and his acceptance speech mentioned something that I had done, or more precisely, something I had not done. The subject matter concerns Fred's riding of Galloway Braes in the King George VI Chase at Kempton's Boxing Day meeting. It was after he retired that Fred admitted that he had been caught napping and was beaten by Limber Hill. I felt sure he had given the race away and wrote an article suggesting this, but was uneasy about the matter and showed what I had written to Fred. He admitted his mistake and said that given the choice he would prefer it not to appear in print, adding that I had a job to do. It did not appear in print, but in his biography, by the late David Hedges, his views concerning his mistake were repeated, and I quote:

It was nice to attend a Tribute Dinner for all of the surviving jockeys who had won the Gold Cup.
Standing L to R: D.L. Jones, G.W. Robinson, W. Rees, M. Scudamore, J. Power, T. Cusack, D.V. Dick, A. Brabazon, M. Molony, A. Grantham, J. Burke, F. Winter, P. Taaffe, R. Black. Seated: H. Nicholson, D. Morgan, E. Williams, T. Hyde, J. Hamey, G. Owen, R. Burford. Sitting on the floor: T.W. Biddlecombe, R. Barry, P. Kellaway

Presenting award to champion NH jockey Ron Barry with Jack Solomon and Charlie Chester in foreground

The one rather wonderful thing that came out of it was that one of the Press, Bob Butchers of the *Daily Mirror*, came to me afterwards and showed me what he had written about the incident and said did I mind him publishing it. I think he must have been the only person on the racecourse who realised what a mess I had made of it. Certainly he was the only person who mentioned it to me. I said I couldn't stop him printing it, although I obviously would be happier if he didn't, and when I looked at the paper the next day he had in fact left it out. I must say that the press as a whole were very kind to me, but I thought this was one of the nicest things anyone ever did for me in racing.

This revelation caused Sir David Llewellyn to write that this was poor journalism. I totally agreed with him, but none of us are the same and it so happens that we have different priorities. Mine remains the same to this day. As far as the *Daily Mirror* is concerned, I think they had their full value from me over a very long period. In an effort to get my feet firmly under the table, I did not take a holiday for the first eleven years and for a much longer period worked seven days a week.

Major John Watts and Sir Kenneth Gibson, Clerks of the Course at Epsom and Sandown respectively

John 'Towser' Gosden was a splendid trainer in Lewes and we were good friends who liked to have a go at each other. This was always done with a laugh. It was regrettable that he died before Charlottstown won the Derby, as he had been responsible for the first season training of the colt. It must also be said that his successor, Gordon Smyth, finished the job in good style. With the jump jockey Andy Jarvis having been with Gosden since leaving school, I suppose it was natural that his son Michael joined the trainer at an early age. It was, in fact, Michael who looked after Charlottstown and 'led him up' for the Derby. Michael still reckons that experience as exciting as any of his big race wins as a trainer. His last two Derby runners have been unlucky. One broke down badly when seeming sure of a place at least while his 2006 runner swerved badly in the final yards when, in my opinion, it seemed sure to win even if only narrowly.

When I was tipping for the *Daily Mirror* I napped many of Gosden's winners and although I knew several of his employees I never once sought any information. At the end of one flat race season I had napped ten winners from the stable and some at very good prices. It was a real laugh when he sent a bundle of documents bound with pink ribbon. All the details were included with an account for the odds to £10 for each winner. One of those winners was Uncle Bones in an apprentice race at Birmingham. The horse was ridden by Bill Rees who later became the stable jockey for Peter Cazalet and, of course, the Queen Mother. In that 1950 race Bill was sixteen and rode at 6st 7lb. As we left the stands after this 9/1 win, Gosden slung a playful right hook at my chin, or at least I hope it was playful or else he would have made a very poor boxer!

Another bit of banter was exchanged on the Lewes Downs. Towser had his horses circling around him as I was returning on one of Don's animals. Towser had evidently witnessed our schooling session a little earlier and shouted, 'You're brave, riding schooling without a hat.' I had an instant reply and simply said, 'I've got hair on my head.' The reference, of course, was to his baldness but the banter continued that afternoon at Brighton races. He sorted me out and said, 'I know it's a bit late, but though I may not have much on my head, I've got something in it.' He was not short of a few tricks and saddled Nicean, owned by the gambler Leslie Redfern, in a hurdle race at Plumpton. As it cantered to the start its forelegs were heavily bandaged with a vast amount of cottonwool on display. The horse, ridden by Andy Jarvis, was backed from 4/1 to 2/1 and duly obliged but without anything on its legs. The bandages and cotton wool had been removed at the start and I wrote about the incident in the next day's paper. Shortly after I was laid up and as Towser had not seen me riding out he asked Don where I was. When told I was unwell he said, 'He's probably got cottonwool on the brain.' So much for those who never read the *Daily Mirror* but always know what's in it! Those who think that only the so-called working class read the *Mirror* are mistaken. I once wrote something about a hurdler trained by Fulke Walwyn for the Duke of Devonshire which had let me down a couple of times and soon after was invited for drinks on the terrace of the House of Commons overlooking the Thames. It was a lovely day and the first person to approach me was the Duke who said he had read my article and that I was to continue tipping his horse as it was sure to win and it did just that.

After winning the *Sporting Chronicle*'s Nap Table, I was given a dinner at the Café Royal and one of the guests was Towser Gosden. After receiving the Cup, I made reference to the number of naps trained by him and as an afterthought said, 'By the way, the nap tomorrow is the

'Towser' Gosden chats to Doug Smith

Gosden trained Impatient in the Tudor Stakes.' It won at 15/8, but Jimmy Lindley had to pull out all the stops to win by a short head. It was at that dinner, given by the *Daily Mirror*, that we had owners, trainers, jockeys, racing officials and paper representatives. The *Daily Mirror* spared no expense and even laid on a private plane to fly some of the jockeys back from Ludlow races. It was still a rush for these boys, who changed into their dinner jackets on the plane, which was just as well as traffic jams caused further delay to the cars that brought them from Croydon Airport. An informal dinner was enjoyed by all and while the wine still flowed freely Lord Derby's presentation of the Gold Cup was screened live on Independent Television. As a mark of appreciation, the *Daily Mirror* gave Lord Derby a set of his famous black and white racing silks, complete with one white button, and also a new racing whip for his jockey, Doug Smith. Most people in racing know the story of one white button but I will relate the reason for those who don't. Jockeys used to have a silk scarf round their necks with the loose ends hanging down inside the jacket of their silks. This gave the neck line a smarter appearance. It was Tommy Weston who unknowingly covered a button with part of his scarf when doing up his jacket before going out to win the Derby on Sansovino. The white button was plain to see so it was regarded as lucky and has been incorporated in every new set of colours. The evening was most enjoyable and to round off the occasion a crowd of us went on to a London nightclub for further jollification. The racing crowd are normally a happy bunch who celebrate their successes and tend to drown their sorrows when the inevitable reverses take place. One thing never lacking is good company.

As I mentioned earlier, my Uncle Alec did the secretarial work for Gosden and liked to have a bet, but unfortunately mostly on losers. He got the idea that one of the stable's runners was a good thing at Yarmouth and decided to make the trip. On the train he wore a trilby hat and dark glasses as a disguise. Alec was in for a shock: while waiting for the train to move off. Gosden walked along the corridor, opened the door and said, 'Hello, Alec. What are you up to?'

Alex Bird had horses in the stable and while I was having a drink with Towser he said it was sink or swim with Precious Heather in the Ayr Gold Cup. It was not a case of running a good race because Alex Bird wanted to know it was a near certainty. I'm pleased for all concerned that it won that 1956 race at 5/1 with Edward Hide in the saddle. It all had to be secretive when there was to be a plunge on a horse owned by Alex Bird and my uncle. Alec was liable to spout to his friends if he suspected there was something in the offing, With this in mind, Gosden dictated a letter for Alec to send to the owner saying a horse due to run shortly was not 100 per cent and advising him not to have a bet. The animal duly won leaving my uncle convinced that trainers are not always right. What he didn't know was that Gosden rang the owner and told him to destroy the letter when it arrived. I am pleased I knew Gosden for so long.

Owning a racehorse has never been among my wishes unless, of course, I had a few million pounds to spare. It would then be my pleasure to have three or four flat horses with James Eustace and three or four jumpers with Andy Turnell. Providing they would have me I would leave everything to them and ask only for a phone call when they were due to run. That would make me the perfect owner.

No doubt I followed that procedure with the one horse I did own for a season. That ownership came about when I was having a drink with Paul Smyth at Windsor. We were joined by a London publican who I had met on the odd occasion. He asked me to buy a yearling and agreed that Paul would be the trainer. The yearling was duly purchased and I

Gypsy Mine (Pat Eddery) was the only horse owned

rang to tell the new owner it was named Gypsy Mine. It was a bit of a blow when he said he had changed his mind. That meant the 'Gypsy' was now 'Mine'. Thanks a bundle was my reaction. I was well and truly lumbered so decided to keep the filly and hope for a fairytale ending, which of course it wasn't. She ran four times and although not entirely disgraced on a couple of occasions, I held little hope that she could win anything. Paul managed to sell her for exactly the price I paid so the venture cost me a season's training fees. The most enjoyable part was seeing my grandfather's brown and orange colours which I had registered. It was fortunate that the colours were still available even though the original colours were chocolate and orange. For some years now only a limited number of basic colours are allowed but the range has been widened by introducing a variety of designs such as diabolo.

30

BEHIND THE SCENES

I have no idea of the antics, if any, of the present day jockeys but fifty or sixty years ago there were many cases of wild goings-on and I refer to the jump jockeys because it was they with whom I associated. Kevin Gilsenan came from Ireland to join Tom Masson in the late forties, and it was not long before we became good friends. I was, in fact, best man at his marriage to local Lewes girl Pam, with my daughter Lesley as bridesmaid. As Kevin was a non-driver we often went racing together and he was also a regular visitor to my home. He rode Cloncarrig in the 1949

Best man at wedding of Kevin Gilsenan. The smallest one is Lesley

Grand National and the horse was fourth favourite. That prompted a visit as he had been offered £500 to ensure it didn't win. It took only a few minutes for the Irishman to make up his mind. He reasoned that it was easy money as the horse would be more than likely to fall and if it happened to be in there with a chance he would be unable to resist riding a Grand National winner. Cloncarrig fell at the seventh fence which is the small one after Becher's Brook and now known as the Foinavon as he was the shock winner of the 1967 race in which there was devastation at that obstacle. I never did ask Kevin for his final decision but I'm pretty sure of the answer.

A couple of crackpot ideas were put to me and I disagreed with both of them. One involved me, and the other was one that Kevin perpetrated. On the morning he came to my house he said he had been awake for more than twenty-four hours after taking a tablet and asked me to try one, but that was out of the question. Kevin said he knew the horse that would do well if he administered a couple of them. The horse was well known to me and once belonged to Miss Dorothy Paget. The animal had a lot of ability and would most likely be a 'good thing' if doing his best. There were only a few runners in a race at Lingfield which seemed an ideal opportunity. I told Kevin that he was playing with fire and I didn't

Jockeys Ron Atkins (L) and Joe Guest (R) among our party

want to know for obvious reasons. The horse won at 50/1 but I didn't ask if any tablets were given and I didn't need to know because what I didn't know I couldn't tell.

The other plot that Kevin had put together in his dreams was to take place at Plumpton. It was before any rebuilding when the first three horses used to be unsaddled opposite the entrance to the old wooden weighing room which was a bit of a bottle-neck. People naturally thronged to this area so it was the ideal setting for Kevin's plan. He suggested leaving the weight cloth off a horse which he used to saddle and ride. I would be at the saddling stall and take the weight cloth and smuggle it under my overcoat or mackintosh depending on the weather. When the horse had either won or been placed I would join the throng and purposely bump into Kevin as he walked past and drop the weight cloth to the ground. Kevin would pick it up as if it was he who had dropped it and weigh in at the correct weight. Nice one, Kevin, but not for me or, most certainly, anyone else with a brain.

Kevin was a bit wild but it was difficult to dislike him. He, together with Pam, Marian and me, used to go to some of the dances of which there were several during the winter. There was, of course, plenty of drinking at these affairs and Kevin had his share, but never became anything but jovial. It must have been something extraordinary that happened one night because he couldn't remember any details. When he called on me the following morning, it was to tell me he was taken to the police station as he had been seen running down the High Street in his underwear. No action was taken and I have never found out all the details because Kevin didn't know them either.

The Belle Vue Hotel in Cheltenham was a favourite place to stay and the jockeys never considered an early night. Kevin and I joined several in the bar one evening and it was a joyful gang that eventually retired. There were a few with hangovers the next morning, but none worse than Kevin. He thought it best to walk the couple of miles or so to the racecourse as it might help to clear his head and asked if I would keep him company. Just as well I did because it was not long before a shoelace came undone. It was me who had to tie it as any bending made the world go round. This is no fairytale but just a real life story. I saw Kevin as he walked to the parade ring to ride Porter's Call in a three-mile steeplechase. He was still feeling groggy and I really felt for him. It is surprising how resilient some people are, and our Kevin rode like a demon to beat the outstanding Martin Molony by three-quarters of a length. The winner was 100/7 and just the cure that Kevin needed. Anyone wishing to confirm the details of that race: it was at Cheltenham in January 1950.

I have a great liking for the Irish and have friends from both sides of the border. Their quaint charm, and some eccentricity, can brighten a dull day. Driving through the Irish countryside is pleasant and often you may see a grand gated entrance which is surplus to requirements because the boundary fences are broken down.

On a visit to Gowran Park I stayed in a hotel in Carlow and my room was opposite a little shop which seemingly never closed. It was not short of customers, a fact related to me by the incessant ringing of the shop's bell as I lay in bed. Had it been a rat-a-tat instead of a ring my suspicions would have been aroused.

It came as no surprise when I ordered tea and toast at this hotel to get just the toast. When I asked about the butter the waiter brought half a pound. I've had some enjoyable trips to Ireland and some quite extraordinary.

John Hughes and I stayed with a friend who managed a large stud in Mullingar and our visit included a day's racing at Leopardstown. Our host gave us a valuable lesson in how not to drive a car. In his drunken state he scraped a car coming in the opposite direction when leaving the course and zig-zagged his way back to Mullingar. We were grateful that he travelled at a crawl but the surprising thing about the journey was that neither our driver nor the driver of the car he scraped bothered to stop. I think we may draw our own conclusions The stud was certainly remote and I saw women carrying buckets to get water from a standpipe as it was not laid on to their dwellings.

The Grand National meeting sees the hotels in Liverpool and Southport buzzing with activity, and, of course, a huge crowd of the delightful Irish. I have known drink and card parties to go on into the early hours with no repercussions. One jockey I know had little sleep after playing cards till the early hours and then making up to his girlfriend. It was not too long before he rode three winners that afternoon.

Years ago Sean Magee was battling against the bottle at the end of his riding days and Matt Feakes gave him a few mounts. One of these was at Sandown, and when Matt gave him a leg-up Sean fell off the other side, but still rode in an obviously unfit state. Our old friend Jock Langlands, believe it or not, rode in an amateur's steeplechase at Liverpool. It was after the race that Jock, in breeches and colours, walked into the bar carrying his saddle and ordered a large brandy. Of course not all jockeys are the same. I remember the evening before Oxo won the Grand National in 1959. Michael Scudamore rode that winner and on the eve of the race he suggested we go to the cinema to see *The King and I*. After a short time, Michael asked if I was enjoying the film. The answer was 'No', so we left the cinema and had a few drinks instead. On this occasion it was not a booze-up or a late night.

Dave Dick was another high flyer and it is difficult to imagine him doing 7st 4lb when winning the 1941 Lincolnshire Handicap on Gloaming. Also hard to believe is Staff Ingham winning the Royal Hunt Cup on Weathervane, who carried 6st 12lb in the 1923 race at Royal Ascot. That horse was owned by King George V. Both jockeys grew to over six feet tall. Dave died suddenly of a heart attack. Sadly he did not live to see his daughter, Daisy, win a major eventing title. He had nurtured her career with a passion.

Shedding huge amounts of weight was something jockeys had to do almost daily. It was after a period of starvation that Dave asked for a lift back to Epsom where I was living at the time. He had ridden at his lowest at Newbury, and on the way home he asked me to stop in Odiham, another of my homes at a later date. The reason for this stop was the International Stores from where he emerged with a load of ham, a loaf of bread and a jar of Branston pickle. About the only bits he didn't eat were those dropped on the floor. Dave was a good doer when able and I remember going with him into Wheelers in Old Compton Street in London. We both had Dover soles and just walked out with Dave saying, 'Put it down to Bernard.' Bernard Walsh was the restaurant owner who usually had a horse or two in training. Dave did not have quite the mentality of Gilsenan but did put forward a proposition. It was for me to libel him in the *Daily Mirror* so that he could sue me and go fifty-fifty when the damages had been awarded. I reminded him that all stories were vetted by the lawyer and this half-hearted proposal was quickly kicked into touch.

Comparing jockeys from different generations is difficult but I believe there are many who stand out with that little bit extra. Between the two world wars F.B. Rees and George Duller were outstanding and Bill Stott and Bill Speck were very successful but not so stylish. Stott had a son, also Billy, who rode winners when apprenticed to Frank Hartigan. This cheeky little devil once told Gordon Richards to 'move over, grandad' as they were lining up at the start before the use of stalls. When the jockeys' championship ran from New Year's Day to 31 December, F.B. was the first to register a century of winners. Occasionally there is a surprise champion and before the war it was Eric Foster. In 1925 Eric won it with seventy-six winners.

F.B. Rees was champion five times with his century achieved in 1924. That was the year of my birth and it was also the year that Fontwell staged its first meeting with F.B. riding the first winner. The format for deciding the champion was changed for the 1925/26 season and it is the one in use now.

In the 1946/47 season, the surprise packet was Jack Dowdeswell and he won the title with just fifty-eight wins. There have been no surprises since and Jack earned his wins as he would ride anything and that led to him having more than his fair share of falls and, of course, injuries. There were others in the same mould. Bill Redmond must have walked away from the site of his falls more often than he rode winners. At one stage the fences at Windsor had been re-built and, following a walk back from a fall, Bill described the new fences as 'like jumping pianos'. After Bill had called it a day a similar role was taken over by Tom Mabbut. Tom was a popular jockey who was seldom without a smile even after his many bone-crushing falls.

In bygone days there were those who rode only over hurdles. George Duller, Staff Ingham and George Pellerin were among them and Pellerin's one ride over fences ended in a fall. Johnny Gilbert, Dennis Dillon and Harry Sprague were later hurdle-race specialists. Dennis and Harry were small with very short legs. This, however, did not stop Harry riding over the Aintree fences and later winning the Whitbread Gold Cup at Sandown on Done Up. Ryan Prince knew what he was doing when he persuaded Harry to take the mount. Done Up was a hard ride who needed getting at almost from the start. He won by a short head due entirely to Harry's masterful ride.

Johnny Gilbert was one of the 'Wootton Boys' and when he joined Alex Kilpatrick, who concentrated on chasers, Johnny had no option. When he rode the winner of a four mile chase at Cheltenham he was over the moon and hosted a dinner for a few of us staying at the same hotel. Johnny, who could talk for England, was very amusing and professed to being scared throughout the race, which in reality, of course, was only half true.

Fred Winter, Martin Molony and Bryan Marshall were jockeys of the highest class who, like many others, were not always in favour of amateur

With friend and top jockey Harry Sprague

jockeys. These days most of the amateurs ride like professionals but in 1919 Harry Brown, an outstanding amateur, won the jockeys' championship with forty-eight winners. Harry Brown trained Didoric who was Don Butchers' only ride in the Grand National and his name crops up in the next chapter. He was the last amateur to be champion but in 1914 Jack Anthony won the title with sixty and in 1922 was champion as a professional with seventy-eight wins. The only other amateur to be champion in the twentieth century was Mr H. Sidney whose fifty-three wins in 1900 earned him the title.

At the other end of the scale was Mr Philip Turner. This little bespectacled man was nearly as broad as he was tall. He first came to my notice when he was walking around at Lingfield wearing breeches, boots, colours and cap plus his whip. It transpired that he was not riding until a much later race. Sorry to say, he looked out of place when mounted and so it proved as he fell at the first hurdle and brought down five of the runners. He had previously ridden in the Puissance (high jump) at one of the major horseshows in London. I am sorry to say that he was killed when falling in a race soon afterwards.

31

GOOD FRIENDS

Friends and acquaintances come by the lorryload if you go racing every day. It goes without saying that acquaintances greatly outnumber the friends and real friends are even rarer. I am lucky to have a few of the rare type and they are not all among the racing fraternity. A couple of the 'just friends' category were for many years visited on the journeys to Goodwood. The first came in the whiskered shape of the old England cricketer Godfrey Evans, who was landlord of the Jolly Drover near Liss. I invariably had passengers and the usual order was a bottle of Champagne. Without exception Godfrey would pour himself a glass without being invited. We all took it as a joke because his personality and charm were disarming. Further down the road at Chilgrove was the White Horse, kept at the time by Barry Phillips. He had a wine cellar that won prizes regularly. It was also a wonderful place to eat. Years ago Barry discovered a Champagne that he considered outstanding and bemoaned the fact that he had overstocked his cellar. To good customers, of which I was one, Barry recommended this Champagne and let us have it for £5 a bottle. I believe that Louis Roederer Cristal costs a little more these days. It is now contained in a clear bottle and the price on my last enquiry was £110. It seems we got a bargain!

Barry and his wife, Dorothea, always had a smiling welcome. On one occasion while having dinner I remarked that savouries were now seldom seen on the menu. Barry said, 'Name it, and you shall have it.' I have forgotten the names of all the savouries, such as Angels on Horseback, but I remember the four of us at dinner that night enjoyed the alternative to a dessert. The diners at this rural eatery were given two wine lists. One had wines that went up to the highest at £850 and the other was for ordinary folk like us. It really was no good me looking at the list and I used to ask Barry to choose me a wine at no more than £15. It was amazing how he would supply a beauty at half the price.

Bob with John Hughes

There are lots of races when nothing wants to make the running and as a result starts at a crawl. A similar human race took place on the approach to the Bedford Lodge Hotel in Newmarket. The runners, or should I say dawdlers, were Robin Terry, of the chocolate family, Humphrey Cottrill, a trainer, and myself. The trip from the car park to the hotel bar was probably about fifty yards. Humphrey's stride was very short and he whispered in my ear, 'Hang back, Robin will get the drinks.' I reckon Robin had the same idea and it was obviously a three-runner race with three non-triers. What I remember is that the round cost me a good few quid.

One of my dearest friends was John Hughes who tragically died of a heart attack while returning on the train from London. John started his career in racing as Assistant Clerk of the Course to Major John Watts at Epsom. He then became Clerk of the Course at Leicester, Chepstow, Haydock and Liverpool, but naturally not all at the same time. John played a huge part in restoring Liverpool and the Grand National to its present importance. He was a man who regarded life to be enjoyed to the full and it would not be too difficult to fill a book on his life alone. His father set up and ran PTS, which stood for Postal Tote Service, with a sixpenny minimum bet. It proved to be a huge success and it was left

A suite of Waterford glass given by Chepstow Racecourse for being top tipster.
L to R: Barbara Frances, John Hughes, Marian, George Frances, author

to John on the death of his father. Eventually the business was sold to a bigger company. John was responsible for gaining many sponsorships including Waterford and other big name firms.

I made so many friends thanks to John's introductions. His second wife, Suzy, is a sweetheart and was a great help to John. Both Marian and I have joined in so many occasions with them at home and various places such as Chepstow and Aintree. Perhaps there were many times when John and I acted like silly schoolboys but no harm was done. My daughter went to Parson's Mead School in Ashtead and it was an open day when John joined Marian and me on the visit. He did a little harmless flirting with the girls and then produced the tube from a toilet roll and used it as a telescope. It caused a lot of amusement as he put it to his eye, took aim, and announced, 'I can see your headmistress.' John was a little bit tipsy and uninvited but always most welcome.

Another racecourse executive with whom many happy times were shared was the Kempton supremo, Henry Hyde. He was a kindly,

With Geoff Webster in Ireland

warm-hearted, down-to-earth man and after Arkle was injured at Kempton on Boxing Day the horse went to the racecourse stables and remained there for some time. When the Duchess of Westminster made a visit to see her beloved Arkle, Henry and his wife June invited Geoff Webster and me to join them for lunch as friends, which we were, and not as journalists. Needless to say, the visit by Arkle's owner did not appear in the *Daily Mirror*. It was always my intention to keep my private life and my business life separate. No doubt I missed several scoops because of it but I have always valued my friends. It was a pleasure to be among a small group who gave Henry and June a surprise dinner at the Berkeley Hotel in London to mark his retirement. June's connection with racing came through her father, Sir Charles Moore, who was racing manager to King George VI.

It was a long time before I would eat anything except English food and I stuck to this when Henry invited me and football pundit Jimmy Hill to dinner at an Indian restaurant. I ordered scrambled eggs and have still to experience an 'Indian' and probably never will. I am, however, always free for invitations to Italian, French and Chinese eateries! The meetings at

Kempton were high on my list of favourites simply because of Henry's hospitality. We used to go to the so-called cellar where the caterers held all of their stock and the only thing better than the free drinks was Henry's companionship.

Mark O'Connor bought the International Racing Bureau from David Hedges, whose brainchild it was, and was involved in many of the happy occasions. Denis O'Dell was in the film-making business, which included the first Beatles film, and had fun and humour high on his list of priorities. Denis was very friendly with Charles Drake, the one time American heart-throb, not to be confused with Charlie Drake the comedian. It was during one summer that Denis turned up at our house with Charles. It transpired that Denis had been working in the States and Charles went aboard the *Queen Elizabeth* to see him off. When warned that it was time to disembark, Charles remained aboard and said, 'This is a real send-off – I'm coming with you.' Charles and Denis were keen racegoers and Denis has owned a horse or two in his time.

A few years ago he and his wife Donna invited us to lunch as Charles had come over to stay and it was a happy reunion with David Elsworth and his wife joining the party. That evening David had a runner at Windsor which was expected to win, and we deliberated over the idea of going but finally decided to go straight home. It turned out to be the right decision as the horse was second.

At a time when Denis had a house in London, it was offered to me and David Hedges to use because we had a dinner in town and they were going away. He made just one stipulation and that was not to let the cat out. On opening the door, the cat got a 'flyer' and we spent a long time looking under all the cars parked in the square. We never did find the moggy but it must have returned as we heard nothing to suggest otherwise.

I have no intention of searching my mind for the many escapades with John Hughes but once he and a mutual friend, John Watt, turned up at our house a little the worse for wear. They were hungry and wanted to take us out for dinner: not an easy job to find a table on a Saturday evening with so little notice. That was not a good enough excuse for them who thought I should have enough influence. In actual fact, I did know I could get a table at an Italian restaurant. On arrival it was a surprise to find so few tables taken and we were in a side room and a young couple were the only others there. The two Johns were being highly amusing, even if a bit loud and using a little colourful language. I

Sister Fay with mother and Lesley

decided to go to the other table and apologise on behalf of my friends, but the young couple said it had turned a boring evening into one that they were thoroughly enjoying. They added that a bottle of Champagne was on the way to our table as thanks.

John Hughes is greatly missed by me and many, many others. He and Suzy have, like us, a son named Guy and they are friends too. John was extremely helpful in forming my son's career, and he was a man of fun and great integrity. To me, John was a one-off.

At this point let me add that when it came to business John put his heart and soul into everything and I'm sure his fun and mischief acted as a safety net. Generosity came naturally to him and as an example I relate a case when we were both looking at racing-connected art at Kempton. There was an original painting of Harry Brown who ranked among the very best amateur jockeys before the war, and later was a trainer. My interest was in the subject as he trained Didoric who was the only mount that Don had in the Grand National. Without a word John produced his cheque book and bought it for £200. When it had been carefully wrapped he handed it to me and said, 'Give that to Guy.'

I used to write a piece for a publication, for which John was responsible, called *Winning Ways* and one year John called in and said jokingly that my piece was rubbish. My response was: 'That's what you get for a tenner.' He immediately doubled it to £20 for me and all the other writers.

The reference to the painting of Harry Brown and Don Butchers' ride on Didoric reminds me that jockeys of that period used to ask for £100 on top of their normal fee to ride in the Grand National. Owners and trainers who did not offer the bonus were usually asked for it by the jockey. I remember Don being asked to ride a horse owned by a wealthy member of a aristocratic family. It resulted in stalemate, no £100, no jockey.

32

SADNESS AND JOY

Bill Jennings was the man responsible for me joining the *Daily Mirror* less than three weeks after being demobbed from the RAF. His meeting with Don in Lewes raised the question of who would replace George Kreiner as racing correspondent. George was eighty and waiting to retire. 'Bouverie' was the nom-de-plume of the paper's racing man but when I joined, the chief correspondent became 'Newsboy'. Bill Jennings, the company secretary, gave me a list of five names to choose from, but I left it to him. His choice was 'Newsboy', and not because it was so obviously connected to the press. His choice was the name of a favourite horse owned by Sir Blundell Maple. If I have mentioned this before it shows that I am getting like the old man who couldn't remember whether he had been in a Teashop in Horsham or a Whoreshop in Teasham!

When Bill retired, his greatest pleasure was coming away with me to meetings that involved an overnight stay. For all the Newmarket meetings I would pick him up at a designated pub. Other meetings he attended were Newbury and Ascot. He was very good company with a huge taste for whisky. While on the paper, he and the then Chairman, affectionately known as Bart, would get to the office soon after eight o'clock, and between them drink a bottle of whisky before ten. There appeared to be no limit to the amount he could drink and it was never anything but whisky. He said of brandy, 'What do you drink when that becomes insipid?' I think the simple reason he could drink so much was because he had regular meals.

At Newmarket over the years I stayed in a variety of hotels and lodgings. At one particular house the landlady would cook for us on one of the nights because Bill used to bring a steak and kidney pudding, courtesy of his wife. Other nights we ate mainly at the Ancient Shepherd in Fen Ditton where Bill would invite all and sundry to 'bathe their lips' at his expense. Bill was popular with everyone and he had a ready-made audience when he went through his repertoire of songs, which included 'Mary the 'addock smoker's daughter' and many other old numbers, some of which were for men only. He used to sing a chorus of an old song and ask: 'Who sang that?' Nine times out of ten the answer would be George Lashwood who was unknown to most of his audience. When on the racecourse, he would put five £1 notes in each of the many pockets of a three-piece suit. He reasoned that pickpockets would not get much if they chose him.

The Ailesbury Arms in Marlborough was another favourite place where we stayed for Newbury meetings. It was at this hotel that sadness reigned one evening. Bill was always punctual but after racing on this occasion he failed to turn up at the car ready for leaving. I searched every bar on the racecourse but there was no sign of Bill. As a last resort I went to the office of the Clerk of the Course and asked if any accidents or incidents had been reported. It was a huge shock when I was told that an elderly gentleman had fallen down the stands. My next move was to go to the hospital in Newbury and my worse fears were confirmed. Poor Bill had died and the bar that night was a different place. A footnote to this sad event is that the diamond tie sticker he was wearing went missing. The fact is that the tie sticker and two others were left to me in his will, but I still have the pearl and sapphire stickers as a reminder of a jolly, generous man who loved life. Perhaps it was the perfect ending. He used to boast that his father was a heavy whisky drinker when, at the age of ninety, he was knocked over and killed by a double-decker bus.

While on the subject of social happenings it is strange how many times the name of Sir Malcolm McAlpine has cropped up. He owned Shaun Spadah, who won the Grand National, he owned most of the winners that Don Butchers rode for Jim Bell and he owned Truckle who gave Ken Mullins his first win. On looking at the table plan for a luncheon in London, I saw that I had been placed next to him. We had an interesting conversation about all manner of things. When it was time to part Sir Malcolm, knowing I lived in Hampshire, said if I wanted to fish on the River Test simply to go to his water bailiff and 'tell him I sent you'. As it happens I don't fish but there were plenty who would have liked that invitation.

Although I don't fish in the true sense of the word, I have been on a couple of fishing holidays in Norway at the kind invitation of 'Hurly' and Lydia Hurlstone. The first time Marian and our son Guy were invited and Robin Hurlstone was there with his parents. Hurly rented a mile and

Guy on Norway's River Stryn

a half of the River Stryn. To get there involved a plane to Oslo and then an internal flight to Ålesund, which is an island. We took a ferry to the mainland where cars were waiting to take us on a two-hour drive to the fishing lodge. It was more like a big house out in the wilds and on the road to the glacier. It had its own freezing unit in the cellar. Hurly and Lydia received a big welcome from the gillies, Hans and Anders, and the cook, Tarla. As soon as we had put our luggage in our room, I went out with Hurly and started spinning for salmon. Unbelievably, there was a salmon on the hook within minutes. I played it for a while and when it got tired I was able to get it to the bank where we discovered it was only just on the hook. It was certainly a thrill and Hurly asked me how long I thought it was before it was landed. My guess was fifteen minutes, but it was in fact forty-five minutes. I won't give you the fisherman's tale about the weight, but it was around twenty pounds, which is not that big on the Stryn.

Lydia was a superb fisherlady who went fly-fishing with great success. I went with her, as a spectator, when she hooked a salmon while fishing for trout on a light line. She played this one for more than an hour as it went behind rocks and it called for great patience amid the fear of a broken line.

The Hurlstones' fishing lodge. Marian with our hosts and their son Robin

We had wonderful evenings with food and drink and a log burning fire. Although I did not get another salmon, Marian landed a thirty-five pound beauty. Guy, aged eight, caught smaller fish from a rowing boat which is called 'harling' as a line is dragged through the water. An aged employee rowed the boat, which Guy managed to overturn in his excitement.

That holiday was unforgettable and there was a repeat performance for me a couple of years later. One big difference involved money. On the day before leaving I backed Sky Pilot to win the Steward's Cup and put around £250 in a pocket inside the waistband of my trousers. This pocket was put in at my request by the tailor for safety. On a visit to the bar to celebrate not only my win but also a 100/8 nap, I found my secret pocket was empty. The only explanation I had was that the wad of cash missed the pocket and escaped down my trouser leg. If that was the case I must have been anaesthetised! Obviously it was not a good start to a holiday but it was not going to spoil the visit. This time Michael Phillips, the then racing correspondent of *The Times*, was a guest while Hurlstone's son Robin had Harry Herbert as his guest. They were school friends and still at Eton.

Robin deals in art and for several years had Joan Collins as his partner. Harry Herbert is now a very successful organiser of racing syndicates. The Highclere and Royal Ascot syndicates have had high-class winners,

Guy at Oslo Airport

including the Derby with Motivator. Harry, the son of the late Lord Porchester, was a cheerful soul, and he and I climbed to the top of a mountain behind our lodge. I collected a piece of coloured rock that I built into a decorative garden wall. The only reason I made the climb was because Robin was not in the mood.

Michael Phillips and I had plenty of fun except for one incident. We wandered off to try a bit of fly-fishing. I say we, but Michael was the only one with a rod, kindly lent by Hurly. The rod was the expensive type that came from Hardy's in London. It, and others, had recently been serviced and after a short time it was minus a tip, having come off second best after a collision with a rock! Michael was in a nervous state and I kept him company as he was trying to get some Dutch courage before breaking the news to Hurly. Naturally the owner was not overjoyed but it was not too long before there was jollification all round. On the final evening Michael and I performed a double act by request but the nature of the show is now very obscure. Sadly, Michael seemed to be poorly treated by his newspaper but he had the guts to start a wet fish round instead of bemoaning his fate.

I'm sure that fishing is very relaxing but at times a little too much so. My policeman friend, Jimmy Leader, once persuaded me to go night fishing offshore as we would be certain to catch sea bass. After several hours we returned home without ever having a nibble. As a small boy of around 8 or 9 years of age I was taken in a rowing boat by an uncle for a fishing trip off the coast of Newhaven. He was hoping to catch something for supper when suddenly the line was wrenched with unusual strength. The boat rocked dangerously and the fun began. After some while the catch was revealed and it turned out to be a conger eel that was six feet long (well, I'll spoil a good story and admit it was actually five feet) and we have a picture as proof.

The most enjoyable of my limited fishing ventures was prawning. Ted Clarke, a professional fisherman and also a fishmonger in Eastbourne, used to take me and my uncle, Frank Lucas, to Birling Gap from where we would scramble over jagged rocks to the foot of Beachy Head and drop our nets into the deep pools. We did not have to wait long before lifting the nets and removing the prawns which, being transparent, could easily be missed. Within a short while we all had enough for a meal and would go back to the Fisherman's Club and boil them in sea water. They went down well with a glass of beer and, ashamedly, our families never saw the proof that we had been prawning! It was a venture that needed a guide who knew the tides because it was a slow journey across the rocks and it was easy to be cut off.

Our host, Ted Clarke, was a keen racing fan who would attend the local meetings whenever possible but as far as I know never once had a winning day. He said on a return trip from another such day that 'I shall have to put the knife as well as my thumb on the scales tomorrow.' He was a good-hearted man and once took me on a working trip on his boat and knew the exact spot a mile offshore to get his catch of plaice for the day. It was not unusual for him to ring me at around half past seven in the morning and say there was a box of plaice for me to collect at Lewes station If there was only one type of restaurant available, for me it would have to be for fish but without me doing the catching!

33

GEORGE TODD REMEMBERED

It wasn't until I started writing about Mr Hurlstone that it came as a surprise to discover that I didn't know his Christian name. He has always been called Hurly, but I do know that his initial was A and I suspect it stood for Arthur. The only reason I know that is because their racehorses ran in the name of Mrs A. Hurlstone. The subject never arose so Hurly it is, even though both he and Lydia are sadly no longer with us. Their horses were trained by George Todd and they had a steady run of wins from their small string. The biggest success came in the Morland Brewery Trophy at Newbury when Hornet, ridden by Tommy Carter, gave cause for celebration. The Hurlstones were really in racing for the social side and any win was a bonus. My meeting of them was by George Todd's introduction and we had a lasting friendship. At the races the first thing they did was to find a table and order the Champagne. It was a party made up of George and Audrey Todd, Marian and me and on many occasions, Bill Williamson and his wife Zel. Bill would always ride their horses if available.

It was a great feeling to know that my association with George Todd was renewed. I had ridden for him as a sixteen-year-old and at his invitation went to the famous Manton stables for his Champagne cocktails more than once. George really enjoyed making this drink with a little brown sugar, a trace of brandy and his favourite ingredient, a slice of peach. The house at Manton was a rambling place with the living room joined to the kitchen by a corridor that must have been thirty yards long. When he and Audrey first moved there, he would pull the sash that rang a bell in the kitchen until it was pointed out that there was nobody there to answer. There was plenty of wall space but when the Hurlstones gave them an original Munnings painting, Lydia found it hanging on the lavatory wall. I don't think George had anything to do with picture hanging!

George Todd at Manton taken by son Guy

For many, many years the travelling head lad was Wally Mills who spent much of his younger days working in Lewes and he, Matt Feakes and Don Butchers were close friends. It was when I took our son Guy to a meeting that we ran into Wally and he asked Guy to spend a week with him at Manton. This he did and had a lovely time. George allowed him to roam around the yard and he even posed for a picture. Considering he had no children, he showed kindness and tolerance to a young boy. I can't find anything negative to say about the man, The Manton establishment had its own chapel and jesters say he went there when he had a fancied runner. George certainly went there but only for the reason it was built.

Apart from race meetings, we had numerous visits to restaurants and then the Hurlstones invited us to join them for a few days at the Imperial Hotel in Torquay. The Todds also came and the first thing George said was: 'Don't buy any Krug Champagne because they have put it up to £11.' Those were the days. There was another occasion when I stayed at the Imperial. I had gone racing at Devon and Exeter and much to my surprise, Hurly and Lydia were there. They persuaded me to join them for dinner, which led to me staying. Silk pyjamas and shaving gear were quickly provided and I remember buying pink Champagne as a thank you. It was not easy to get a chance of buying in their company.

They came to the wedding of our daughter Lesley. When the Rolls-Royce came to pick us up it would not restart. All was not lost because Hurly had his own Rolls-Royce and chauffeur on the scene. The slight panic was over when the hired car decided to behave itself.

When George Todd had a birthday coming up it was Hurly who suggested a surprise party in a private room at Mirabel's in London. We and Julian Wilson were guests and a case of Krug was the present from us all even though we were not allowed to contribute any money. The hardest part was to get George to town for a black tie occasion. I have forgotten the details but Hurly concocted a fairly important reason. George was not a good traveller. He fought in France in the First World War and must have had a shocking experience. He was wounded and refused to leave these shores ever again but I would never ask and he never volunteered the reason. The gathering proved highly successful and George and Audrey were shocked, to say the least, when the secret

Dinner with Bill and Zel Williamson in Melbourne

205

Grandson Jack on his pony

was out. An enjoyable evening was had by all. George was a lovely man whose first job was that of an ostler and later as an assistant to that fine trainer, Tom Caulthwaite. Todd's shrewdness as a trainer was emphasised when he backed his Dramatic to win a small fortune in the 1950 Lincoln Handicap. It enabled him to buy the famous Manton stables for £90,000. He landed many more coups and was an expert at getting horses to stay even though their breeding suggested something different.

The successful trainer Paul Cole was assistant to Todd and said to me one day, 'You don't spend time with him without learning something,' and that came from the heart. Patrick Haslam was also assistant at some stage and echoed Paul's sentiments. Todd attended to detail and when I was working there the horses always had clean mangers. The reason for that was because he had been in every box before anyone else arrived. The evening feed was also done by Todd himself. On just a few occasions he asked me to stay behind and perhaps take the feed to only two or three horses.

It was through the Hurlstones that we met Bill Williamson and Zel. Bill was a quiet character with a lovely sense of humour. Our friendship grew and when we went to Australia Bill was the first to greet us and took us to dinner at Eliza's in St Kilda. We returned the compliment with a visit to the Walnut Tree in Melbourne. He gave a friendly smile when he received a parking fine for leaving his car outside while picking us up at the Southern Cross Hotel.

Bill has to be among some of the best jockeys whose gentle touch brought magical results. Some of the top trainers in the UK and elsewhere can't all be wrong. When Lester Piggott replaced Bill on Roberto two days before winning the 1972 Derby there was not a ripple of resentment. I spoke to Bill soon after the news broke and he simply said, 'It's just one of those things and I wish them the best of luck.' He was a gentleman who sadly died of a brain tumour. When they lived in England, Zel decked out their house with some exquisite pieces of French furniture. She had good taste, not only for furniture, but in the man she married.

34

ADDICTIONS

Generally speaking, gambling is a mug's game but, despite being aware of the facts, the mugs carry on. Without doubt betting is a thrill and at the same time, wonderful and detested. Those who gamble regularly will know the feeling. I was one of the mugs who found it addictive. If I had put as much thought into gambling as I did my tipping there would probably have been a profit. The two addictions in my life were betting and smoking. The first I gave up in 1980 and the second a couple of years later. 'There is no such word as can't,' has been one of my guidelines and I have always tried even if I failed. Away from the racecourse the betting was not a problem and the idea of spending time in a betting shop fills me with dread.

The smoking was a different matter. I smoked sixty cigarettes a day and vowed I would never give up, until one day my chest began to hurt quite badly. It was just before midnight that I smoked the one remaining cigarette in my packet despite the discomfort. That was the clue to stopping. With nothing to smoke it meant I couldn't, so I made the decision not to buy any more. Instead I bought sweets and within a week the habit disappeared. I loved sweets, and still do, but not as regular as a habit-breaker. Now I don't want to be anywhere near a smoker. Believe me when I say it needs only will-power to kick the habit.

You usually hear about the winners people have backed. That may take a few minutes but the majority won't have enough time to tell you about the losers. I had never invested £400 on a horse until one day at Lingfield I won that amount on the first race so the £400 went on the favourite at 7/4 in the next race. Merry April was the horse, but it didn't bring me any joy. Of course, I've had some good wins but got carried away very easily. My hours with the formbook produced many winners for the *Daily Mirror* but I was easily led, not in my profession of tipping but solely in my betting, and often backed a horse only to see my paper tip succeed.

A very close friend of mine was requested to attend an Inland Revenue tribunal to inquire into the reason why there was more money in an account than allowable at the time. It was something to do with Post Office savings. Before the tribunal took place he said the money came from betting and that a lot of the winners were supplied by me. Several of the winners were named and backed up by the racecard of that day. When the tribunal took place the Inland Revenue produced several issues of the *Daily Mirror* that coincided with the alleged wagers. It was found that some of the horses that I told him to back were not the horses I had tipped in the paper. My friend said that the tips had to go into print the day before the races and there was always late information. The result? No action taken.

Just like smoking, there were times when I tried to stop betting and it seemed that when I lowered my stake the wins were more frequent. For example, I had a reliable tip for Lucky Jordan who won the 1947 Wokingham Handicap at Royal Ascot. Alec Boyd sent him from Yorkshire and with Jack Sirett riding won at 33/1. Instead of having £1000/30, I had £66/2. Unfortunately, I had not started tipping in the paper then.

Soon after the photo-finish camera was used, I had reason to rejoice. I always stood in the same position on the Press stand at Newmarket and was well used to the angles. I had a bet of £1000/60 on Queen's Beeches in the Cambridgeshire and there was a photo finish between Queen's Beeches and Minstrel. To me there was no doubt which had won and I dashed to the betting ring, and to my surprise heard 3/1 Minstrel being offered. My bet was £150/50 Minstrel so I showed a £90 profit. Incidentally, the winning distance was a neck but bookmakers are better informed these days but oh!, how I wanted the other one to win.

Winning was exciting and at Lingfield one day I had £50 each-way on a 20/1 winner trained by Clive Brittain and followed up with £800/100 on my nap, trained by Martin Pipe. £800/100 on a Piggott winner at Newbury and £500/400 on another Piggott winner at Sandown were not unusual happenings and the Sandown bet got me level on the week's betting. Although winning is fun, the losers can bring heartbreak if you're on a losing spell. Losing is one thing but losing a bundle is a different kettle of fish and the effects can prove disastrous. There is not enough room in this book to list the losers I have backed. If you are betting for fun you should not grumble if it costs money because most hobbies are expensive and with betting you can, at least, control the amount you wish to lose. I don't wish to preach but a solid piece of advice is bet only that which you are prepared to lose. That, I know, is easier said than done.

A dear late friend was a heavy gambler whose generosity knew no bounds. It was this friend, Geoff Greenwood, who asked me at Ascot one day if I knew the results from an away meeting. Having given him the result of the race he wanted, he did a quick calculation of a multiple bet. The win came to around £8,000 whereupon Geoff smiled and said, 'Good, I'm nearly level on the day now.'

The late Gil Bennett was another fearless backer. At Royal Ascot he bet £10,000/£11,000 on Krakatoa on whom Gordon Richards scored. He was the man who promised me £10 at Plumpton and failed to honour that promise. Betting losses are not recoverable in law but that may change and it is bound to be a deterrent to many gamblers. I must add that bets of around £10,000 look like a little flutter these days.

One near miss, one abstention and one success all supplied by three different trainers. The near miss was at Newbury where I strongly fancied a favourite trained by John Winter. Within minutes of placing a £200 bet I met David Elsworth who said his would win but not to shout it about. There was nothing I could do but watch as it won at 100/8.

At the Cheltenham Festival, I was leaving before the last race to miss the traffic when I ran into David Baron. He was adamant that his would win and when I thanked him and said I wouldn't be betting he told me to tell my friends. This I did and a 100/8 winner enabled a heavy backer to retrieve his Cheltenham losses.

The third incident involved Jack Holt who had been a friend of mine for many years and it was at a meeting at Newbury in December that he finally tracked me down after saddling his runner in the last race. 'I've been looking for you everywhere,' said Jack and then, 'You can get the Christmas money on mine.' This time it was a better ending as my bet of £500/£40 was a winner. Strangely each of these incidents involved the last race, all were 100/8 chances and the word came from three trainers who were not in the habit of tipping their horses to anyone.

I stood beside a regular punter in years gone by whose expression never changed and it was impossible to detect whether he had won or lost. When I queried his reaction, or lack of it, he said, 'I just break blood vessels internally.'

To add some more cheerful notes. I relate a bet that was shared with Derek Barker, who wrote for the *Evening Standard*. The Quad bet on the

Tote involved the four races nominated. We took both Derek's tips and mine for the races. We often had reasonable wins, but at Ascot we had different horses in the final race. The pair dead-heated and when the dividend was announced as £800 odd, we were happy to have a half of that each. We were even happier when, surprisingly, we drew £800 for each of the dead-heaters, which if I had thought, was pretty obvious.

Another occasion that sticks in my mind started on a lovely summer's day at my hometown racecourse at Lewes. I stood by the parade ring and, without looking at the racecard, decided to have £1 on the horse that caught my eye. The animal finished fourth and then ran at Folkestone when I was not at the meeting. In both races it seemed as though he needed a longer trip. It was another sunny day at Ascot where this horse was due to run in the Brown Jack Handicap over a distance of two and three quarter miles. The only thing in his favour was the extreme distance, but he was up against some very useful stayers. Nevertheless, I again threw away £1 on the Tote. The race was a thriller with little separating the first three and the judge calling for a photo. My horse was involved but I was clueless as to which had won. It was like a miracle when he called Neville Lodge as the winner, he being the horse that caught my eye at Lewes. The distances were a short head and a head. I sat on a seat in front of the Totalisator awaiting the dividends that would appear in a bright orange colour. At last they came and the win paid £21 9s. to a two shillings stake. For my £1 investment I collected £214 19s. That was in 1948 and is what I call fun betting. There was, however, a twist in the tail.

Neville Lodge was trained in Lewes by Harry Lawrence and he was the owner of Loch Royal, mentioned earlier as the horse I straightened out because he would not go anywhere. I was also second on him at Cheltenham. The real joy, however, was the huge payout which, many times over, paid me for Harry Lawrence's refusal to reimburse my expenses from Gloucester to Wye. I was on an airman's pay and made the long journey at his request to ride a couple of no-hopers.

Perhaps my happiest betting experience was at Hurst Park. My nap was The Bog trained by Towser Gosden in the third race. It was during the time of one of my reduced stakes betting and I didn't want to lay out a large amount on The Bog, so I decided to start with a £2 bet on La Joyeuse at 9/2. She obliged so I now had £11 to play with. In the second race I had £40 to £10 on Red Hackle, trained by George Todd, and then £500 to £50 on The Bog who scraped home by a head. She was out of

211

Mother Ireland which accounts for her name. The sequel to this was a walk round to Mother's to give her £500 which I owed her for something to do with our first house purchase.

I don't want to make an issue of jockeys backing horses, but it obviously goes on and in certain cases it is an incentive when they have backed their own mount. Much more worrying is when jockeys are paid to lose. Before the war I know of one of the biggest rails bookmaker who sent an agent to offer £500 to jockeys for losing. What goes on now is beyond me but I would be surprised if it amounted to more than a very, very minute proportion. As we know action is, and has been, taken over such cases in recent times.

I remember Johnny Haine asking me to place quite a hefty sum on his mount as he was leaving the paddock at Windsor. It was not in the first three which proves a point. It was Johnny who came to a flat race meeting at Goodwood and asked me to put £200 on a runner in a four-horse race. He was surprised when I refused and said that he had picked the wrong horse. He agreed that I should put the money on my choice and the result was a twelve lengths win at 2/1.

Johnny was a fine jockey and a good man whose only objective was to win. Not a lot of harm in that, but as far as the authorities are concerned it could be a case of 'give an inch and take a yard'.

I remember Matt Feakes telling me of an occasion when he sat next to Staff Ingham before going out to ride in a hurdle race at Gatwick. Staff asked Matt about the chance of his mount and followed by saying he was having his last £200 on his. As most people know, Staff was a highly successful trainer who landed many huge gambles including Chantry in the Cesarewitch and Richer in the Cambridgeshire. It can be argued that any man with a huge incentive is going to make a super effort to succeed.

Another memorable wager was on Philominsky in the 1975 Triumph Hurdle at Cheltenham. I had backed him at some long odds and he eventually started favourite at 4/1. There was nothing going better as they raced to the second-last hurdle. A blunder at that dashed my hopes and I put down my binoculars. Seconds later, I could see with naked eyes that the horse still had a chance. Inch by inch he was making ground on the leader but failed by a head to catch the outsider, Royal Epic.

Philominsky was trained by Bill Marshall and it is about this extraordinary man that I wish to write. He was a fighter pilot during the war and awarded the DFC. That would be enough for any normal man but Bill wasn't normal. He was in a small plane that crashed on Newbury racecourse, sadly killing the pilot. Despite injuries, Bill risked his life in freeing others that included the jockey Joe Mercer.

As well as training, Bill rode as both an amateur and professional and was good enough when the money was down. He trained loads of winners but will be remembered for his handling of the sprinter Raffingora, who was one of the fastest in modern times. Modesty was an endearing part of his make-up and, for me, his most heroic act was at Fontwell when a known savage horse got loose in the paddock just outside the old weighing room. The name of the animal, trained by Tom Gates, was Bistro or something near to that but whatever the name, Bill Marshall jumped in where angels fear to tread. The animal had grabbed a man by the groin and it is usual for them to shake their prey or kneel on them. In cold blood, Bill was in like a shot, secured the horse to a near-by post and started beating him across the nose until he let go of his prey. The man, a local jockey, was hospitalised for some time but made a full recovery.

The handling of this incident may seem logical but it took a very, very brave man to do what Bill did. Everyone knew that Bill enjoyed a few drinks and surely nobody deserved them more. It was after one meeting that he was stopped on the motorway by police, not for speeding but for going too slow. He was just moving at 15 mph and when stopped was asked to breathe into the instrument but declined. At the police station he also refused a request for blood and urine samples saying all the blood he had, he needed and he didn't want a pee. I know these facts because the following day he asked me to introduce him to a solicitor who I knew specialised in such cases. The introduction took place but the solicitor could do nothing as Bill had 'dug his own grave' by refusing to use the breathalyser.

The obituary of his death in Barbados at the age of 87 could have been written by Ian Fleming for a Bond film. It was an extraordinary life, packed full of bravery and fun.

35

TIPPING EXCITEMENT

The merit of newspaper tipsters is usually judged on the result of their 'nap' selection, supposedly the best bet of the day, and to create a competitive atmosphere a profit and loss table based on the nap selection was run by a couple of sporting papers. The *Sporting Life* awarded a Silver Cup, while the *Sporting Chronicle* gave a Gold Cup and both papers offered a cash prize of £100. While the winning of either of these tables is good for publicity it is often anything but a fair reflection of a tipster's performance over a season. The table is now run by the *Racing Post* and in an effort to win, a tipster is liable to nap horses with little real chance towards the end of the season in the hope of a fluky big priced winner. The late Clive Graham threatened, if he won, to hold a party in London and then pitch the wretched Cup into the Thames. I have no doubt that Clive would have carried out his threat.

Despite the drawback, the competition creates an interest but the day is sure to arrive when the winner succeeds because he has shown a smaller loss than any of his rivals. If the table was based on all selections, rather than just the naps, the winner would almost certainly be the one with the smallest loss. This fact is based on my many years of compiling such statistics. It is indeed rare for any tipster to show a profit, at level stakes, on all his choices. This is quite understandable and anyone who shows a loss of less than £100 during the flat race season on all his tips has performed a pretty good job. I was able to keep that margin of loss a few times, while during one National Hunt season I managed to show a profit of over £80 but the merit of the Naps Table is illustrated by the fact that in that very season I finished only thirteenth in the table with a loss of £2 18s. 3d.

Even though I do not entirely agree with the principle of these competitions they cause a bit of excitement. When I first won the *Sporting Life* Cup in 1951 my prospects had seemed hopeless with little more than six weeks of the season left. The naps were showing a loss of over £2 and Bill Curling, 'Hotspur' of the *Daily Telegraph*, was close on £50 ahead of me. Then a winning run began and in less than three weeks I found myself at the head of the list with a profit of over £40. My sympathies were with Bill Curling who had been in the lead practically throughout the long season but racing is a game of fluctuating fortunes and one becomes hardened to reverses and blasé about success.

By far the most exciting win to come my way was in the 1952–53 National Hunt season. With only three days left, the idea of winning was non-existent but on the Thursday Hadlow landed me a 100/8 nap at Nottingham, which put me right in the picture, and it became a challenge. 'The Duke' and 'Captain Heath' were both still ahead of me and it became a matter of tactics. Should I nap a couple of short-priced horses during the two remaining days and rely on my rivals napping losers, or should I anticipate their success and try and find better priced winners? After deep thought I decided that the former policy offered the better chance of success. My nap on the Friday was Glenbeigh who won at Newbury at 11/10, while the two leaders chose losers. The tension had now risen for that win put me in second place and with just one day remaining the *Sporting Life* table read, 'The Duke' showing a profit of £10 12s. 9d., 'Newsboy' £9 3s. 0d. and 'Captain Heath' £8 19s. 8d. There were three meetings from which to choose my final nap so I stayed at home to put in a bit of overtime with the formbook. The result of my studies was a list of five possible horses to nap on the Saturday.

I figured that three of the list might possibly be the nap of 'The Duke' so, to avoid stalemate, my final decision revolved round a couple of horses at Chepstow. One of them, Turn-A-Penny, seemed a certainty but could not always be relied on to run an honest race while the other, Glenandri, was trained by a good friend of mine, Ben Lay. With victory in sight I rang Ben and asked for his guidance. He was only too delighted to tell me that he thought his horse was sure to win and what is more I should make him my nap. Having made the big decision I was anxious to see the morning papers and discover which horses 'The Duke' and 'Captain Heath' had sorted out. Luckily neither of their naps was any of the five I had listed for my own choice. Thus the results of three races taking place within forty-five minutes of each other at Ayr, Chepstow and Newbury would decide the destination of the Cup.

While I do not normally get flustered over such matters, I must admit to a feeling of high excitement that afternoon as I sat with a friend who

Nursing the two cups won in the same season

rang his bookmaker and listened to the running commentaries of each of the three races in question.

First on the list was 'The Duke''s nap, Persian Hunt, at Ayr. It was a relief to hear that he had been easily beaten into second place but then it was the turn of Glenandri at Chepstow. His success at 11/8 called for another cup of tea because half an hour later Fighting Line would be out to land 'Captain Heath''s nap at Newbury and my calculations told me this one had to win at odds of only 13/8 or more for him to beat me. I stood by my friend's side at the telephone and learned that Fighting Line was a 3/1 chance. When the field set off for this three-mile chase, the commentary was repeated to me. For what seemed an interminable time Fighting Line was mentioned among the leaders but suddenly my friend grinned, and putting down the receiver with thanks, turned to me and uttered, 'He's fallen.'

This friend was the late Ted Morgan, a great sport, who kept the Crown Hotel in Lewes. I arranged a dinner party in his hotel for the following week and twenty of us sat among Champagne bottles for a feast for which Ted simply refused to let me foot the bill. Only when I protested did he tell me that he had backed the list of five horses from which I chose my nap and, believe it or not, each obliged at prices ranging from 2/5 to 2/1.

The winners of these tipping trophies were expected to treat their press colleagues and the usual custom is for the winner to have Champagne or other alcoholic beverage laid on in both the southern and northern press rooms the following weekend. By the time you had celebrated with other friends it was usually a case of the winner being the loser. I know that I finished well out of pocket when I won the *Sporting Chronicle* Cup in the 1957–58 season and once again it was a last-minute dash that put me in front on the next to last day. Stalbridge Park won the Grand Military Gold Cup at 100/8 and while that win placed me at the top of one table I was still only second to 'Solon' in the *Sporting Life* competition.

A 10/1 winner was needed for me to complete the double and I knew my fate before my last nap, Farmer's Boy, ran in the Imperial Cup. He opened at 10/1 in the betting but was backed down to favourite at 13/2. A win would not have been enough to win the second of two cups and it was no consolation to see Farmer's Boy win the Imperial Cup at 25/1 a couple of years later.

I am not going to bore readers, most of whom will probably be my family, with further details of nap competitions, except to say that I won the *Sporting Life* Cup four times and the *Sporting Chronicle* Cup twice. A win at 11/4 by Ron Smyth's Menton at Plumpton gave me another last day win to land both trophies with only a few coppers to spare. Statistics have always appealed to me and my many years of tipping produced the following figures:

Winners	43,440	30.45%
Seconds	25,926	18.17%
Thirds	18,662	13.08%
Unplaced	54,671	38.30%
Placed	88,028	61.70%

Among those winners are two that gave me great satisfaction. I had seen Light Flame run at Newmarket and what I saw prompted me to say when next he ran was, 'Light Flame is not the best bet of the day, week, or month but the bet of the year.' He obliged at 2/1 which I reckoned was stealing money. The other one that pleased me was Ridge Wood, on whom Michael Beary won the 1949 St Leger at 100/7. This three-length winner was one of two Noel Murless runners in the race and Gordon Richards opted for Krakatoa. My pre-race headline read, 'Gordon has chosen the wrong one.'

I suppose tipping all seven winners at a Wolverhampton meeting was satisfying as it earned me a spot in the *Guinness Book of Records*.

Noel Whitcomb had a long career in journalism in almost every branch but horseracing was always a love. It was he whose brainwave resulted in the *Daily Mirror* Punter's Club. Ably assisted by Bob Rodney, the scheme was launched and with free membership the public joined in their thousands. I had nothing whatsoever to do with the club except mingling with the members at the various happenings. The Andy Capp Handicap at Redcar was one of the original events, but the real interest was at its highest when horses were acquired to run in the club's black and white jacket and red cap.

The first of them was Steel Bridge, leased to run in the 1969 Grand National. A young Richard Pitman put himself about and secured the ride. Steel Bridge was trained by the formidable Mrs Lockhart-Smith but no doubt Noel Whitcombe was quite capable of charming his way through her defences. The operation was a success, and Steel Bridge ran a great race to finish a twelve lengths second to Highland Wedding at the rewarding price of 50/1. Four years later, Richard Pitman had a more publicised and heartbreaking second on Crisp.

36

JOY, SADNESS AND PRISON

Heidelberg did well for the Punter's Club but the star turn was Even Up. Noel had sounded Ryan Price about a likely place to buy a prospective chaser. Northern Ireland was the answer and four of us flew across to Belfast and on to the yard of Will Rooney. His was a family in the thick of jump racing and his daughter Rosemary rode a lot of jumping winners. Noel's party consisted of Ryan Price, Alan Oughton and myself. Alan was going to be the trainer, a condition made by Ryan, which showed the generous and unselfish side of Ryan. Even Up was brought out and trotted round by Rosemary and then it was the turn of one of us, that being Alan or me, to ride him in his quicker paces. Neither of us was keen to get our suits mucky but I had the trump card and said, 'You're going to train him, so you ride him.' There was never any chance of him not being bought even though Noel dithered a little.

To liven up the flight home I suggested we each put a fiver in the kitty and have a guess at the colour of the knickers worn by a chosen hostess. This was agreed but when the plane landed we were all shying away from the next step. Who is going to ask the vital question of the colour? Alan completed the double. I pushed him into riding Even Up and now I pushed him into asking. There was no quick reply as the young lady said she had done an extra shift and had to borrow knickers from a colleague. She sportingly went somewhere to check and I can't remember the colour or who won, but I do know that I didn't. This light-hearted escapade was sadly the last occasion on which Alan and I had a bit of fun. It was not long after Even Up had run a couple of times that Alan became unwell. He was in hospital when Even Up began to fulfil his potential and, with Graham Thorner riding, won a Sandown hurdle race at 25/1. There was nothing one could do to console Alan. Words were not enough so Noel immediately rang his wine merchant to dispatch a case of Champagne in half-bottles as a tangible thank you for Alan's part in the win. I paid him a visit in his London hospital and Alan was incredibly brave.

Even Up went on to bigger and better things but was liable to take liberties with some of the fences. He ran in the 1998 Grand National but refused at the eighteenth, which is the second fence on the second circuit. Some of his wins were very impressive but a four-pound penalty may have prevented him winning the Welsh National. Under a big weight he failed by two and a half lengths to beat Rag Trade. Even Up certainly did well for the Punter's Club, winning twelve of his fifty races, and being placed in eleven more. The Club also had trips abroad organised for them at affordable prices. The January meeting at Cagnes-sur-Mer usually attracted British runners as part of their preparation for the British flat season. My wife and I went on a couple of these trips and stayed at the Carlton Hotel in Cannes. We acted as hosts and also went to a Casino at the request of a friend. That was not the kind of gambling I enjoyed, but I went with the promise that I would lose no more than £10. Unfortunately, you have to add another nought to that.

The *Daily Mirror* was never slow to arrange functions to attract readers and quite often one of their named writers was requested to attend. I had no hesitation in helping a good cause. One such meeting was with several Chelsea Pensioners who had been invited to the *Mirror*'s Function room. There was also a children's tea party with The Shadows providing the music.

One of the saddest visits was to the Star and Garter home at Richmond. Peter Laker and I were part of a panel chaired by Eamonn Andrews, who at that time hosted *This Is Your Life*. Most of the patients were bed-ridden or walking wounded from two wars. After the panel game we mingled with the men and chatted about everything and nothing. It was an eye-opener. Some bed-ridden patients even played table tennis from their wheeled beds.

Incidentally, Peter Laker was the chief cricket correspondent of the *Daily Mirror* and the son of Guy Laker, my friendly landlord at the Pelham Arms in Lewes. Like me he got his job on the paper via the Company Secretary, Bill Jennings. Peter was younger than me and an all-round sportsman. He was on the Sussex CCC staff and had the unusual experience of bowling out Denis Compton with no-balls on two occasions.

One of the early television panel games was *Pencil and Paper* hosted by Shaw Taylor. The Computer Programmers had won for several successive weeks and now they were to play against the Racing Correspondents. The show was live with an audience at the Aston Studio in Birmingham. Our team was Peter Willett, Tim Fitzgeorge-Parker, and myself. We had all been racing, and working, at Kempton so were unable to set off until after the last race at four-thirty. Peter drove us at high speed and when we entered the lady director gasped, 'What kept you?' She received a short answer, 'Work.' The game was based on IQ and other odd shapes and symbols. It must have been on the commercial channel because Shaw Taylor told us to look over a colleague's paper during the break if we were stuck. We were well trounced and handed an envelope as we left. Each one contained seven guineas.

The writing of this book has had me working my memory overtime. One thing leads to another and when Wormwood Scrubs came up in conversation recently it reminded me that I have been inside twice. Not as a prisoner but as a panel member once, and then as a speaker. The first was with George Swinden, the Arsenal goalkeeper, and Peter Wilson, the *Daily Mirror* columnist. It was a question and answer evening which went down well. My second visit involved a short introductory talk and then questions. It went on for some time and then the prisoners had a period to chat. One asked if he could speak to me and he turned out to be a solicitor who had dealt with many people I knew but he did not say if he was inside for any connection with them. While having sandwiches and drinks with the governor, he said I must have gone down well or otherwise I'd have been booed off!

The strange thing about those visits to Wormwood Scrubs was the fact that getting inside was much more difficult than getting out.

37

THE TURNELLS

One of my closest friends in racing was Bob Turnell whom I first met in the very early forties. He had been riding at Plumpton and, with his wife Betty, came to my local, the Pelham Arms, after racing. I remember the occasion because Bob had an unusual experience. It was when the water jump was in front of the stands and after jumping the last fence it was necessary to swerve round the water which was dolled off. Bob was either squeezed out or his horse ducked out but whatever the reason they jumped the water and despite passing the winning post in front were disqualified.

Bob was in the Army and I was in the RAF when next we met socially although we had ridden in the same races. It was at Hereford and although I had no rides I sneaked off from my camp. Some things are hazy but I remember Bob asking if I needed a lift to anywhere. It must have been while stationed at Staverton because Bob and Betty not only drove me to Cheltenham but insisted on taking me to dinner. From that day, we became friends and I distinctly remember him coming out of his way to say, 'Well done,' after I had ridden a winner at Fontwell. When I started work for the paper, I used to stay at the Ailsbury Arms in Marlborough for the Newbury meetings and later for Cheltenham. Bob trained a few miles away at Ogbourne and he and Betty would come down and invariably we had dinner together.

The Turnell family consisted of Jean, Ann and the twin boys, Andy and Robert, who sadly died at a young age, and of course Grandma. Robert was allergic to horses and had to quit his original training as a saddler. He and a friend had established a high quality soft furnishings business in London when he died. The two boys were away at school but it didn't appeal to Andy and there was a time when he went missing. It turned out that he was hiding in a barn at the stables. Apparently he was receiving food and drinks from some lads in the yard. Grandma was

Fun with the Turnells, Ancils and Beers on the Algarve

Betty's mother and a wonderful old lady. She was at dinner with us on her birthday soon after *Peyton Place* was a risqué serial on TV. I gave her the book of that series which she thought was great fun. She lived with Bob and Betty and had a fall one evening which resulted in a broken hip. She didn't want a fuss and said, 'Don't trouble the doctor at this time, just throw a rug over me and wait until the morning.' Her consideration was, of course, ignored. Her daughter came from the same mould. When the children had flown the nest I used to stay with Bob and Betty and, for the Cheltenham Festival, Marian used to stay as well. The routine was to have 'gin and It' before leaving for Cheltenham and dinner out at various places on our return.

As I have explained earlier, the Rees family in Lewes were always part of the social scene. Young Bill was the latest to join in and many an evening he knocked on the door when he knew something was going on. Bill did his national service in a cavalry regiment, as did several other jockeys. They were welcomed by the sergeant instructor whose outbursts were on the lines of, 'You think you can bloody ride, you will after I've finished with you.' Bill was forced to start riding under National Hunt Rules owing to increased weight. It was not long before he made his mark and his early success came his way via Snowy Parker. Things were

223

very hush-hush when Snowy laid out a horse for a gamble. Bill would never tell and I would never ask.

I had a phone call from Bob Turnell one evening and he wanted to know something about Bill with a view to offering him the job of stable jockey. Someone had told him that Bill was a drinker. I was able to assure him that he was nothing of the kind and that half a pint of bitter might pass his lips because he was a normal young man who liked a bit of fun. That was exactly the kind of jockey he wanted, a man with no extremes. The combination of Bob and Bill worked splendidly for several years. Jeff King and Johnny Haine were up and coming boys in the yard and not far behind was the trainer's son Andy. When Bill Rees was offered the job as stable jockey to Peter Cazalet the time was ripe to accept. Bill was highly successful in his new job, which meant he rode many winners for the Queen Mother.

The mention of Peter Cazalet reminds me of the day my pal Tony Grantham said he had been offered the job of stable jockey by Ryan Price and Peter Cazalet, and what did I think. I said Cazalet was the obvious choice as Price was only winning small races with moderate horses. Little did I know that Price was going to sprout wings. When Tony joined the Fairlawne stable there were lots of horses owned and ridden by Lord Mildmay. Tony used to be paid £1 for each horse he schooled and Lord Mildmay was also generous to Tony for 'pinching' the rides on his own horses. Before taking the Cazalet job, Bill married the Turnells' daughter Ann. Having been with the Rees family practically all my life I felt almost like a relation.

Bob Turnell was not a lover of the media and refused to appear before the TV cameras. He was civil to the racing press but seldom in agreement with what they wrote. It was, thus, unusual for us to be such close friends. Whenever there were black tie dinners in London, Bob would ring and ask if I was going. It was usually the two of us or neither of us. One of the best occasions was the Bollinger dinner for the champion National Hunt jockey. It was light-hearted with no lengthy speeches, good company and, of course, no shortage of the Bolly.

The last dinner given to me for winning both the tipping trophies was made up of many friends rather than obscure bodies. I have Dave Phillips, the racing editor, to thank for that as he drew up the list. I and two local friends including Bob Mayes, alias Tim Handel, from the Jeffery Bernard incident, caught the train to London and a kind lady friend, Olga Stringfellow, no relation to Peter, drove my car to pick us up in the early hours. Bob Mayes and my other local friend Ted Rawlings, together with Bob Turnell and Derek Ancil, went into the Ladbrokes Club where Derek played at the table and won enough for the evening and left immediately. We went on to a respectable club where the four of us drank and talked whilst Bob Mayes was on the dance floor with a partner he referred to as a 'Dusky Maiden'. It is impossible for me to remember all the social activities Bob and I attended together but they included the Hunt Ball at Chippenham, which we attended several years running. There were also dances at the Ailsbury Arms. A dance was also put on in the Town Hall, which I did not know about so had no dinner jacket. Where there's a will, there's a way, and my way on this occasion was to borrow the garb from the hotel's headwaiter.

In the days when there was a six week break between the jumping seasons, holidays were possible. The Turnells used to go away with Derek and Yvonne Ancil, and Fred and Lucy Beer. It came at a busy time for me, but they asked Marian and me to join them at the Dona Filipa at Vale De Lobo on the Algarve. They were able to play a lot of golf at this Portuguese resort and were staying for a fortnight. That was impossible for us, but we managed to wangle a stay of a week between the Derby and Royal Ascot. It seems usual to meet people you know on these holidays and the first was Di Nicholson, mother of David, who was staying in Faro while the wife of W.A. Stephenson and one of their owners were a couple of ladies in our hotel. Our party of six went into Faro one evening where they had arranged to meet Dick Saunders and his wife for dinner at a well-known restaurant. This was before Dick became the oldest man to win the Grand National when riding Grittar.

In seek of a change, we went to a nearby club one evening and on leaving I said to the girl who owned the club that we hadn't enough money to pay the bill. She didn't appear too worried and, thinking I was serious, asked where we were staying and what was my business. I simply said journalist, and she said that she was going out with a journalist but that I wouldn't know him because he was in racing. It turned out to be John Hamner who was a friend and colleague. With that distraction we actually left without paying. We went there for lunch the next day and settled our account. A very trusting young lady.

Bob Turnell was a punter and like all of us had his good and bad days. He came to a flat race meeting at Ascot one summer and asked if there was anything I fancied. It just so happened that I knew one that looked sure to win. We stood on the grass by the rails to watch the race and the horse obliged. It came as a shock when Bob said it made a bad week a good one as he had had £2,000 on the 2/1 winner.

We always had good times with the Turnells and when the wives had retired to bed, Bob and I would have a few drinks and put the world to rights. We talked about people and horses, not what chances they had but horses in general. One night he said whisky and milk was a good drink so we got stuck in but Betty wasn't too pleased the next morning when there was no milk for tea. That was my first taste of whisky since it had made me ill several years before and although I have had the occasional tot since, it is not my favourite tipple. Soon after that Bob suggested we try gin and sherry. We did, but a couple was enough for both of us. It had to be Champagne when some owners came early one evening and Bob went to the chest in the hall where it was kept. He popped the cork in a second bottle and found it was not up to scratch. He opened another in readiness and poured the dud one out of the window. Bad luck Bob, you chose the wrong one in a two-horse race. I hope the plants thrived on the good bottle! It was reason enough for another entertaining evening.

It was on one of the TV racing programmes that Richard Pitman told viewers that they should take notice when 'Newsboy' tipped a Turnell runner because I was in the know. Nothing could be further from the truth. Every horse that ran was trying for its life and Bob's assessment of its chances may or may not have coincided with my reckoning. From the outset I made it a rule that my tips were made on my interpretation of the form, and not to be influenced by outside parties or publications such as the *Black Book* assessments which, after all, were the ratings of people who had the same fallibility as myself. It was a rule that I adhered to, with very few exceptions. At best it was a chatline for Pitman, who I liked as a man. I used to make visits to the Conservative Club in Marlborough to have a game of snooker, which I played very badly. Richard came in one night but there was a queue for the table so we played table tennis upstairs. He was not too steady on his feet and the last I saw of him was lying under the table after very few rallies. I hoped his hangover was not too bad! Richard seemed to have an on-off relationship with his first wife, Jenny. It was after the Welsh Grand National dinner that Richard, tongue in cheek, blamed me for a final separation. Soon after the opening of the new stand at Newbury I was standing next to Jenny and remarked that the new layout made it difficult to find one's friends. Her immediate retort was: 'You're lucky to have any.' I have never found out whether she was referring to me or herself!

As you will have gathered, Bob Turnell loved a bet and had a frustrating experience at Worcester when he fancied one of his runners more than a little. It was in the parade ring that Bob told an elderly, and deaf, owner that his horse would win. At the fourth attempt, with ever-increasing volume, the owner heard this confidential message and so too had nearly everyone on the racecourse! Bob missed all the 4/1 and had to take 2/1 but the horse won to make it a fairly happy ending.

38

LOST FRIENDS

Bob Turnell and I never once had a cross word in the considerable time that we knew each other. There was a period when I used to ride out for him if I was in the area. I remember being introduced to John Lawrence, now Lord Oaksey, as we rode out of the yard one morning. John asked questions about life as a racing correspondent, and the rest is history.

One of Bob's chasers was Prince Eyot who was advertised for sale in the *Racing Calendar*. Philip Kindersley, the father of Gay, was looking for a reasonably priced chaser and Don rang to ask about him. I was staying with Bob at the time and rode Prince Eyot that morning. It turned out that there was a reason as Bob sent me and Bill Rees to school over a couple of fences. We didn't mess about and really raced at them. At breakfast, Don rang to ask if he was a safe conveyance as Gay was to ride him and, quite rightly, Don was going to safeguard his owner even though Gay would ride anything. In mid bacon and eggs, Bob said you had better speak to me. I assured Don that Prince Eyot did everything right and the deal was concluded. Price Eyot, with Gay aboard, won at the first time of asking at Fontwell, and it was not their only win.

Bob was a fair man and loyal to his owners, jockeys and lads in his yard. I was sitting next to him when he answered a call from the Earl of Carnarvon, of Tutankhamen fame and grandfather of Harry Herbert who manages the Highclere and Royal Ascot Syndicates. The Earl had a useful young chaser named Blessington Esquire and said he would send it and that Bill Rees would ride it. Bob disliked the dictatorial manner and said he had other horses and that Bill was not certain to be available. The final words came from Bob who suggested that he send the horse elsewhere and with that replaced the receiver.

Unless the rules have been changed, apprentices on the flat receive half the riding fee while the other half goes to the employer. The half fee for apprentices was paid into a separate account and remained there until his time ended. I think arrangements for conditional jockeys, the equivalent under National Hunt Rules, are between them and the trainer. Bob had no flat race apprentices but insisted that any jockey riding for him should receive the full fee. In days gone by, some jockeys would offer themselves at a lower fee in order to get their feet on a rung of the ladder. It was not easy for jump jockeys to make ends meet in those days and you had to love it to stay in the game. I suppose they could be correctly described as masochists.

When Bob had his first heart attack, Marian and I went to see him in Savernake Hospital. He was cheerful as he pulled a bottle of whisky from under the bedclothes. When discharged, he was told to take things easy with as few physical jobs as possible. As you may guess, Bob was straight down to the horses, bending to feel their legs and doing anything that needed doing. It was not long before he had another heart attack that proved fatal. A true friend disappeared and I miss him a great deal.

When it comes to ages we discovered that Bill Rees was ten years younger that me, I was ten years younger than Bob and he was ten years younger than Gordon Richards. This decade incident was also present in my family. My daughter Lesley was born in 1950 and my son Guy arrived in 1960. I tell people that I master-minded this so that calculating their ages would be easy. Now that's what I call riding a waiting race!

For several years before his death, Bob had a habit of tapping his chest because of discomfort. His wife, Betty, told me that she was sure Bob knew his end was coming by something he said. He had purchased a house and a yard with boxes at Rockleigh from Gordon Richards. It was a remote place on Marlborough Downs where Richard Hannon 'hid' Mon Fils before this colt won the Two Thousand Guineas. It was also the name of a round gallop which George Todd used when preparing his Cesarewitch winner, French Design, and, of course, other stayers, which were a speciality of this trainer. However, back to Betty. She and Bob were driving on a quiet road near the house when Bob, out of the blue, said, 'I don't want you to live at Rockleigh when I've gone.' Betty didn't live there and it was sold.

The yard at Ogbourne was rented and his son, Andy, took over the string. After a short while he bought a yard at East Hendred formerly owned by Eddie Reavey. It was from there that Andy sent out the 1987 Grand National winner Maori Venture ridden by Steve Knight. Luckily, Betty was able to buy a house not far away from The Green in Marlborough. One of Bob's best horses was Bird's Nest and, displaying

With Betty Turnell outside 'Bird's Nest'

a nice sense of humour, she named her lovely little house just that. We had the pleasure of having a name-plate made as a moving-in present. All the family were very supportive of Betty and the nearest one in distance was Jean who lived only a couple of miles away but has a leather shop in the centre of town. She is married to Roger Upton and they are the parents of Guy and Mark. Guy did well as a jockey and now has a busy livery yard. Mark is an artist of some ability and his Christmas and other anniversary cards frequently catch my eye. Mark also does commissioned paintings and we had the pleasure of looking round his studio which contains work covering a variety of subjects but mainly equestrian. Ann and Bill live at Shalbourne and Ann made regular visits to her mother, as they were only ten miles apart. We used to visit her and go out to lunch and gossip about all and sundry. Betty died aged ninety-two, but neither looked nor acted her age.

When Bob died the funeral was for family only but the memorial service in Marlborough drew a huge crowd. Betty's funeral was at Ogbourne St Andrew. Again there was a packed church followed by a gathering at the Red Lion in Axford. It was in this village, just outside

Marlborough, that Betty gave a party for her ninetieth birthday. We all had a wonderful time with names from the past cropping up all around. John Oaksey delivered a few chosen words that paid tribute to a lovely lady. Betty confessed that she was going to leave money for friends to have a big party after she had died, but changed her mind with the sentiment, 'Why should I miss out?' The times were always cheerful whether it was winners or losers, but our friendship of nearly sixty years now has a legacy in the form of their offspring and subsequent issue.

The children were responsible for another happy assembly on the lawn at Bill and Ann's house for Betty's eightieth birthday. Although her birthday was in March the party took place in July and in one of the loose boxes were untold cases of Champagne. It was a glorious day and later that evening some of the details were being drowned in Champagne. I'm sure there is no better way of drowning.

39

HAPPY OCCASIONS

The lawn at Bill and Ann's house was the scene of another huge gathering thirteen years later when their daughter Joanna married Charles Curtis. It was, however, a hugely contrasting occasion. Whereas it was scorching hot for Betty's birthday, the heavens opened for the wedding party even though it was in the middle of May. It was fine arriving at the church and during the ceremony but then it started in no uncertain manner. The bride and groom were taken to the reception by horse and carriage and the rain did nothing to brighten their journey. There were two marquees. The first was for Champagne drinking, followed by a short walk to the second marquee where the wedding breakfast followed the five o'clock ceremony. It was a glorious affair and the rain outside was not allowed to spoil anything.

Joanna, known as Do since a small child, has done well as a lady amateur jockey and won several races on Final Divided owned by her husband. She has also ridden point-to-point winners while her brother James has won a steeplechase at Cheltenham. His career was cut short by a very bad injury when a horse, owned and trained by Brian Gubby, fell while doing a routine piece of work. Her other brother, David, was keen on horses but has ended up as an accountant. Do was a very little girl when I first knew her and I remember taking her to school when all other chauffeurs were unavailable. As you may imagine, the reception was full of racing people and it was a treat to see so many friends from years past and, of course, the younger ones.

We stayed a couple of nights at the Ivy Hotel in Marlborough and by arrangement so did Peggy Heriot and her friend Tom McMillam. Peggy is the middle daughter of F.B. Rees and was married to the late Martin Heriot who owned the Shelleys Hotel in Lewes. That was another happy reunion.

Ann Rees was despairing of having the grandchild she longed for, but now Do and Charlie have come up trumps with a daughter named Rose

Peggy Heriot and Marian with Bill Rees at his daughter Do's wedding

and twin boys, Freddie and William. Ann is very friendly with Gay Eustace who is the niece of Ann's husband, Bill. James and Gay Eustace own the famous Park Lodge Stables in Newmarket where Sir Jack Jarvis trained so successfully for Lord Rosebery. The Derby winner Blue Peter came from the yard and his name remains over the box he occupied.

It is at Newmarket where I have hung on to the 'apron strings' of racing. This is made possible by the kindness of James and Gay. They run the Blue Peter syndicates and have open days to which we are invited. We also go to their owners' day, which takes place during Guineas week, and Easter Sunday is the day that we enjoy a particularly long lunch! Originally it was the Easter Partnership which laid out £20 a head and entered the Tote competition run by the *Racing Post*. Owing to various events we have not entered for two or three years but the lunch continues. Apart from the hosts, the gatherings comprise Michael and Gay Jarvis, Chris and Carol Wall, Willie Jarvis and Charles and Do Curtis. At the most recent gathering William and Maureen Haggas joined in to give even more fun to the occasion. All the children have the space to enjoy themselves and have their own party.

James Eustace and Willie Jarvis are Harrovians and their friendship remains. The two boys, Harry and David Eustace, are, not surprisingly, also Harrovians. Michael Jarvis, no relation to Willie or Sir Jack, and I have Lewes as common ground and we have countless memories. It really is a treat and, as well as the roast lunch, there is non-stop conversation and wine, wine, wine in the most friendly of atmospheres.

Andy Jarvis, father of Michael, was a friend of mine and in retirement drove a dray for the local Harvey's Brewery. He was not the sort for retirement and we kept in touch by phone. Michael was one of three private trainers to David Robinson, and was able to tell his father the progress of his string, especially as the owner was not a betting man. As Andy provided some successful opinions our racing editor, David Phillips, thought it was an opportunity to put him on the payroll. Poor Andy had some bad falls as a jockey and I'm sorry to say I had a close up view of one tumble. It was in a hurdle race at Plumpton when Royal Joy fell and Andy rolled under the animal I was riding. I was in mid-air and powerless to avoid him. His skullcap was cut through and during a long recovery period he had to have a hole bored in his skull to relieve the pressure. It was in the twenties that skullcaps were introduced but they were inadequate and, of course, there were no body protectors. I am so pleased that Michael Jarvis has done wonderfully well and I'm sure James will have more winners as time goes by. He does not waste his owner's money with multiple entries but treats them individually and makes owning a horse a pleasure.

The Blue Peter syndicates were a great idea and the participants really get the red carpet treatment, as, of course, do all the other owners. Nothing is too much trouble and as an organiser and hostess, Gay is worthy of great praise.

Weddings and marquees are usually memorable, and so it was when James and Gay got married in Findon. Willie Jarvis was best man and I was honoured when the bride's mother, Diane Oughton, rang to ask if I would speak as a friend of the family. Neither Willie nor I are keen speakers but we were able to get a little courage via the Champagne. It was another wonderful occasion with one missing ingredient, and that was Gay's father, Alan. He was a real family man and would have been so proud to lead Gay down the aisle.

More fun and great company was the order of the day when we stayed at the Swan Hotel in Southwold. It was a joyous occasion with James and Gay and also Martin Mitchell of Tattersalls. It was shortly before Christmas and the snow started to fall in the morning and by teatime it was several inches deep. All agreed that we would go to the carol service

With James and Gay Eustace at the reception

at the local church and, dressed appropriately, trudged through the snow. On returning to the hotel a healthy glow made our pre-dinner drinks even more enjoyable. With our party well fed, it was back to the roaring log fire in the lounge and outside the large window was a wonderful Christmas scene. The little market square was decked out with Christmas trees, coloured lights and a gathering of young and old dancing, singing, and snowballing. Inside the music from a fiddle band was drifting in from a private party and audible to those outside. It was a case of 'good everything'. Good company, good food, good drink and a really good Christmas feel. It was a situation that could not have been bettered even if stage-managed. Usually snow is an enemy of the racing fraternity, but on this occasion it was fairly localised and did not affect the race meetings. That stay on the Suffolk coast will be remembered forever. Romance is not dead even though a few worn out parts prevented me from dancing!

The two Rees brothers, F.B. and L.B., laid the foundation of what has been, and still is, a line of offspring who have provided so many happy times for Marian and me. Of course there has been sadness as well, but I'm afraid that has to be a part of all families.

Having witnessed the complexities of the present-day trainers it reminds me of how different it used to be. The *Racing Calendar* and the form-book were necessary but expensive and not all trainers had them. Mine were paid for by the *Daily Mirror* and while in Lewes there were frequent visitors wanting to peruse these publications.

Entries for races were made weeks ahead followed by the weights for handicaps and one or two forfeit stages. The handicaps were made by various handicappers and the difference of opinions was astounding. It made hard work of deciding where to run a horse. That hard work has lessened with the ratings system. It is worth relating an absurd happening with the old method. The handicapper made a genuine mistake which gave a runner at Lingfield Park a turn-over advantage of something like 42lb or it may have been 50lb. Whatever the figure this hideous mistake was widely publicised and you can guess the next part: the animal was beaten. It is often said that something always comes to rescue the handicapper but this one had all his birthdays at once.

Comparison of horses and humans of different generations is to my mind not difficult but almost impossible. Ratings, handicaps, time figures and any other method of assessing horses boils down to someone's opinion and as everyone knows, opinions can differ enormously. Any

Marian, Guy and Jack

236

Step-grandson Daniel on his New Forest pony

mention of time figures make me think of Belisarius who once held the record for seven furlongs at Brighton and may still do so. His time was in a selling race which is the lowest type of event. That is extraordinary when we know that far superior horses have run over that course and distance time and time again.

We all have our opinions in whatever category and, if we are truthful, are usually biased. I had great pleasure in following the career of Golden Miller but whether he was better than Arkle or Best Mate we will never know. Everyone will probably shout 'rubbish' at the mere thought of anything beating Arkle and they may be right but there is no way that it can be proved.

Every time I was asked which is the best horse I have seen my answer has been: 'Ribot was pretty good.' That Italian horse was unbeaten in 16 races and I saw him win the King George VI and Queen Elizabeth Stakes as well as two wins in the Prix de l'Arc de Triomphe. He was no oil painting but handsome is as handsome does. Sea Bird was a very impressive Derby winner but how he compares with the runaway winners, Shergar and Troy, nobody can say for certain. I usually say 'suspect' because that is all anyone can do. Sir Ivor was no slouch either but one can go on and on with the names of good horses and you will never be able to furnish enough evidence to prove which is the best.

40

SIR GORDON RICHARDS

I was a huge fan of Gordon Richards and his record speaks for itself. Champion jockey twenty-six times and 269 winners in 1947. Bear in mind that there were no evening meetings during his career, and also there were several blank days. Those who never saw him in action missed out in a big way. I, and many others, had a real thrill when Gordon won the 1953 Derby on Pinza. It was his only Derby win and what a wait he had! It was the year before Sir Gordon retired, and I understand the Queen said, 'Racing will not be the same without you.' That was a sentiment echoed by thousands, including those of a certain age, who knew him as 'Moppy' because of his shock of black hair. The reception given to Gordon was heartfelt and enormous but not on the scale of that accorded Frankie Dettori after his win on Authorized. As I have said before, overreactions were not part of the scene in Gordon's day and, quite frankly, I was embarrassed by the post-Derby events. In mitigation it must be remembered that Frankie is an excitable Italian. The pecking order after the Derby used to be the horse, the owner, the trainer and lastly the jockey. Now, owing to the media, we have these 'celebrities' in all walks of life who seem to wallow in self-importance. It appears to be backed up by the honours list with awards for many people who are doing only the job for which they are paid. As a result the awards are cheapened and it is an insult to those many worthy people who really deserve recognition. Such happenings seem the norm these days and my undoubtedly old-fashioned ideas will probably earn me the label of 'a miserable old sod'. I can live with that.

Jockeys such as Charlie Smirke, Charlie Elliott, Harry Wragg, the Smiths, Eph and Doug, and a score of other exceptional jockeys were in opposition. When Gordon retired his colleagues gave him a dinner at the Savoy Hotel on 15 November 1954. They waited until the end of the season so that as many jockeys as possible could attend. It was an honour to be invited in my capacity of a pressman. Members of the Jockey Club and the jockeys mingled freely in a relaxed atmosphere and it was a genuine tribute to a fine jockey and a fine man even though some of the jockeys were merely celebrating the fact that the 'Little Man' would no longer be around to ride the lion's share of the winners! It is always a pleasure to listen to Sir Gordon's speeches and he can be guaranteed to hold his audience with well-balanced humour and the odd back-hander aimed at higher authority with perfectly good taste.

Unlike many dinners these days the only wine was Champagne by the bucketful. It may be of interest to many that the Champagne was Bollinger, Extra Quality, Very Dry 1947. After dinner it was Crofts Port 1922, bottled 1924. Doug Smith made a presentation on behalf of the jockeys. I still have the menu for that great occasion and it is signed by fifty-four of the guests. The following day I made a list of all who signed, which is just as well because some signatures are difficult to decipher, especially by anyone who was not around at that time. That dinner took place when another champion jockey, Willie Carson, was a twelve-year-old schoolboy.

Willie himself gave me a worrying time when we were dining out. I asked him and his first wife, Carol, out to dinner and to book a table at a restaurant of his choice except for that 'arm and a leg job' near Cambridge. Willie said to come to his house for a drink before we went. Willie drove, and as we approached the restaurant I noticed that it was the 'arm and a leg job'. Naturally, I took it in my stride and didn't turn a hair when I discovered that Clive and Maureen Brittain were joining us! There was no point in worrying about the bill or I would be put off my dinner and, after all, the bill would probably be less than I might lose in the first race at Newmarket the next day. There were no credit or debit cards at that time so payment was by cash or cheque, but not all places would accept cheques. I excused myself and went to settle the bill before it was presented by the headwaiter. I had a pleasant surprise when told that 'Mr Carson has taken care of the bill.' Willie obviously had an account or made prior arrangements. Thanks, Willie!

If luck was with me over that dinner, I was unlucky when staying at Ye Olde Bell at Bawtry for the big Doncaster meeting. On making my way there after racing I saw smoke in the distance and as I got nearer there was a feeling that it might be the hotel, and it was. One wing was completely burnt out, and there were a few residents looking rather

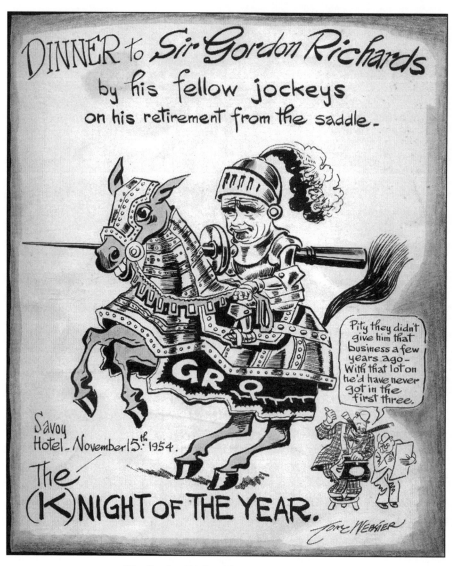

Sir Gordon Richards' retirement dinner

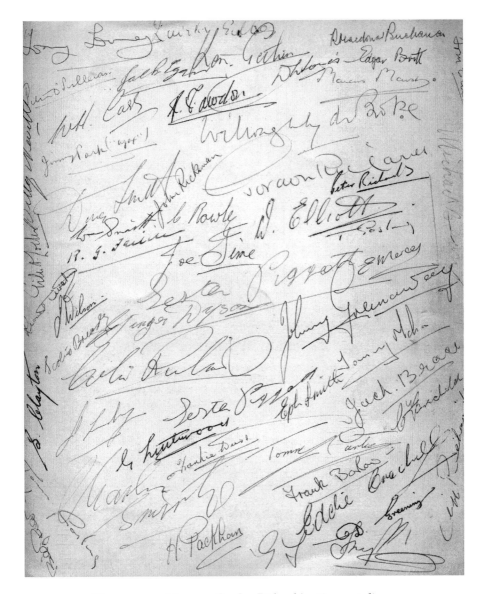

Signatures on Menu at Gordon Richards' retirement dinner

Jockeys: *Sir Gordon Richards, Colin Richards, Cliff Richards, Tommy Lowrey, Jack Egan, Ken Gethin, Davy Jones, Edgar Britt, Michael Beary, Lester Piggott, Charlie Smirke, Harry Carr, Bill Elliott, 'Snowy' Fawdon, Cyril Rowley, Doug Smith, Eph Smith, Tommy Gosling, John Greenaway, Tommy Mahon, 'Ginger' Dyson, Joe Sime, Willie Snaith, Billy Nevett, Jock Wilson, Manny Mercer, Joe Mercer, Jimmy Lindley, Scobie Breasley, Stan Clayton, Bill Rickaby, Geoff Littlewood, Frankie Durr, Tommy Carter, Bert Packham, Eddie Cracknell, Frank Barlow, Jack Brace, 'Micky' Greening.* Jockey Club: *Sir R. MacDonald-Buchanan, Lord Willoughby de Broke, Lt-Col. Giles Loder, Sir Randle Fielden.* Racing Press: *Quinnie Gilbey, Peter O'Sullevan, Jimmy Park, Bob Butchers, John Rickman, 'Fairy' Fairchild, Lionel Cureton, Tom Webster.* Trainer: *Marcus Marsh.* Others: *Peter Richards (son), George Smyth (Gordon's valet)* happy. It was interesting to discover how many expensive suits and Turnbull and Asser shirts they lost in the fire! Unfortunately, I was in the part that was unharmed.

That evening, after dinner, I and Lionel Cureton, 'Templegate' of the old *Daily Herald*, used to potter a few hundred yards to the local pub where H.J. (Jim) Joel's driver and valet were staying. They were very fond of their employer, but the valet did relate a funny incident. It was his job to lay out the clothes, including underwear. All Mr Joel had to do was slip them on as laid out. It wasn't until nature called that he realised that his pants were on back to front. Jim Joel was staying at our hotel but I never set eyes on him. It was while staying here that I got into conversation with a couple of strangers who were sitting by themselves in the lounge. They must have recognised me because one asked me what I had napped for the next day's racing. I said there was a certainty, trained by the shrewd Les Hall. They seemed quite amused and revealed that they were the owners. For the record, it obliged.

In an earlier chapter I said that I didn't listen to tips but went entirely on my own judgement. I should have said with two notable exceptions that proved absolutely vital. When Glenandri won me the naps competition it was his trainer Ben Lay who pushed me into making it the nap. For those not familiar with names from the past, Ben Lay was a jockey who rode as P. Lay and usually had more rides in a season than any other jump jockey.

The second was when Stalbridge Park won at the Sandown's Military meeting. It was Bert Morrow, and he alone, who was responsible for me napping him. Bert, who rode as R. Morrow, was stable jockey to Alex Kilpatrick who trained Stalbridge Park. Obviously Bert knew more than I did and literally begged me to make him the nap. I actually watched the race with him and it was a happy moment, and the starting price of 100/8 was a bonus. It took a little persuasion to get the *Daily Mirror* to send Bert a dozen bottles of whisky.

For no reason, it has just crossed my mind that jumping jockeys hardly ever walked from the weighing room to the parade ring without wearing an overcoat or mackintosh. When the time came to mount it was either carried by the trainer or thrown to the ground. Somehow or other they usually found their way back to the weighing room. Maybe they didn't all have expensive items for use as a doormat, or worse, but they received exactly the same treatment, and remember, it included days when the fee was five guineas a ride and three guineas when the race was worth less than £80. There have been many more changes.

Pretty Obvious and Don take a tumble at Plumpton. The course Inspector would today close the venue if it had the chestnut-paling fence and no plastic rails

Once upon a time jockeys used to have a white neckerchief but I have noticed that they now wear a white garment with a turtleneck under their colours. Another item of their dress code was to have the cuffs of the colours gathered and held in place by elastic bands. No doubt this is still the case but I have noticed that Ryan Moore's sleeves often slip up the arm. Perhaps it will become a Ryan Moore trademark, much as losing his cap was the trademark of Lord Derby's jockey, Tommy Weston. These days, one set of Lord Derby's colours appear to be a bit skimpy. When Olivier Peslier won on Ouija Board at Ascot one sleeve ended up near his elbow and it was the same when Frankie Dettori won on her at Goodwood. I understand a less skimpy set of colours will be evident in future. Perhaps a three-quarter length sleeve set of silks should be made as a reminder of that great filly!

The strictness of stable routine was commonplace years ago and many trainers insisted that staff turned up in jodhpurs or breeches. Fred Darling stood out as a disciplinarian and was feared by many in the yard and outside. I was among half a dozen pressmen to be invited to look round the horses before the start of the season. It certainly came as a bolt from the blue in a stable where the horses stood to attention when Fred Darling appeared. I have no idea how present-day trainers carry on their business, but from what I have read, Sir Mark Prescott is from the old school. It seems obvious that the staffing these days is difficult and from watching television some of the lads who lead up look more suited to heavyweight boxing. It is probably true to say girls outnumber the men in the parade ring.

Jack Watts, who trained for Lord Derby, was another from the old school, and a very pleasant and professional man. At Newmarket races one day, Jack told me a *Daily Mirror* photographer had been to his yard and asked to take photos for some reason or other. To make conversation Jack asked if he knew Bob Butchers. 'Who's he?' was the reply. That was enough for Jack to say, 'If you don't know your paper's racing correspondent, you can f—— off.' I told you he was professional!

It is also difficult to make comparisons with today's jockeys and those of forty or fifty years ago. I suppose a poll would result in Lester Piggott being a clear winner but we don't know for sure if he was any better than Gordon Richards or whether Gordon was better than Fred Archer. Lester won the Derby on Roberto after the intended rider, Bill Williamson, was replaced. Those two jockeys had completely different styles and perhaps the gentle approach of Williamson may have resulted in Roberto winning more easily. It is easy to say that nobody else would have won on him but it is simply one of millions of facts that cannot be substantiated.

Over the years, I have seen hundreds of jockeys and apart from Gordon Richards my favourite was Scobie Breasley. He really knew what was going on in a race and his judgement of pace was uncanny. So often I saw him in seemingly impossible positions only for him to be returned the winner. Scobie knew those up front had gone too fast and would come back to him.

I have not forgotten the jumping boys but their job is more diverse. They have a variety of styles which suit individuals. Pat Taaffe had a style that was far from pretty but it was very effective. Among present-day jockeys, Andrew Thornton and Richard McGrath ride with a longer length of stirrup leather than the vast majority and can be easily spotted in a race. Tony McCoy is a wonder and would shine in any company. I am sure that Fred Winter would also fit in anywhere as he was determined and had a brain. There are many more who were in the top class but I am not going to name any for fear of leaving out some worthy of mention.

Fred Winter senior introduced me to young Fred soon after he had finished his National Service and was about to begin his career as a jumping jockey. 'I have never ridden over a jump, not even a dandy brush,' said young Fred and he had hardly started when he broke his back at Newton Abbot. It was his guts and determination that put him in the 'super class'.

The girls are facing an uphill struggle which makes the success of Hayley Turner even more praiseworthy. It was a great performance to dead-heat with Saleem Golam for the 2006 Champion Apprentice title and she is now being used by more and more trainers. Those who thought the girls would never make it are having to modify their views. Even without being able to claim a weight allowance Hayley is getting plenty of rides from a wide range of trainers.

Currently I follow the fortunes of those I know well, such as the trainers Gary Moore, Michael and Willie Jarvis, James Eustace and Andy Turnell. Naturally I also keep an eye on Gary's boys Ryan and Jamie.

Ryan became champion jockey in 2006 and what a shame that his grandad Charlie was not around to witness his successes. Ryan has achieved something that no other champion has matched. He was the champion amateur on the flat and his very first win came in a hurdle-race.

Marian with Lorna Moore, grandma of the successful jockeys

What a shame that a broken arm delayed his start to the 2007 season by three months. He still finished a creditable third to the dead-heaters Jamie Spencer and Seb Sanders.

Despite the number of safety measures now in place there will always be serious accidents in racing.

41

SOMETHING GOING ON

Gay Kindersley has for long been a popular figure not only in racing but also with anyone who comes in contact with him. He is also the tops when it comes to giving a party and when attending one. When living at East Chiltington, near Lewes, he had to lose two or three pounds in order to do the correct weight the next day. He rang and asked if I would keep him company on a run. I was happy to oblige and so was another friend. Typical of Gay, he said bring Marian and have supper. There were no chores to worry about as his 'Man Friday' was looking after things as he had been doing happily for a long time. Gay looked fit to withstand a hurricane with sweaters and mackintosh as his attire while we wore just tops and shorts. All went well with the run, which the following day I measured in the car. The fact that it was almost ten miles was no great surprise. On reflection, it was amazing that we could run along country roads in the dark without some fluorescent clothing.

Jogging that distance was not so bad once you caught your second breath. Even so, it was quite nice to get back and sink a few gin and tonics. Gay got into a steaming hot bath and then joined his guests looking fighting fit. Next on the list was steaks all round except, of course, for the host. It was a lovely evening, inside if not outside, and made more satisfying when Gay announced that he had achieved the necessary weight loss. The get-together continued until Gay said, 'Sod this,' or words to that effect. Within a short time he had downed a few gins and asked for a steak. A good night was had by all, even though Gay's weight had by the next day returned to what it was before the run. It mattered little as Clearing, the reason for the exercise, still won at Newbury.

When Don moved to Epsom, Gay was living at Beare Green and much closer to his horses. It was here that he gave a party in aid of local charities, and what a party it was. A large lined marquee, wall lights, dance floor and a live band, and naturally food and drink. It went with a buzz right from the start and I am not going to name-drop except to say that Rupert Davies was having a good time. I mention him because his brother, Evan, is a good friend of mine and when I stood down as President of Odiham and Greywell Cricket Club I asked him to fill that position. Rupert, who played the leading role in *Maigret*, was in great form and at one stage took over from the band's drummer. He also tried a little '*amour*' with the hostess, Magsie, but to her relief he fell asleep.

David Hedges, who founded the International Racing Bureau, was staying with us in Epsom and, like most of us, had quenched his thirst sufficiently. On the way home from Gay's I saw David standing by his open-top car near traffic lights in Dorking. There was damage to the offside of his car. Wisely, he chose to leave his car and continue in mine. After very little sleep I drove him to his car in which the police had left a note saying that his binoculars were in safe keeping at the station. David was now in a real stew and told the police that his car had stalled and wouldn't start again. The binoculars were returned and nothing more was said. We retraced the route back to Beare Green looking for anything he might have hit, such as bollards. There was no sign and my theory was that he hit a car coming towards him with a driver in the same state as himself.

Soon after Don moved to Epsom we moved as well because my mother was in poor health. We had plenty of friends but I didn't like Epsom as a place to live. Riding out on Epsom Downs was rather boring compared to other racing centres. There was, however, a bonus as I had a regular supply of field mushrooms which are a particular favourite of mine. This came about when I ran into Freddie Laker at our local meeting. It was his mother's birthday and he had brought her racing as a treat. He said she was a follower of 'Newsboy' and would I go and have a drink with them. I was more than happy to oblige and it turned out to be something of a 'knees-up'. On departing, Freddie asked if I liked mushrooms and if so to gather as many as I liked at his Woodcote Stud. It was quite local to me and when I got there he showed me the paddock and remarked: 'Try not to tread on too many.' That was easier said than done and I filled a shopping basket without moving many yards. They were beautiful and I never went short of them and neither did our neighbours!

There were plenty of things to celebrate in Lewes when it was a real training centre. Our trusty landlord, Guy, was one of the gang that comprised Ken Oughton, Ben Wise and Harry Hannon, father of

Richard. Harry, whose right eye was a different colour to the other, had set up as a trainer after he had been working for Tom Masson. He was sensitive about his eyes for what reason I don't know. For me it was like betting each way. A lot of so-called secrets were mulled over in the local including Coppards, who was Don's last winning ride.

The incident that sticks in my mind though concerns Industrious Lass. She was a mud-lark and there had been plenty of rain at Lingfield where the going could be very heavy and a large drainage programme appears not to have solved the problem completely. The previous evening, our gang was in the local and one or other of us was constantly checking to see if it was still raining. The more rain, the more drink, and the bigger certainty was the mare. Michael Rees had the mount and racing down the hill before the straight she was many lengths clear and the further she went, the longer the lead became. It was a sight for sore eyes. If that wasn't enough, there was more to come. We could not believe her starting price of 100/6. As I have said earlier, there were plenty of losers but let us wallow in the good days. After wins like that it was yellow Chartreuse night at the Pelham Arms, but it was sufficient to say, 'Top shelf, landlord,' where an ample supply of both yellow and green was kept. Don't ask me why, but it was always yellow and usually after 'time' had been called.

Harry Hannon proved himself a more than capable trainer and when he moved to Everleigh he was laying the foundations for Richard. He was always a bit of a prankster and at one stage of the war Tom Masson made a temporary move to Cheltenham and Harry went as well. A local veteran was 'Deafy' whose name was for that reason. He cleaned the tack and did other jobs around the yard. While he was cleaning the bridles, Doris, the only girl in the yard, went in to get a rug from the chest. As she was bending over, Harry crept in and impolitely touched her bottom. The sprightly Harry was out as quickly as he entered and poor old 'Deafy' was the unlucky recipient of a clout around the head.

It was always Harry's boast that he made me nap Champagne Charlie at 20/1 to win the *Sporting Life*'s nap competition. My memory is good enough to know that was untrue, but it was a good line for Harry and I never contradicted him. I had known him for many years and even did baby talk to Richard in his pram. I was sadly unable to go to Harry's funeral but Marian was taken by a mutual friend, Bill Graham. Harry repeatedly told me Marian was the best looking girl in Lewes, which I always passed on to get myself a few Brownie points!

Those days in Lewes were fun and something different seemed to happen quite frequently. At short notice, Ray Pulford wanted me to ride in a gallop at Goodwood racecourse on a horse that he was training for the Northern Cesarewitch. It was an experience to ride over every inch of that course. It was then off with Don to ride work for Bob Willett. He was the uncle of the journalist Peter, and had colours of white, black cap, the opposite of Lord Derby's black, white cap. All I remember about that was going through a couple of gateways where it was knee deep in mud. I don't remember much more about Simon Demitriadi collecting me to ride Diabutsu in a bit of work at his father's home near Plumpton. What I do recall though is the extremely steep hill at the end of the work ground. It crossed my mind that this would be the ideal place to ride a runaway. I reckon that would be one contest in which the rider would be a hot favourite.

Much later, Alan Oughton was going to ride schooling for Gerry Langford and wanted a companion. I was silly enough to volunteer because schooling there was a mixture of racecourse, hunting and eventing obstacles. The first to be jumped was the wing of a hurdle. Mine landed so steeply that my thumb was pushed back to near dislocation and prevented further participation. There was nothing ordinary about schooling there.

Earlier I mentioned the fact that I had been on the back of horses that finished first, second and third in the Grand National. It has now crossed my mind that I came very close to the 1951 winner, Nickel Coin. I had been riding something at work on Grand National morning and was about to leave when Jack O'Donoghue collared me and asked if I would ride a runner of his to keep Nickel Coin company in a sharp pipe-opener. Happy, happy days.

42

THANKS, HUGH

Hugh Cudlipp had a lifetime in the newspaper industry and could be cruel on occasions. He wanted the best from his workforce and that was certainly the case when he became Chairman of the *Daily Mirror*. Fortunately, I was seldom in the office, but on one occasion my presence was required at a luncheon with Cudlipp in the Chair. There were no more than ten of us and I never discovered why I was there. It was not a celebration but very much the opposite. He tore into the Sports Editor, who at the time was the kindly Jack Hutchinson. I am not an admirer of the newspaper business with little or no respect and hurtful actions foolishly justified simply as it's a 'tough world'.

Brian Chapman was also present and he had a title, which I can't recall but it was fairly important. My first dealing with Brian was a telephone call. He had altered part of an article to make it nonsensical and I'm afraid I lost my cool. I asked him what he was doing interfering with something he knew nothing about. When he was able to get a word in it was to say, 'I'll see you in my office tomorrow.' Naturally, I didn't go to see him. It was at Cudlipp's luncheon that I first saw Brian again. He spoke about internal affairs and staring straight at me said, 'There are some people who say Black's black, and White's white.'

One year, at the Variety Club meeting at Sandown, the *Daily Mirror* had a small hospitality tent that was full all the time with my racing friends. One of the people from the advertising department said that Hugh Cudlipp was at the meeting but would not be able to get in but when Hugh saw the situation he said, 'That's fine, after all it's there for Bob to entertain his racing friends.' He was hard but fair and certainly disliked anyone licking his boots.

When the *Mirror* was in a circulation battle with the *Sun*, I met Hugh who said he knew tipping was not easy but if I could win a prize it could not come at a more important time. That was just a wish and not an expectation, unlike one editor who asked why I didn't nap twenty short-priced winners in succession. The wish was answered and I won not one Cup but two. There was a big dinner to mark the occasion and Cudlipp actually attended, which was unusual. When it was port and brandy time, he got to his feet and after a few complimentary words said, 'I was going to give Bob a rise or two first-class tickets to anywhere in the world with his wife.' After a pause he said, 'He can have both.' That was in the spring, and I was loath to miss the important races in the flat season. The *Mirror* gave me a pretty large dinner party on each occasion that I won the 'Naps Trophy'.

It was December before I made arrangements for the trip. I asked for tickets to Australia, thinking it was the furthest away but New Zealand was a bit further. The tickets were ongoing which meant just that. Now it was simply a case of deciding which way round the world we should go and in which countries we would like to stay. There was also a business allowance of £800, which in 1973 was quite good. We set off on 3 January 1973 and made Hong Kong our first stay, which was 8,657 miles and took seventeen hours. I thought some silly individuals like me might be interested in such details, and I can also tell you that timepieces had to be advanced eight hours. It was a wonderfully clear day, as our flight progressed, and we were able to see the Ganges, Himalayas and the Burmese jungles. It was a really amazing sight and the vastness of the jungle was unbelievable.

Friends of ours, Mac Old and Audrey Westerdick, were going to be in Hong Kong at the same time so we naturally arranged to meet. We were guests of Sir Douglas and Lady Clague. He was Chairman of the Royal Hong Kong Jockey Club and we met several interesting people in his box. The course was Happy Valley, as Shatin had not yet been built. Our hosts gave us a wonderful day and Major-General Penfold took me to meet stewards and officials and then to the jockeys' room, which was securely guarded, and had a lounge with armchairs and TV. It was surprising how many I knew. Sir Douglas, wearing his business hat, had a lot to do with the building of the bridge that linked Kowloon to the island of Hong Kong. It was officially opened while we were there and our host asked what I thought of it and my answer was: 'It's wonderful but why are they trying to get the money back in the first week?' The charge for a single crossing was the equivalent of 7s. 6d. or 37½p in today's currency which I considered excessive at that time. The money to build the bridge had come from the Hong Kong Bank in which Sir Douglas was the 'bigwig'.

We did all the tourist things and I had a couple of suits and four shirts made while Marian bought pearls, but gave me the bill! The next stage of our journey was to Melbourne, which was another 5,100 miles and eight hours in the plane.

Marian's older sister, Kay, lived in Australia and that was the reason for taking this route. Kay was a nursing Sister in England and during the war she nursed a wounded Australian soldier, Don Bruton, whom she later married. Don farmed in Swan Hill, which is about 200 miles from Melbourne. They came down and drove us to Swan Hill but we chose to return by train and take in the countryside. We were loaded with luggage, as we did not know how long we would be away. There were two huge cases plus smaller ones because we had to take dinner jacket and evening dresses just in case.

The *Mirror* said they would book and pay for our first hotel. We chose the Peninsular in Hong Kong but that was being refurbished and was fully booked. The paper then booked the Astor in Kowloon, very much less comfortable but you don't look a gift horse in the mouth. Before leaving for Australia I booked a room at the Graham Hotel in Melbourne. The taxi from the airport was unable to stop outside for reasons best known to the authorities. We were dropped some fifty yards away and our luggage dumped on the pavement. It meant me carrying some baggage to the hotel while Marian stood guard over the rest. Apart from a case, I had clothing over my arm and one of the hangers got caught up in a girl's dress, causing a rip. She did not seem keen to accept my apology.

It was a scorching hot day and we were looking forward to getting settled in, but there was more drama. Within a few yards of our hotel I saw a man thrown out, and I mean thrown. It looked a roughish place so I trampled back to Marian and hailed a taxi. 'To the Southern Cross please,' was the instruction and it was a relief to settle into what was then the best hotel in town.

Before leaving home we were told we must go to Fanny's so we went there for dinner on our first night. Oysters had caused me grief in England but I was told that Sydney rock oysters were different. 'In for a penny, in for a pound' was my cavalier approach and I reckoned I might as well be ill on a dozen as I would be on six. They were smaller than in this country and a real treat. I ate plenty more down-under but never again in this country. The meals we had with the Williamsons and elsewhere were wonderful, and so was everything we did or saw. Friends from Lewes, Harry and Margaret Clapperton, had emigrated to Australia so we met up with them for a day. Harry took me to Young and Jackson's pub to see the notorious painting of the nude, Chloe. I can't say it excited me over-much. This was the same Harry who took me to Trundle Hill as an eleven-year-old to see Greenore win the 1935 Steward's Cup. It was also he for whom I arranged the winning ticket on the *Daily Herald*'s Templegate Trio. Before the war Harry joined the Territorial Army together with a few others as they thought it would be fun. Poor Harry did not think it so funny as he made his way back from Dunkirk.

In Hampshire, our friends, Frank and Joyce Morris, had a large barn structure in his builders yard. The nephew of Joyce was in a group working their way across from Australia. They had been some of the entertainers aboard ship. They eventually arrived and Frank and Joyce invited friends to hear this group play in the barn. They were very good and stayed around for several weeks trying to get an opportunity over here. The nephew, Bruce Woodley, a member of the group, arranged for us to meet his father, Bill, who worked for the police in Melbourne and we had a very enjoyable day. The group got the breaks, and with Judith Durham as their vocalist, went to the top as The Seekers.

The hot weather in Australia was breaking all records but did not inconvenience us. We crammed in so many things including a visit to the theatre. While travelling over, one of the passengers was Robert Morley. He was, like us, in first class, so had access to free drinks. It broke the monotony when you could go up a few stairs to the lounge on the Jumbo Jet and ask for Champagne. We were wondering why Robert Morley was visiting and found it when we saw his play advertised. It was *How the Other Half Loves* which we had wanted to see in England. It was very amusing and when we went outside during the 10 p.m. interval it was still 98 degrees. How he survived wearing an overcoat and scarf for much of the play was amazing. I wore one of the light suits made in Hong Kong and strolled from our hotel to the theatre. After being in a hot building and walking back to our hotel my suit was drenched and I had to take it to the cleaners the next day. An example of the heat was rammed home while we were in Swan Hill. Marian's sister broke an egg on the stone step to the kitchen and it was cooked in no time.

43

MOVING ON

The racing in Hong Kong and Australia was of major interest. Sir Randle Feilden, the Senior Steward of the Jockey Club at the time, had kindly written to John O'Reilly of the Royal Victoria Jockey Club asking him to do as much as possible for me. He supplied all the right tickets and we were invited to lunch with the Committee at Sandown. It had not been so long ago that the ladies and men were separated for lunch but on this occasion it was for tea only that there was a separation. We met all sorts of people including Sir Philip Jones who was the head of TV and the biggest newspaper group. He told me that he had been with my boss, Hugh Cudlipp, only a fortnight previously While Marian was still having tea, I went with the jockeys Bill Williamson and Ron Hutchinson to meet some of their old pals. Ron said he would ring to arrange a visit to his stud in Adelaide. That would have been marvellous but we were too busy to make it possible.

Bill and Zel were really kind to us. They drove us everywhere and we went to their home in the suburb of Brighton. On the Sunday after Sandown, Bill and I were invited to go on television, not together but on separate channels. Bill was on the commercial programme. Peter Lovitt had asked me a week previous if I would come on to his programme and rang to say they were sending a car to take us to the television studios at Burwood, about fourteen miles away. Although I had been in TV studios before, it was the first time I had been made-up but with only a little, thank goodness. The programme was an hour long and my interview lasted eight minutes. There were questions in general, and then how I thought Stewards in Britain would act if they were dealing with an incident that took place at the previous day's race meeting. It was explained that the programme was very informal and Marian, sitting on the set, said I seemed more relaxed than on other occasions. Bill Williamson rang to see how I got on and to make arrangements for meeting. He received a few goodies on the commercial programme and quipped, 'You got nothing. Not even underpants?' which was a reference to a conversation when Marian told them I had packed twenty-eight pairs of underpants for our trip.

A couple of days later Peter Lovitt and his wife Helen drove us to the Arundel Stud at Keilor run by Wally Cockram. He was Vice-Chairman of the Race Committee and it was he who had invited us to the Sandown meeting. We rang our friends to say our goodbyes and thanks, and flew to New Zealand. As we had not booked our ticket to that destination, we had to pay £25 each which seemed very reasonable. The visit was to see my dear Uncle Ern, his wife Wyn and daughter Patricia.

Wyn had had a stroke and lost her speech, but she could smile and just about walk. I knew this would be the last chance of seeing them. It was Ern who had played Santa Claus to the many children at Grandad and Grandma's Christmas parties. He did everything with great enthusiasm and drove us all around Auckland and to the top of Mount Eden, from where you have a wonderful view including the International Cricket Ground. Although there was no racing, we visited Ellerslie racecourse where two of the fences were so close together that it made the railway fences at Sandown look very normal. After showing us many interesting sights and four days of non-stop talking Ern, aged seventy-eight, confessed to being hoarse. When we said our goodbyes Ern handed us a note. The note was from Wyn saying how nice it was to see us and hoped we had enjoyed ourselves.

Before leaving for the airport, we went to the Vista Bar at the top of our hotel which had a 360-degree view. The airport had poor memories because when we landed very late in the evening the customs asked if we had been anywhere near farms or horses. We confessed to having been near both and had to have our luggage searched because of some fruit disease. It was a long process and when the good-hearted search was over, he laughed and said, 'That will teach you to tell the truth.' It was well after midnight when we booked into the Intercontinental Hotel.

The next journey was to Fiji, but there were delays after we had landed. It was something to do with a civic reception for the first Jumbo Jet to join their airline. We were booked into a bungalow type hotel and everything was provided, lunch, a car into Nandi, the nearest town, dinner and entertainment. There was also a native dance on the lawn of the hotel when we arrived as a traditional welcome.

Honolulu awaited us and as we crossed the International Dateline it meant we had two Saturdays. We came in to land over Pearl Harbour, which we later walked around. This US Naval base was attacked by Japanese planes in 1941 and resulted in the US entering the war. On reaching the Reef Hotel, it was packed and it turned out that it was holiday time and similar to the throngs that used to descend on Blackpool. It was bad luck as Bill Williamson had told us it was the best place to stay. We were at Waikiki on the island of Oahu. Immigration was strict as this was the fiftieth state of America. It was a seaside resort and Marian paddled just for the sake of saying she had done so. The first night we ate at an Italian *trattoria* because we didn't fancy the hotel. Our room and view was acceptable but when we went down to breakfast the Americans on package holidays were in a queue stretching yards outside the entrance. We chose a coffee shop and discussed the venue for dinner. I bought a guide and decided we would go to the best place on the island.

The choice was Michel's at the Colony Surf, Diamond Head. Luckily, they were open on a Sunday so we rang to book a table. We took a cab and enjoyed a superb meal. I remember that one of the dishes was lobster tails in abundance and they were delicacies. After the meal and wine we found a cocktail type drink, as opposed to a liqueur, that was very satisfying. We had feasted very well and when I got the bill I found I had not got enough money. We were short of sleep owing to delays, dateline and a noisy hotel. The amount of money I had was enough for an average bill but this was not an average restaurant. I had the equivalent of £28 in dollars. The only thing to do was to see the owner or manager and put my cards on the table. I went to his office and explained the situation. He was a German and said not to worry and insisted that I have a drink with him.

I had been gone a long time and Marian was obviously looking worried. On the next table was a Canadian couple and they asked if there was anything they could do to help. Marian told them the problem and they offered to lend us money, a very kind and unusual act when we were complete strangers. When I returned to the table smiling it was naturally a relief. The manager had said, 'You're English. I trust the English. You can bring the money tomorrow.' He didn't even want what I had, and sterling traveller's cheques were definite non-starters over there. We went back the next day, had a delicious lunch and a walk on the private beach. I'm not too sure the English are so easily trusted these days. If you might wonder how I remember some of these details, the answer is that I kept an explicit diary just in case. We topped up a lovely evening with a few dances back at our hotel.

It was now decision time. We had the option of going to San Francisco or New York, or even both. As Marian had not been to America before, we decided on New York but there was little to celebrate as we approached the airport. There was snow on the ground and it was freezing. There was no customs hold-up as we had come from an American state so it was a coach to Grand Central Station and a yellow cab to the Park Shereton Hotel. We couldn't wait to get into some warm clothes, including overcoats.

We ventured out and walked down Broadway to Times Square. We spent a lot of time looking round Macy's Store, especially as it was in the warm. I had to show Marian the Empire State Building and we took the express lift to the top. Luckily the visibility was unlimited but neither of us is keen on heights so we didn't linger. Marian found Fifth Avenue much more interesting and we walked twenty-two blocks and noted several landmarks. Neither of us had experienced such cold weather which tended to limit our activities. The hotel was grotty and unclean and that included the bedding. After a long delay we managed to get clean sheets, but nobody came to clean the room. The hotel and the cold were enough for us to look forward to the last leg of our jaunt around the world.

First class on the BOAC Jumbo Jet to London was extremely comfortable with Champagne and the thought of home making it extra special. Touchdown at Heathrow was 9.30 p.m. and we were met by our daughter Lesley who had been driven by Geoff Webster, a friend who at the time worked on the *Daily Herald*. Our son Guy was at boarding school. He had only just started and became so homesick that he finished up in the sanatorium.

It was very late by the time we got home, but I was anxious to know how my deputies had been tipping under my 'Newsboy' nom-de-plume. I sat with all the *Mirror*s and all the *Sporting Life*s and entered up all the details as was my habit. They did nothing spectacular, and in my heart that was about right with me. It was almost six o'clock when I went to bed but it mattered little as my mind's clock was in a muddle.

For those of you who don't like statistics, my apologies, but you are still going to get them.

Days away	33
Miles in planes	28,408
Time spent in flight	53 hours and 53 minutes
Two first class tickets	£2,103
Hotels	£300

All in all, it was a great experience and the kindness of so many people was much appreciated. If I could live anywhere in the world it would, surprise, surprise, be England.

44

ART IN THE FAMILY

We know how prolific George Butchers was as a sire of jockeys and athletes, but art crept in somehow with a bit of help from elsewhere. His youngest daughter, Edna, was bright and spent all her working life in a library, but the arty streak came from her husband's side. She married Frank Lucas who was an engineer but could draw more than a straight line. It was, however, his father Edward who was the dab hand. He designed stained glass windows and his work can be seen in many of the churches and cathedrals in Britain. Perhaps his skills missed a generation and were passed on to his grandchildren, Gill and Paul. Neither of them have pushed their way to the front but they are very talented. Paul was commissioned to paint Brigadier Gerard for the Canadian Jockey Club and Peter Walwyn commissioned him to paint his Derby winner Grundy. Incidentally, Paul has now had equestrian art accepted by a London gallery.

Unfortunately, he has been diabetic since he was a small boy and obviously it has not made his life any easier. He took early retirement to help his wife Jackie run an excellent bed and breakfast establishment in Lewes which has now been sold as a private residence. Not surprisingly, Paul worked as a graphic designer, and it was he who created the cover of this book.

Paul's older sister, Gill, works in pastels as well as oils and there seems no limit to her skills with embroidery and exquisite lampshades. Gill, who has produced greetings cards, suddenly gets the urge to use her skills and when she decides to exhibit it is usually a success. Another of my cousins, Betty Phillips, the daughter of Reg Butchers, is also a dab hand at painting.

Our grand-daughters, Jo and Emma, had the patience when they were in their very early teens to do a cross-stitch of a picture of themselves as youngsters. It took many months and many, many stitches but the result made a much appreciated birthday present for their Grandma.

Grandaughters Emma and Jo

This is not an autobiography in the true sense but more like a ramble through a field of memories which I know are likely to be of little interest to outsiders. That said, I can now relate an amusing incident at the races on a very muddy day. Frank Lucas, the father of Gill and Paul, loved his racing and came with me to Wincanton. He was not a gambler and ten shillings on the Tote was just about enough for him. As we were walking in the paddock he noticed a £5 note stuck to the heel of a man ahead. It is easy to imagine the scene. As the man walked, Frank was attempting to get his toe on the note. There were near misses and side steps and it was rapidly turning into a comic opera. Frank, with his head down and determination, finally transferred the note to his shoe just before the man stopped. He picked up the £5, looked up, and to his dismay found he was second in line at the Tote's £5 window. Suitably embarrassed, he hadn't the nerve to push his way through the queue that had gathered behind him and was forced to have the biggest bet of his life. Sorry to say there was no happy ending.

Frank may not have gained from his 'paper-chase', but a lady friend, Olive Morrison, had her bad luck turned into good, following her first visit to Royal Ascot. For convenience she opened an account with the Tote. Her first ever bets were fifty pence on each race but there was no beginner's luck. Imagine her alarm when she received her account

Daughter Lesley with husband David

showing she owed £300. Luckily, Olive and her doctor husband, Jack, were friends and, through us, also acquaintances of Geoff Webster who moved from the *Daily Herald* to be the Press Officer for the Tote. It was clearly a mistake when she wrote 50 in the space for pounds and Geoff kindly rectified the error. You may well ask what would have happened if one, or more, had been winners? The answer to that is also clear to me. She would have found out how it could be refunded.

Becoming parents is the easy part, but bringing up the issue is as hard as it gets. We all hope to have done the right thing but most parents, in their hearts, find it difficult to let go. Marian and I are born worriers and even though Lesley and Guy are settled and happy we invent something to worry about, but have probably failed in keeping it a secret. Lesley worked as a dental nurse, but then passed numerous exams to become a registered childminder, with higher qualifications than necessary. It is a relief that she is able to work considering she was diagnosed as having multiple sclerosis in her late teens. We lived with that hanging over us for some time until a specialist announced that a GP had made a faulty diagnosis. Even if she has not got the strongest of constitutions, she makes up for it in endeavour and our reward is two loving grand-daughters.

Guy worked on a stud for six months before joining the International Racing Bureau. After several years with the IRB he joined the racing staff

Guy as captain of the Lord Wandsworth College u/14s

of the *Daily Express*. He took redundancy after thirteen years and became Marketing Manager of the National Stud, a job he relinquished to set up his own business. He and his partner, Juliet, live in Hampshire where they have horses including a couple of foals from the New Forest. Guy has a stepson, Daniel, who is a keen sportsman, and a younger son, Jack, who is also mad on sport. Both of the boys ride but not with any intention of making it a career. If sport was to be a career it would be as footballers as they have both been 'spotted' by scouts from professional clubs.

I am thankful to Emma who turned my pages of scribble into computer print and to Guy who took it a stage further. I am quite happy to be computer ignorant but I have done a bit of work on a laptop borrowed from Joanna. Guy is a better writer than I could ever be and has produced articles on a variety of subjects. Guy is keen on most sports and played rugby to a good standard. He is now paying the penalty with troublesome knees.

45

FOOTBALL AND CRICKET

The opportunity to play football or cricket was greatly limited as I was working a seven-day week. After several years with the paper I decided that it was about time to have some Saturdays off during the football season. I joined the Lewes club, known as the Rooks because these birds seemed to like life at the Dripping Pan, presumably named such as the ground on the four sides has a steep bank similar to an amphitheatre.

I became captain of the Lewes third eleven who were in the Brighton and District League that had a host of divisions with ours fairly high up. We played our home matches at the Stanley Turner ground and had great fun and gained promotion on one occasion. My position was centre-half and the one who invariably had the task of heading a wet leather ball while hoping that the laces did not make contact. My friend, David Hole, was six feet nine inches tall and played in goal. Surprisingly, he was able to deal with low balls and obviously dealt with anything in the air.

I didn't have a football brain but was speedy enough to make a run down the touchline even though my cross was usually too near the goalkeeper. The best part of my game was gaining possession and laying it off to the wing-half Dicky Dorrington. He had played better class football and it was he who set up the attacks.

On many occasions I played after a late night on Fridays when the Hunt, Rugby and Police Balls and many other events took place. They were high on our list of priorities but not the ideal preparation. Nevertheless, I enjoyed every minute of both the football and the dancing. My legs were swathed in crepe bandages for the football and not the dancing but, on second thoughts, it might have been wise to keep them on when tripping the 'light fantastic'.

It was said that my place in the team was secure as not many of the lads had cars in those days. With David's and my cars we got the side to away games. The only goal I scored was against Falmer. I squeezed between a couple of cowpats, swerved round another and lobbed the goalkeeper! Those facts are only very slightly exaggerated. That pitch is where Brighton and Hove Albion are hoping to have their new stadium built eventually. There must have been a spate of illness or injuries at the only time I was selected to play for the Lewes second eleven! The mention of football reminds me of the old Tottenham and Welsh International, Willie Evans. When he retired from the game he worked for the Daily *Mirror* and told me he got £2 for playing for Wales but, like the rest of the team, would have willingly played for his country without pay. as it was the honour that counted. That is another example of how attitudes have changed and in my opinion, as you would expect, for the worse.

Cricket was not so easy to fit into my schedule but I was a social member of the Odiham and Greywell Cricket Club known by the initials of OGCC. They played on part of the common plus a bit of land given by Captain Bobby Petre, who won the 1946 Grand National on Lovely Cottage. He was President, and the Chairman was Mike Conville. Things were about to change, as the Odiham bypass was to go through the ground. Mike had done his stint and suggested to the committee that I should take his place. This was agreed and it led to an interesting and challenging period as Chairman.

Malcolm Hooker had resurrected the club, which vies with Hambledon as being the oldest. Now we had to find a new ground and there was a field only two or three hundred yards from our house but there was a problem about the ownership. After that was solved the Hampshire County Council gave us the go-ahead. It was now a case of 'all systems go'. Malcolm as a solicitor, with me dealing with the practical side of things worked well. The Hampshire CC were duty bound to see us rehoused and it turned out that our chosen field was not quite big enough. After a deal of negotiating with the owner of the adjacent land our problem was solved. He would lease forty yards to Hampshire CC who agreed for us to have a hedge removed and a ditch filled in at their expense.

We now had a field big enough for the game of cricket but the next job was to make a square. The field sloped with the fall from one boundary to another being twelve feet. Specialists who do county grounds were brought in and did a marvellous job. A stockproof post and rails fence was erected all round the ground and the process was now getting quite exciting. We had a ground and a really professional square, all paid for by Hampshire CC and leased to OGCC for a peppercorn payment of nothing.

With the ground replacement settled, it was now the matter of building a pavilion and a building for our machinery. Malcolm settled the price we would be given and any shortfall would be made up by a loan from Courage's Brewery, providing we stocked their products. Everything was going smoothly, and the next job was to have a pavilion erected. This was done by En-tu-Cas in atrocious weather. Marian was kept busy making endless flasks of tea and coffee for the work force that came from the Leicester area. Prior to the building being installed, there had to be a raised base constructed to detailed specification, plus sewers, drains, electricity and telephone services. It was a case of Hampshire CC owning the ground with the pavilion being the property of the club.

When the building was put up it was a shell with just the various partitions erected. Electricians and plumbers did their jobs but the hard work was still to be done. I would get up at five o'clock and work on the building until it was time to go racing. After dinner it was back to the club to work until ten or, quite often, much later. Some of the partitions were moved so as we could construct the bar and the showers in the two changing rooms were improved. Boxing in yards of piping and fitting locks to all windows were among a hundred and one other things to do.

Some local residents who were club members helped with the decorating. It was now the time to build a bar from scratch and a young carpenter and cricket player, Paul Monk, did the structure, with me as his helper. When it came to the bar top and security shutters we worked until two in the morning. To make the shutters fit we had to saw through steel. Nevertheless, it gave us great satisfaction and inside a wooden clad pillar we put all manner of items that may or may not be found.

A lady member, Audrey Horne, dealt in pine furniture and we bought what was needed at a favourable cost. She also advised us on colouring and curtains. On the day before the club was to be officially opened, I was putting finishing touches to the bar when my saw slipped and a sliced hand needed several stitches.

By careful planning and negotiating we had a superb ground and pavilion, which was a great asset to Odiham. The loan from Courage's was repaid in amounts that were barely noticeable. I wrote, and had printed, a booklet that detailed the whole process of our move and the benefits that were available, such as functions for local communities. It told how it was done with little cost to the club, whose membership was roughly seventy. The fittings and furnishings were our responsibility and in the literature we invited people to make a loan with a promise that it would be repaid within a year. There was also a form to complete for those who would like to join as a social or playing member at a cost of £3 and a little more for players. Our membership rose to 375 and most of those who lent money didn't need repaying while others had their loans repaid within a very few weeks.

It really was a success story and all those who so kindly helped were invited to a cheese and wine party as a token of appreciation. The booklet was distributed on a Saturday and at the bar of the old ground after the match a member handed me a cheque for £200 to set the appeal in motion. The donors were Maurice Hooper and his wife Margaret, who are sadly no longer with us. They never missed an opportunity to help the club and they certainly kept the bar profits in a healthy state.

I was able to play cricket on so few occasions since leaving school that I was really a non-cricketer. It was, however, very enjoyable to turn out for Odiham against the Odiham Society. Both sides were almost entirely members of the Club and the Society. It was an evening match with the bar and nibbles doing a roaring trade. I had made thirty-two for the Cricket Club off some poor bowling, but it was my fielding position on the boundary that pleased me. Alan Wood and Charles Orme opened for the Society and were big hitters. Charles was first to go and right on the boundary line I caught him at knee height. It was getting chilly when I asked for a sweater to be brought. I was in the midst of putting it on when Alan had a massive hit in my direction. With the sweater half on and half off I caught him with no fuss. The wicket keeper reported that Alan, with the ball in full flight, had said, 'The old boy won't catch that one.' In an earlier charity match I opened the innings and took a cheeky single off the first ball and at the other end I was caught in the slips off a rising ball that I knew I should have left alone but the temptation was too great! All very enjoyable and immensely satisfying.

46

A GRAND OPENING

Through Malcolm Hooker, our cricket club was closely associated with the Hampshire County Club and it was their long serving Peter Sainsbury who officially opened the new ground. It was then Odiham and Greywell Cricket Club versus the Hampshire County side in the opening match. The County players praised the cricket square and the strip on which they played.

Nothing could have gone better on the day and there was a surprise presentation to me, which was very emotional. Mary Hooker, the then wife of Malcolm, had found two appropriate Stevengraphs. One was of Fred Archer in the Royal Colours and the other was titled 'The Struggle'. The silk pictures are much sought after and in addition I was given a large greetings card signed by everyone connected with the club. The names and messages made me very proud. I was in a run-down state following weeks of working such long hours but the effort produced what we all wanted: a super ground, a pavilion and a good social gathering.

The first non-cricket occasion was the Odiham Society's fancy dress evening which was anything with a French Connection, and the next year the theme was Shipwrecked. Since the opening in 1980 the Clubhouse has staged many and various occasions unconnected to cricket.

Following a long stint as Chairman I decided to step down and was then made President. Living so close to the club resulted in me running the bar, banking, keeping the books, cleaning, stocking up from the Cash and Carry, ordering from Courage's, buying spirits locally and any manner of odd jobs. It was very difficult to let go and the Club was taking over my life. We were having regular incidents of breaking in, especially when we had a cigarette machine. Eventually the supplier refused any further business. The bar was another target but the shutters kept them out until we had a small extension built to hold barrels and other items that needed to be stored. That became a target almost immediately and

Receiving an award at the new Odiham and Greywell Cricket Club

Guy hits a 4 at the new ground

269

the wooden cladding was prized off and the breezeblocks pushed in before the cement had hardened. I think that may have been an inside job. There are usually a few rotten apples in the barrel and we had wine stolen and fingers in the till. We could hear the burglar alarm clearly from home and it meant me, as keyholder, going to the club, quite often as late as 2 a.m. After several occasions the police told me not to go there on my own. It was scary and on one occasion I knew the burglars were still there. It was depressing, but the cricket was a success. Sir Tim Rice brought his team, the Heartaches, to our old ground and it has been a regular fixture at the new premises even though Sir Tim has given up playing.

Before our move, I arranged a match for a local charity which raised close on £1,000 in 1976. Looking back at the team is interesting.

Odiham, batting first, scored 186 with de Moraville taking 4 for 21 and Duval taking 4 for 52. Dyer and Brooks dismissed the tail-enders. Several pupils from Lord Mayor Treloar Colleges for handicapped children attended the match for their benefit and Mick Channon was a hero. He signed autographs while fielding on the boundary and in that position received applause when sprinting many yards to take two spectacular catches. My charity eleven with their scores were:

Robin Dyer (Warwick CCC)	10
Jeff King (Jockey/trainer)	13
Mick Channon (England)	9
Michael Phillips (*The Times*)	1
Bob Haynes (Course commentator)	21
Peter Willett (*Sporting Chronicle*)	6
Peter Bromley (BBC)	20
Chris Lander (*Daily Mirror*)	0
Claude Duval (*The Sun*)	36
Charles Brooks (Marlborough)	25 not out
John de Moraville (*Daily Express*)	11
Extras	16

There was a crowd of youngsters waiting for Mick Channon to emerge from the changing room but when the players were respectable Mick asked me to let them in, after which he signed autograph books and chatted to them.

It was a wonderful gesture from a man who was a celebrity but still able to give his time so freely. When Mick finally emerged and entered the bar, his first act was to buy bottles of Champagne for anyone whose taste it was. Mick is now a celebrity in the racing world and it is rare for a man to have been right at the top of two professions.

The following year, I arranged another match for the College before we moved to the new ground. This time my charity team scored 209 for 6 declared which set Odiham a stiff task and they could reach only 145 for 9 at the close. They scored as follows:.

Jim Standen (Worcester CCC, West Ham and Arsenal)	56
Jeff King (Jockey/trainer)	3
Bryan Timms (Hampshire and Warwick CCCs)	40
Tommy Langley (Chelsea)	44
Peter Taylor (England and Tottenham)	25
Michael Phillips (*The Times*)	21 not out
Martin Hinshelwood (Crystal Palace)	9
Dave Swindelhurst (Crystal Palace)	4 not out

Did not bat: Steve Perryman (Tottenham), Claude Duval (*The Sun*) Bill Ives (Dorset CCC).

It is not easy to get eleven players in mid-summer as so many have prior commitments. Approaches were made to well known individuals who were unable to play. Of those who turned out, none requested payment. The only one to ask for a fee of £25 was our old pal and 'Champagne taster' Godfrey Evans. Needless to say we had to do without this entertaining character.

The old ground was adequate but really needed some modernisation and better car parking. Following any downpour of rain the car park was a sea of mud and needed a tractor or manpower to get the cars out. The police did not like cars parking on the road and everything possible was done to ensure that there was plenty of hard-standing at the new ground.

I had wonderful times at both grounds. A notable difference was the lack of moles at the new one. A recent President, Doug Smith, who died in the summer of 2006, was captain of the second XI which he had formed to play cricket as a fun-loving social side and labelled them 'The Moles'. The mounds left by the moles were sacked up by the grounds-man and used for repairing the wicket ends so they had some use. When Doug Smith fielded the President's XI he had the England Ladies Test Team as the opposition. Later on, my son Guy became captain of the Moles and encouraged a lot of the Colts – many of whom are now playing at a much higher level.

There were many exciting moments with Odiham winning promotion on several occasions and also winning various Cups. Bob Hooker, father of Malcolm, was a first-class umpire and a wonderful supporter of everything the club took on. Bob was also a director of the Aldershot Football Club and arranged annual games of cricket between the footballers and Odiham as part of their pre-season training. It was in one of these games that I took pleasure in seeing my then 15-year-old son knock the Aldershot bowling all over the place only to be caught on the boundary for 49.

Another exciting episode concerned Dave Barker and Brian Timms. While we were all in the bar after a match, Dave Barker said, 'I feel a century coming on,' and ex-professional Brian Timms voiced the opinion that Dave would never score a hundred. That set the ball rolling and Dave, who would bet on anything, asked what odds he would offer. Brian quoted 10/1 and Dave handed over a tenner and shook on the bet of £100 to £10.

It was only a few weeks later that Dave was getting among the runs and when I arrived to watch the match he was in the fifties. The word had spread that the lovable and popular Dave was going well and quite a crowd turned up as the wager was common knowledge. Slowly but surely he inched towards the century. The time came when he needed just a couple and as he swept the ball to the boundary the crowd went crazy. Dave was unmoved bar a wide grin.

We celebrated in style after the match but Dave had forgotten the wager. Not long afterwards Timms came to the club but refused to settle as the opposing team, Long Sutton, was the village in which Dave lived and it was Timms' belief that they let Dave reach his century. Our modest and laid back century maker took it in his stride and didn't even ask for his £10 stake to be returned. We all knew his century was not contrived but well deserved.

47

NEW FACES

It was a Sunday when we said goodbye to the ground by the Basingstoke Canal. We gained permission from the police to have a procession up the High Street to the new ground and it included a tractor and a sit-on tandem roller. We also gained approval for the motorised vehicles to use the road unlicensed. The number of accessories needed to run a cricket club is not realised until you have to move. There was a lorry carrying things such as a safe and refrigerator while members were shouldering some of the smaller items. Malcolm Hooker had given the tractor to the club while Paddy Gallagher gave the tandem roller. Paddy, a contractor, was a friend who owned some horses, and the tractor is still going strong. Club member John Rawlings kindly fetched it from Wales on his firm's low-loader.

We were now able to be more ambitious and our annual cricket dinners, held in the clubhouse, were quickly a sell-out. None of the guest speakers was paid which was a bonus considering many were household names. As chairman it was my duty to receive them and be at their side during dinner. Guests included Sir Tim Rice, Sir Trevor McDonald, cricketers Geoff Miller, John Morris and Hugh Morris, footballer Peter Osgood, TV stars Terry Scott and Michael Robbins plus impersonator Kevin Connolly whose take-off of Lord Oaksey made me think the 'Lord' was really in the room.

In our first season we raised £1,000 for the Hampshire batsman David Turner, whose brother Chris is a long-serving Odiham player and now a committee member. After David Turner, we had dinners or events for several of the Hampshire players in their benefit year. It really is a great help to have the County Club as close allies and they have responded every time we have asked for anything. Richard Gilliat, a relation of Sir Martin, Trevor Jesty, Michael Marshall, Gordon Greenidge, Nigel Cowley, Bobby Parks and Robin Smith are a few that Odiham have helped in a modest way.

Undoubtedly the highest profile match on this ground was that between Hampshire CCC and Old England, sponsored by Whitbread, with Samuel of that family attending. The ground was decked out with local business firms lending support, some with marquees. The ground was also seen fit for a minor counties match. Basil D'Olivera was among the well known players for Old England while Fred Titmus was there in a official capacity.

A lot of girls have played important parts in the success of the club. Sally McGaughrin has been a great organiser of catering and Sir Tim Rice has for long praised her lunches when the Heartaches have attended.

When Evan Davies was President his team included Freddie Forsyth and he thoroughly enjoyed his day, particularly as he was left to enjoy himself without being hounded by autograph hunters. All cricket lovers will know the name of 'Richie' Richardson, the West Indies opening batsman. It was thanks to him for attending one of the President's matches and handing over a bottle of Champagne to 'Man of the Match', Darren Robinson. The photo of the award will no doubt be cherished.

Plenty of big-hitters have graced the square. A few balls have been hit out of the ground but the clubhouse was really christened when John Inverarity, an Australian player, sent one through the glass of the entrance door without a bounce.

I am naturally proud of the club and all it has achieved. The Colts get proper coaching and several have gone on to play, not only with us, but with other clubs. Bobby Parks, for long the Hampshire wicket-keeper, helps with the coaching. I have often teased him for being a Hampshire player instead of Sussex like his father and grandfather. For several years, a Racing World XI were visitors and on these occasions the winner was the bar whose profits got a real boost. In addition to touring teams, there is a visit from a team calling themselves 'Not the MCC' which is made up of musicians. Apart from well-known cricketers, I have seen the likes of Ludovic Kennedy, broadcaster Michael Nicholson and, on many occasions, Alan Ball who has actually played at the Club.

Most clubs have a period when their fortunes take a dip and it happened to Odiham. I am pleased to say that local businessman Peter Fountain has become chairman and the club is again prosperous. As soon as our clubhouse was habitable the Royal British Legion used it for their AGM and other social functions. Even the local Legion had racing overtones. The President for a long time was General Gordon. He was the youngest General in the Second World War and the grandfather of

Jamie Railton who rode with success as an amateur and professional. Also a visitor on Legion nights was Colonel Duggie Gray who was once a director of the National Stud and whose riding career included participation in the Grand National. The Legion also hosted a meeting at the clubhouse attended by Field Marshal Lord Bramall, a former President of the MCC and top man in the Legion organisation. As a Legion member myself I was invited to sit beside him wearing my other 'hat', that of Club Chairman, with a request to talk cricket with him. I would have found horse racing an easier topic.

The cricket club and I were like twins joined at the hip. When I retired it seemed possible that the club would be my sole occupation which would be most unfair on my family. In my view the only safe decision was to move away from Odiham. We moved to a flat in Petworth but I remained President. On paying a visit to the club we noticed a building being converted into a couple of flats. Although we had been in Petworth for only eighteen months we decided to buy the flat which was even closer to the cricket ground than my previous house in Odiham. It was small but unusual with a spectacular view. The move away did the trick because the many jobs I had been doing were, out of necessity, being done by others and I could now go there to have a drink and a game of snooker without interruption.

After five years we moved to Suffolk so we could see our two granddaughters growing up. They are now adults but Guy has now got two sons, Daniel and Jack.

As mentioned earlier, many well-known people have trodden the turf of the club and when Sir Tim Rice featured on the *South Bank Show*, presented by Melvyn Bragg, it was filmed at the Odiham ground and a £200 donation was made to the Club.

The late comedy actor Arthur English was no stranger to the club and I saw Tony Lewis, the ex-England captain, at one of the Heartaches' matches. I have purposely left to last a character by the name of Oliver Reed. It was his ambition to open the batting for Hampshire and we gave him the chance. The County side had come to play against the Club in a benefit match and Mark Nicholas, the captain, sportingly allowed Oliver to open. The first two balls spread-eagled his stumps but were sportingly called 'no-balls' and after falling over on the third delivery he was forced to retire. Naturally, he was drunk most of the time. Later, I saw him 'mooning' on the boundary. He stayed two nights at our local George Hotel and his bar bill was reputed to be £400. Understandably the Hampshire captain, Mark Nicholas, dispensed with him as a fielder. I'm no prude and like a bit of fun but his behaviour did not go down well with me or a lot of families. He did, however, draw a crowd and the bar did well but unfortunately the Hampshire side had to make a quick getaway as they had a Sunday one-day game and had to travel that evening.

48

NOW AND THEN

Before I retired from the *Daily Mirror* in 1985 there had been many changes in the pressroom. There used to be about a dozen scribes who turned up at all the principal meetings. The London dailies had their correspondent with a name and a nom-de-plume plus the *Sporting Life* and *Sporting Chronicle* writers and representatives from those papers who returned the starting prices. A man from the Press Association and a couple of telephonists just about summed up the gathering. What is more, it was fairly silent compared to the present set-up with bodies everywhere. That is just one of the things that has changed since I first started out and, almost certainly, before.

When I first went racing as a member of the press, instead of working under cover, our means of entry was a small folded card and not a metal badge as now. The only way of entering any members' enclosures was to buy a badge or become an annual member. This entailed getting an existing member to sign an application form. For Newmarket it was a little different in that it needed the signatures of two members of the Jockey Club on the form. Soon after the introduction of the metal press badge it became eligible to gain admission to all enclosures. It is still so today but a 'swipe card' is needed to gain entry to the actual course.

A trilby hat or some other headgear was worn by most racegoers but having lost a couple and had one thrown on a coal fire by a prankster, I decided to go bare-headed. This did not meet with the approval of Lord Rosebery who told me to wear a hat when next I was in the enclosure immediately outside the weighing room at Newmarket. What a bloody cheek!

On arriving at a Salisbury meeting I was given a message saying Sir Michael Sobell wished to speak to me. I sorted him out and asked what he wanted. He was curious to know why I tipped a lot of his winners but very few of his losers. My interpretation of his request is that he suspected someone was leaking stable information. The answer was simply, 'That's what I'm paid to do.' Another case of a bloody cheek.

Naturally things have moved on in the racing industry. The old-time stable lads were a proud bunch and it was common practice to take home any of their kit that needed washing. As an example, they would wash the 'rubber' that went under the saddle because they took pride in their job. Now there is a labour problem with the lads and girls having a greater workload and more than just two horses to look after. Having said that, the way they turn out their charges on racedays is worthy of the highest praise. The most visible change is the increasing number of girls working in stable yards.

There were once very few trainers who owned their own horsebox while these days I understand that they can be 'the best horse in the yard'. Without inquiring I assume that horses cannot go by rail any more. When the railway was in regular use the yearlings purchased at the autumn sales had to be led from the station to various stables. People in Lewes, and no doubt in every training centre, used to stand and stare as it was probably the nearest they had been to a racehorse. The yearlings of bygone days were not accustomed to traffic and quite often became frightened enough to make leading them anything but straightforward.

Television has brought about many of the changes and the content of the racing coverage has, in my view, reached saturation point. The way betting in the ring and the exchanges is presented amounts to rapid bafflement that must seem like a foreign language to a large proportion of viewers. With thousands now betting on the exchanges it is probably very popular but with many others a real turn-off.

Winning jockeys are confronted with a mike before they have caught their breath or gathered their thoughts. 'He's a nice horse and did it well,' sums up a jockey's reply, which is something the majority of viewers have seen for themselves. Oh, how I wish the serene style of the late, and loved, Clive Graham could return to soothe the mind. The analysis of every aspect seems superfluous to requirements. This is no reflection on the presenters as they are presumably doing as instructed. It appears to be a necessity for most programmes to be noisy with the increasing use of foul language. I am pleased to say the racing programmes are not guilty of that.

I suppose a lot of trainers do not know the days before televised racing and take intrusion in their stride. Nowhere is sacred these days and a microphone interrupts a group in the parade ring, on the stands and in the winner's enclosure where I think the owner should be left to enjoy his success with the trainer and jockey as the number one priority.

Not once did I see Clive Graham flustered, not even when someone broke into his bedroom while we were staying in the St Pierre Hotel for a Chepstow meeting. Clive and his wife Marie, together with me and Marian, were having a few nightcaps after the Welsh Grand National dinner and Clive went to his room for something or other. He found his binoculars and Marie's jewellery untouched, but her underwear and some bedding were missing.

Call me old-fashioned, or anything you wish, but I prefer the old routine. If you asked a trainer about the chance of a runner or, more blatantly, will it win?, you would have received a rude reply. They start work at the crack of dawn, do their job professionally, worry about one thing or another, travel miles and are then expected to reveal all. There are a dozen runners in a race and the trainer of each is asked about its chance. It is a hypothetical situation but more than likely each will answer, 'I hope it runs a big race.'

As for the betting, it too can be misleading. Some horse drifts from 5/2 to 7/2 and you might believe the world is about to end. The market moves are made out to signify a definite win or lose as fact, but for every hundred market moves that prove to be a true guide there must be as many that contradict.

Channel 4 certainly tries hard but seems to fall between two stools. Is it comic entertainment headed by John McCririck or the seriousness of Jim McGrath that is needed? In short, the coverage appears to be pulling in opposite directions, but I expect the powers that be will call it balanced. At my age I tend to keep opinions to myself as I am living in a different world and obviously don't know the likes and dislikes of the present generation.

I am afraid the BBC, when they occasionally decide to show racing, have a spot when each race is dismembered. What's happened to the theory that things unbroken need not be mended?

Television in general has a lot to answer for. On radio there must not be too many lengthy periods of silence but on TV action programmes viewers can see most things without the need for non-stop gabbling. I am reminded of Lord Hailsham, who, when asked by his barber how he would like his hair cut replied, 'In complete silence.' Perhaps some of the presenters should have 'A Little Silence is Golden' emblazoned across their foreheads.

Of course time has brought about changes for the better and in racing the top of the list must be the helmet. It was only in the twenties that a skullcap was introduced for jump jockeys. That was a flimsy affair that was kept in place only by tightening the strings of the coloured cap and, as the peak got in the way, was much better done by your valet. Now the helmet is securely fastened. The body protectors are also a sensible innovation and I'm sure the weighing rooms must have better facilities. It is many years since I set foot in one but even the mention of the word reminds me of the racecourse at Wye. The facilities there consisted of a washstand and jugs of cold water. It is not difficult to imagine the scene on a muddy day. There was also an outdoor bar which was open to the elements with rusted corrugated iron sheets for a roof. Whisky drinkers had only to hold out their glass on a rainy day to get the water from the leaking roof.

One of the curses used to be the bad weather and the number of lost journeys. Unless you had a radio in the car, or even a car, and not everyone did, there was no way of knowing if a meeting was off. Even then the BBC was not guaranteed to make an announcement. This was an era when the BBC seemed to treat racing as if it was an infectious disease and while giving the results, would not lower themselves by giving the starting prices. Even now they seem to be less and less interested in racing.

Alan Oughton and I drove to Southwell on one Boxing Day only to find that the meeting had been called off some hours before our arrival. The moment you got on a train you were helpless. There were two train services to Birmingham and the one I usually caught left from Euston but just for a change, I decided to go from St Pancreas. It was not until I got in a taxi at Birmingham that I was told about the cancellation. At Euston there had been a large board breaking the news to racegoers.

There were other omissions that became frustrating. A telephone is a vital commodity for a journalist, so the lack of them was a spanner in the works. If the racecourse had a kiosk there was likely to be a queue and if you managed to get in and hogged it for around thirty minutes you were liable to get lynched. The Press Association phone was usually the only one in our rooms so it was often best to drive to a quiet spot away from the course, again assuming you had a car. If travelling by train, it could become irritating. Grabbing a phone on one of the platforms was usually possible, but watching your train leaving while you were still dictating your copy was a blow. In later years, several papers had their own telephone lines which made things a lot easier, but I had left the scene before the introduction of computers. I believe they use what is called a Tandy, unless some other device has been introduced.

Before overnight declarations came in we had to rely on a list compiled by 'Fairy' from the Press Association. He might not have completed his list until after several races had been run but we managed, so I suppose it was a case of what you've never had you never miss.

Today a lot of things are taken for granted and included is the debit or credit card. Without either, life could be difficult as cheques were not accepted in most places unless you were known. I had to stay in Dublin's Gresham Hotel for a few days and when I got out my cheque-book to pay I was told they didn't accept them. In the end it was accepted when I said it's a cheque or nothing, but it made me feel uncomfortable.

Lincoln used to open the Flat race season and it was three days there before a drive across the Pennines for the three-day Grand National meeting at Liverpool and the cash usually needed replenishing. Some-times I would go to a branch and ask them to ring my bank to check identification. Quite often they would ask for the name of the chief cashier, and on one occasion the teller came off the phone and had a broad grin on his face. When I got home I asked Dickie Giles, the chief cashier, what he said to justify the grin. I only said, 'If he's got big ears, that's him.' It is unlikely there are many like Dickie who kept the *Sporting Life* and a bottle of Worthington on the shelf below his counter. What is more, my bank had a lady teller on occasions, unheard of at the time.

My other way of getting cash was to ask the secretary on the sports desk to wire it to the nearest post office. On reflection, those early days were inconvenient to say the least but the general way of life was, in my book, a great deal better.

One of my pet hates in racing is the flying dismount performed by Frankie Dettori. It goes without saying that some of the past trainers would have gone spare, not only with that but any over-the-top exuberance. My dislike for the flying dismount is for the simple reason that it is dangerous. One day Frankie will make a mistake and cause himself an injury but more importantly his valuable Group winner might become alarmed and knock a joint or strike into himself. That reasoning is not piffle but logical. Remember Barry Geraghty failing to gain top points for his attempt to copy Frankie after winning the Cheltenham Gold Cup on Kicking King? He landed on his backside but it might well have resulted in a broken ankle.

My mind frequently goes back to how different things were. Once we had a Starter's Assistant but now he is an Assistant Starter and, more recently, in football the one-time linesman is now the Assistant Referee.

In racing the change seems to be not only in name but also in the type of person so employed. With the advent of starting stalls, the old-time assistant would not be playing his usual role. The best known of the old assistants in the South was Bill Cracknell, a well loved character, who, without being disrespectful, was the rough and ready sort for want of a better description. His dress was breeches, leggings, jacket, trilby hat and the tool of his trade, the 'long tom' by which the hunting crop was generally known. Bill would flick this expertly round the heels of those horses showing reluctance at the start. In his early days he would walk to the start while the starter would arrive astride a hack. It was a regular occurrence for Bill to receive a backhander from a trainer accompanied by the words 'look after mine'. He was part of the furniture, liked a drink and had plenty of punters but, above all, was loyal to his employers. Bill, like nearly all the jockeys, named the genial Major Kenneth Robertson as the best and also their favourite dispatcher.

As I have indicated elsewhere, the weighing rooms were very basic but mobile phones weren't banned because they hadn't been invented. The general means of communication was by telegram and the on-course office was usually busy. The earliest weighing room change I can remember was when a chap named Harry turned up with a tea urn, followed some weeks later by a few sandwiches. That initiative has, of course, been built on.

No crash helmets of today's type, no body protectors and no ladies' tights were to be seen in the old weighing rooms. Tights had not then replaced suspenders but stockings were very much in evidence as breeches and leg-hugging boots slipped over them with ease. In those days you weighed out and in with anything the horse was to carry and included breastgirth, skullcap and whip. The main change is that jockeys now leave off the heavier crash helmet and discard the whip.

When the old style flimsy skullcaps were in use a vigilant steward once visited the changing room and inspected all of the headgear. Those he considered almost useless were thrown to the ground and reduced to pulp with the heel.

Another item of 'racecourse furniture', was the paper-boy. There were two or three regular sellers of the evening additions and each had his clients who received free copies. Mine was called Harry and the arrangement suited both of us and particularly the seller. At fairly frequent intervals the recipient would bung him a few quid which, of course, meant he pocketed many times the value of the papers. It was one of those things that added a bit of harmless charm to the racing scene and Harry was useful in passing messages if I needed to contact people.

Unexpected reminders crop up quite often and not too long ago I was looking at a story on Channel 4 Teletext when I glimpsed my name. It was a piece by David Crow, a nom-de-plume for whom I know not. The relevant passage read 'Summertime blues at the *Daily Mirror* due to Newsboy's plunge to the foot of the *Racing Post*'s 52 runners Nap Table. Many of us Old Codgers were weaned on *Mirror* legends like Bob Butchers and Tim Richards. Halcyon Days!' A good way to remind me of my age but bad luck for Tim, who at 19 years my junior, is a mere boy!

Although I reckon to have retained a reasonable memory there was a quote attributed to me in a book entitled *Lester's Derbys* which I cannot recall writing in the *Mirror*. In describing Lester's win on Sir Ivor in 1968 I wrote: 'One of the greatest performances of race-riding that Lester Piggott, or any other jockey for that matter, has ever executed. The sheer cheek of the champion had to be seen to be believed.' Even though I may not remember penning that piece it was, without a doubt my true thought because the words would have been dictated to the copy-taker very shortly after the finish of that Derby.

49

THE PRESS

My early years in the pressroom were so different to my last years and most of the rooms were small but just big enough for the regulars and a likeable lot they were. Eric Rickman was on the *Daily Mail*, a post taken at a later date by his son John. Norman 'Roly-Poly' Pegg was on the *Daily Sketch* and took life very seriously in contrast to Frank Harvey of the *Sunday Dispatch* who was mischievous to say the least. Dickie Dickinson, of the *News Chronicle*, would never miss an opportunity to sample the hard stuff. Dickie was an officer in the RAF Regiment during the war and it was his task to meet a Squadron at a London station and escort them to their new post. Their sergeant gave the order to fall in and follow the officer. This they did and Dickie led them straight into the station bar and bought them all a drink.

Cyril Luckman was the *Daily Express* man but shortly to retire and make way for Clive Graham. Soon afterwards, Peter O'Sullevan left the Press Association to join the *Express*. Ernie Cureton was replaced by his son Lionel on the PA. and later as 'Templegate' of the *Daily Herald*. Merrick Good was 'Man On The Spot', the chief writer on the *Sporting Life*, and Sam Long wrote as 'Augar' for the same paper. The other specialist paper was the *Sporting Chronicle* for which Quinny Gilbey wrote, probably, the most number of words in a day. Also on that paper was Peter Willett.

Quinny knew everybody worth knowing and from his mouth flowed the most colourful prose and most of it unprintable. At Wolverhampton one day he was busy writing and cursing at the same time when John O'Neil came in and pointed out that Eve Beary was standing nearby. I'm afraid Quinny's gentlemanly behaviour deserted him when he said, 'She shouldn't be in here, she should be at the so-and-so kitchen sink.' Eve, wife of top jockey Michael, was at that time one of only two females on the racing press, the other being Rita Cannon.

Doug Newton, Frank Hill and Lionel Cureton at my retirement party

John O'Neil was one of the most sincere men I knew and fairness should have been his middle name. Although a Northerner, he was better than anyone I know at rhyming slang. 'That beats the lot, I've just seen a pineapple at the airs,' was his outburst as he came into the Birmingham pressroom. It was, of course, the first time he had seen a monk at the races. If it's not obvious, I'm sure you'll work it out.

Also on the *Sporting Chronicle* was Bob Watson who moved south with his family and became a close friend. Bob did not drive and for years he came racing with me. Bob, whose daughter Janet married Michael Rees, was one of the best beer drinkers I have known. It was while we were staying at the Ailsbury Arms in Marlborough that we went to a few pubs and Bob had his fill. The night was bright but freezing as we returned and rang for the night porter to let us in. The delay was too much for Bob who decided to water the shrub guarding the door. As if from nowhere a policeman appeared and pointed to the stream of water that was turning to ice. It seemed a fair cop until Bob said, 'It wasn't me officer, it was my friend.'

Doug Newton joined the *Sporting Life* on leaving school and stayed until his retirement a few years ago. He was another trustworthy friend, and like Bob Watson and Geoff Webster, our friendship extended to our private lives and not just the racecourses. At one of the last meetings at Lewes racecourse, Doug made the journey by train. I had already moved away from Lewes so it was not surprising that I, together with Doug and John Hughes, decided to renew some old acquaintances in the town or, to be more precise, the local pub. One thing led to another and Doug asked to be dropped off at Haywards Heath station to catch the last train to London. He didn't even get to the platform to see the last train departing. A hitherto unknown turn of foot saw Doug in pursuit of my car with arms waving and breathless shouts and a sad ending. That is how I visualised the scene when I was told that he missed the train. I was genuinely sorry for him especially as it must have cost him a few quid to get a cab back to London.

In latter days, the first three people in the pressrooms of all courses were Peter Willett, Michael Phillips and myself. The runners for the following day arrived in the offices at eleven thirty and either Michael or I would phone the paper and tick off the runners in the *Sporting Life*. It was a laborious task, especially when there were several meetings. With that mission accomplished, one of the trio would go to the bar, sometimes there would be one in our room, and return with two large

Vernon Sangster hosted a party of pressmen and jockeys aboard ship in Liverpool Docks

whiskys and a large gin and tonic. Serious work would then begin and only when that was under control did a few of us, generally led by Len Thomas of the *Sporting Life*, decide to bathe our lips once more.

While on the subject of pressroom colleagues there were none nicer than George Ennor and Peter Scott, whose sudden death was a real shock. Now at the age of just 65 dear George has departed. To this pair I have, sadly, to add another dear friend, David Phillips. He was Racing Editor of the *Daily Mirror* and for many years we worked closely and successfully. It was a shock when his wife Betty rang from their Isle of Wight home to say that David had dropped dead after leaving the table at a restaurant where they had been lunching. He took over as 'Newsboy' when I retired. The deaths of these exceptional men caused me much more than normal sadness. For a long time I was hoping to get George Ennor a job on the *Daily Mirror* but for various reasons it was not to be. The departure of these men who were years younger than me just makes me realise how lucky I am.

The other outside man for the *Mirror* was Dick Ratcliffe and it was me who got him the job. The work-load was getting too much for me and I jumped at the chance, when asked, to find somebody else. His job was to write about the day's happenings while I concentrated on what would win the following day. Although it may not have been apparent, I found it difficult working with Dick. He did not work hard enough at his job and had a serious drink problem as well as other difficulties. Things would have run more smoothly had I been able to take George Ennor from the *Sporting Life*. There was Tim Richards in the North and he was a hard worker and reliable as was Charlie Fawcus who came as I was nearing the end of my long stint.

You may wonder if I received the 'golden handshake' that was at one time promised. The answer is no. Robert Maxwell arrived on the scene and grabbed that, together with the pension fund.

I am godfather to one of George Ennor's sons and, ashamedly, have seen him only once since the christening and likewise a son of Sos and Peggy Phillips, non-racing friends. After his christening the next I saw of him was at his twenty-first birthday party. I failed in my duties.

In my very early days on the paper the powers-that-be always took a close look at gimmicks. When they heard of the Lord who dreamed winners they could not resist and so Lord Kilbracken, known to us as John Godley, was employed. He had a great record of war service and was a lovely man even if a wee bit eccentric. Not surprisingly his reign

Bill Gollings hosted a lunch at Claridges to celebrate winning the Cheltenham Gold Cup with Mill House. From the left, John Rickman, Dick Francis and Bob

on the paper ended after a short while with few, if any, of his dreams having come true! Digging into my memories is a good way to remind me of my age and to think that the head of the BBC, and now ITV, was a very young sub on the Sports Desk named Michael Grade. That was when I had been with the paper for many years. It puts things in perspective and it is probably sad that I still regard the seventies as a modern era.

50

RIDERS IN THE STAND

One of my pet hates is, as the chapter title says, 'riders in the stand'. Anyone who has ridden in a race, or even ridden a racehorse, must find them most irksome. Everyone is entitled to an opinion and to be free to criticise jockeys but on most occasions they are talking through their pockets and simply do not understand the technicalities. That said, I don't think jockeys take criticism from this section too seriously as it is a case of being critical just for the sake of it. In football it is even more evident and the 'boo boys' enjoy that part more than the game itself. I reckon it is similar in racing except that the critics are not so vociferous.

There is not a jockey born who has not ridden ill-judged races which in many cases are not apparent. This is something I know because in my limited experience as a jockey I made more misjudgements than I like to admit. Obviously those with experience should make considerably fewer errors but they will never be completely eliminated because it is quite simply human nature. The first thing to remember is the well-worn phrase that horses are not machines and how very true it is. They have no accelerators, gears or brakes even though such words are frequently used to loosely describe their abilities. Each of these so-called reactions is, to say the least, unreliable.

The most common criticism is when horses come from behind, finish fast and fail to win. I am not suggesting that it is never a case of misjudgement but other factors are involved. The horse may not be able to go the early pace without being bustled along and becoming unbalanced. He may be better suited to some cover rather than seeing daylight and thus running too freely and in many cases simply being saved for his known turn of finishing speed. It should be obvious that he cannot use speed at both the beginning and the end of his races.

That being said, there are further facts that have to be taken into account. When asked to quicken some horses take longer to respond than others, that is if they are able to respond at all. Likewise when the steadying function is operated it does not always work as one would wish. These unpredictables are present if a horse is galloping on his own so imagine how different it is when in a race with a field of horses around you.

When setting off you do not know how the race is going to be run and original plans of campaign may have to be ditched. Interference and split-second decisions are ever present and can lead to a horse becoming unbalanced which is one of the worst things to happen. Breaking stride and losing rhythm due to the tightening up of the runners is often unavoidable unless the jockey goes wide in which case he will be accused of riding a bad race because he 'went all round the houses'.

Believe me, a race may not take long to run but the jockeys have more than enough to think about. Another misconception is that horses which appear to be fast finishing is exaggerated because those ahead are actually weakening. There is not a truer saying than 'a jockey cannot come without the horse' and only the man on top can tell how well or poorly his mount is really travelling. Some animals find nothing when asked while others keep digging deep under pressure. Some are very straightforward whereas others take a bit of knowing. Perhaps the most misleading factor concerns those horses which have just one short finishing run and that has to be timed to absolute perfection. If it doesn't come off it is usually the jockey who gets the blame rather than the horse not having the ability. Quite frankly, I am hugely impressed by the high standard of jockeyship.

The art of race-riding has always been a subject that fascinates me and I shy away from those who criticise simply because they don't understand and there is no quick way of explaining. In all probability they wouldn't want to listen in any case. I have only scratched the surface of what race-riding involves so I think a count to ten or, preferably fifty, may be advisable rather than immediate condemnation although I know the champions among the 'riders in the stand' would never heed such advice and I have probably wasted words by even trying to defend the riders. Oh, how I wish they could find themselves on a horse and shut in on the rails with all the jockeys they have slated clustered around them. They would be silenced forever by fear. Fortunately the 'riders in the stand' do no harm to the image of racing and still make a contribution by their betting but it seems to be overlooked these days that the owners of the horses make a much larger contribution. It is time to get off my soap-box but at least I have got it off my chest: that is the topic and not the soap-box!

51

STUCK IN MY MIND

Everybody has happenings, however minor, in their lives that they will never forget. They are not necessarily important things but simply made an impact. Two incidents were long before my age had reached double figures and the Black Horse stables were still there. Right opposite was the grocery shop called T.G. Roberts and I was often sent on errands and as soon as I was spotted the manager came out to see me across the road. It was the same when I was leaving. The traffic in those days was light and also children were safe to roam with no thought of abduction. I remember not only the helping hand but also the staff. The manager was Mr Smyth, the bacon and dairy products were the domain of Mr Fyefield while the junior was Joe Punker, all of whom I addressed as Mister. My most usual mission was to buy Casino and Pat-a-cake biscuits, which were sold loose rather than in today's nasty packaging. An added touch of comfort was the provision of chairs for customers while ordering their goods.

The second of these very young memories was something more serious. From a very early age I spent a lot of time in adult company, especially around the stables, and no doubt the staff were to blame. It was one of those Sundays when Gwyn Evans joined us for lunch. My table manners were good and I politely asked my father to 'pass the f——— vinegar, please.' He did so and simply said I should not use that word again.

I imagine holidays provide fond memories for many of today's young children, but not so for me. The only one I can recall is staying in a boarding house in Eastbourne, with my mother and sister. It was all of sixteen miles from our Lewes home and my recollection is of rain and boredom.

Exotic holidays abroad were not for ordinary folk in those days and when my mother and father went for their only ever holiday, it was to Lyme Regis in Dorset. Even that caused a stir among the locals. For me it was no hardship as I was happier at home among the horses.

It was while living in that same Lewes house that I missed seeing the one and only Derby during my working life It was won by Never Say Die, ridden by the 'boy wonder' Lester Piggott. All the details of that are still perfectly clear. I woke up feeling extremely tired and very weak and there was no way that I could make it to Epsom. I got Marian to ring the paper and tell them the situation. After the boy Piggott had won it was a top story for all newspapers. I was slumped in a chair when the Sports Editor rang and wanted to speak to me. He questioned my inability to work and there was anger in his voice when he said, 'Are you telling me you are too ill to work?' My one word answer was 'Yes' and I replaced the receiver. When the doctor arrived shortly after he took one look at me and said, 'You have got jaundice.' I have never felt so low and it took a long time to feel really well again. The win of Never Say Die did, however, bring a little joy. Many weeks before the Derby, Harold Dixon, the punter/bookmaker, rang me to say he had backed Never Say Die to win a lot of money and to tell Marian that she had got £100 to £1 about the colt. He was as good as his word this time and Marian received a cheque within a few days.

Ascot has been the scene of several incidents over the years but the two I recall were very sad. The death of Manny Mercer was dreadful as explained earlier but the most frightening experiences was when lightning struck the metal fencing near the winning post and directly opposite the stands. The stands were those in situ before the two reconstructions. I had hoped that the latest building would have a more precise angle but it seems there remains a slight problem. On the ground floor of the original structure, at the end near the old parade ring, was a gentlemen's urinal. It was a large convenience with white glazed tiles from floor to ceiling. When the lightning struck, blue flashes bounced from one wall to another, for what seemed quite a long time. How lucky were we occupants who, on leaving, saw the real devastation. It was a distressing sight less than a hundred yards away with many casualties among the crowd.

Sadness of another kind was on the dance floor. It was very slippery and when we fell I landed on top of my partner and she broke her ankle. Despite her pain, she insisted it was not my fault. Something like that is hard to forget. She didn't cry but the water-works were turned on in a big way after I had been the judge of a beauty contest. Reg Akehurst, a trainer who has handed over to his son Jon, invited us to supper prior to the contest in Lambourn and then took us to the Village Hall. I announced my choice, whereupon one of the losers burst into tears and the poor girl's mother was also inconsolable. It was a no win situation and I didn't stay any longer than necessary.

I shed no tears when an innocent deed saw me ejected from a very respectable club in Chester during their big race week in May. I stood by a table where dice were being thrown quite forcibly on the sunken baize of the table. I had not the slightest idea what the game was all about when suddenly a man said it was my throw. The dice came to my unfavoured left hand and my exuberant throw saw the dice hit the curtains at the end of the room. I was ushered out by a burly individual but was re-admitted after a colleague, Laurie Brannan, explained that it was a genuine mistake and that I was not a trouble-maker.

Impending danger is something else that usually sticks in your mind but it was the laughter that I remember most about the following incident. Fighting is not my scene but it came close when I challenged a hefty individual as we passed on the dance floor. Marian told me he had made unacceptable remarks in the street and I understood that he was a great big coward so I invited him outside. It came as a bit of a shock when he seemed more than anxious to oblige. He grew bigger and bigger as we walked to a quiet alley and the 'coward' label was being quickly transferred. My accusations had been made and he asked, 'So what are you going to do about it?' He was moving menacingly close to me and the situation needed some quick thinking. Luckily, an answer came to me in a flash and I blurted out, 'I'll let you off this time.' This was followed by laughter and a handshake.

His name was John Light and we often had drinks together. Another of the Light family was Joe and it was he who sang at our £1 a head party at Southover Grange. He also sang in the Lamb pub which drew quite a crowd on their music night. One evening I went with a couple of mates to heckle Joe in a kindly sort of way. After he had finished his number he shouted, 'Grab that Bob Butchers as he is singing next.' Luckily I beat the would-be grabbers and was out of the door in a flash. Joe was a likeable character with a dry sense of humour. He had a jackass (male donkey) on his bit of land which came to the notice of a titled lady. She asked how much he charged for a service and without hesitation Joe replied, 'I charge a tenner but the donkey does it for nothing.'

Motor vehicles and horses are a poor mix. Glen Kingie is a horse I remember because our association could have ended in a really bad accident. We were in Matt Feakes' string and trotting along the Lewes to Brighton road when a double-decker bus came too close when passing. This caused Glen Kingie to panic and he collided with the side of the vehicle which is a pretty rotten feeling. No harm was done to the horse, and presumably none to the bus. No doubt the most frightened were the bus passengers.

A final memorable incident was also painful. We were all prepared to go to Venice on holiday but the evening before, I decided to fix a canopy that had come loose on the summerhouse. The ladder slipped and I fell some six feet onto concrete. The first parts to hit the ground were my hand and my thigh. I was sure my thigh had been broken and did not want to move but when I called for help nobody heard. I had to do something and it was then that I saw three fingers on my left hand pointing in the opposite direction. With Marian being a non-driver, the search was on to find someone to drive me the eight miles to Basingstoke Hospital. The fingers were x-rayed to see if there was any breakage after which they were pulled into place.

Walking was not easy and my hand was so swollen as to be useless, not that I intended walking on my hands! The doctor came shortly before we were due to leave and strongly advised me not to travel but I had no intention of laying out a lot of money and staying at home. Two local friends were also coming so at least I got out of helping with the luggage. I thought it better to recuperate in Venice rather than at home. I was advised to soak in a bath morning and night, presumably to help the massive bruising. Although restricting, it could have been worse. My theory is that a break can sometimes be less hassle than a dislocation.

On returning home I had physiotherapy for my hand given by a blind man. On telling him I couldn't bend my fingers to make a fist he said, 'Nonsense' and with that, bent my fingers with no difficulty or pain to him. For me – OUCH.

52

PARTING THOUGHTS

While writing this book I have become increasingly aware how attitudes and priorities change with the passing of the years. Even when you feel a 'young-at-heart' octogenarian there is a warning signal in your head, or, at least, there is in mine.

'Act your age', 'there's no fool like an old fool', and 'silly old devil', are among the remarks liable to be muttered behind your back if you step out of line. That's just one of the minor drawbacks of growing old and one tends to have a more serious outlook.

It may surprise a lot of people to know how often older persons can feel uncomfortable when with the younger generation but fortunately there are plenty who go out of their way to make you feel wanted. Not so long ago I came over very dizzy in my local shop and the next thing I remember is lying on the floor with people looking down at me. I had passed out completely and was embarrassed but the kindness of the staff was a welcome reminder that there are still some caring people and in this case both young and old. I must add that my collapse was simply due to some tablets that had lowered my blood pressure a little too much. That's enough of being morbid so I can now rejoice by recounting two happy and greatly appreciated occasions. They are both down to the family and a couple of surprise parties that, apart from the cost, took a lot of time and effort to organise.

The first was on my retirement when I was led to believe we were having a family dinner. On the day I chose to move a telephone from one side of the kitchen to another. It was before the simple plug-in type which meant making a detailed plan of the numerous wires an essential. As a result it took longer than expected and unknowingly I was stopping the kitchen being used for what turned out to be some elaborate preparation. In desperation my son-in-law was called in to challenge me to a game of snooker at the cricket club. They knew that it was something I wouldn't refuse. With the wiring finished, it was up to the club and once there they knew it would not be easy to get me back. This gave them the time to get on but as expected it was not easy to get me home.

On my eventual arrival I cursed the number of cars parked in the road but on entering the sitting-room I understood. There were some twenty friends waiting for me, with glasses that I'm sure had been filled more than once. I could only apologise for delaying the proceedings but it was a genuine surprise and a jolly good party!

There was a larger gathering when the family gave a party for my 80th birthday at Guy's Hampshire home. I knew we were having a couple of friends to join us but the surprise was the number that arrived. We were amazed as cars pulled into the yard and even more amazed as the occupants alighted. There were friends we had not seen for ages, several of whom had travelled long distances. We ate and drank on a lovely summer's evening, albeit under awnings in case it rained. To make sure of the surprise, Marian and I were booked in at a local Country Golf Club with no cost to us. The family organised another fine party at our top-class local restaurant, Theobald's, for Marian's 80th birthday. Proof enough for us that family and friends really do care. It's been a good life and Marian has helped to keep my feet on the ground even though it has been a case of tiptoe on many occasions!

My family and riding have been the highlights of my life but attending an informal drinks party at Buckingham Palace hosted by the Queen, with many other members of the Royal family present, was special. Marian was with me and many more of the racing fraternity. It was a party to celebrate the success of her horses. I have had the good fortune to meet the Queen, a truly wonderful lady, on two other occasions. Marian tells me I may have breached protocol while in conversation about horses by saying 'your mother' instead of 'the Queen Mother'. I was referring to the fact that the Queen Mother had recently had her 300th winner and Her Majesty said she had read my piece on the subject. As mentioned earlier, all sorts of people read the *Mirror* but obviously the Queen has to read them all so it came as no great surprise and I cannot claim it to be a 'feather in my cap' that she had read my column.

My parting thoughts are how lucky I have been. A loving family, good health, good friends and a much bigger share of the good things that so many are denied.

A proud moment

Sharing a laugh with the Queen

P.S. If you find my chapters upside-down, inside-out, in the wrong order or unreadable please refer to my introduction and if it was simply uninteresting I can understand but please don't bother to tell me!

DID YOU KNOW?

Whilst having a drink with the famous golfer, Sam Snead, at our hotel during Ascot week he invited me to go outside. Not for a fight but to prove that if I was to lie down with a ball on my forehead he would drive it with no harm to me. Obviously there was a negative reply.

When the Queen Mother died, the Queen took over one or two of her jumpers and the Royal Colours were on view. It was the first time since they were worn by Danny Morgan when winning on Marconi at Fontwell before World War II. Marconi was owned by King George V.

Bruce Hobbs won the Grand National on Battleship at the age of seventeen. Joe Tizzard rode in the race at a similar age while Bill Payne rode Great Span in the race aged eighteen. It is thought that Great Span would have won had he not fallen two fences from home. It is, however, Bill Payne, father of ex-Newmarket trainer Pip, who rode Turkey Buzzard in the 1924 race, aged fourteen.

The Epsom trainer Vic Smyth specialised in early two-year-old winners and his batch of yearlings were 'ridden away' and 'tried' before Christmas. He reckoned the result of those early trials proved to be greatly consistent throughout the season.

Brienz was third to Trigo in the 1929 Derby and fell in the 1936 Grand National won by Reynoldstown. He was ridden by Tim Hamey. Brienz is a village in Switzerland on the Lake of Brienz hence his name as he was by Blink out of Blue Lake.

A pre-war racehorse was named G.D.It., only because the authorities would not allow God Damn It. Horses with the fewest letters in their name include GB and Ur.

It was at Plumpton that Ron Harrison rode a strong finish to win on Ur but unfortunately it was a circuit too soon. Ron Harrison was fined and so too was the amateur John Dennistoun. The once father-in-law of Lord Oaksey lost a race when the Judge failed to see his mount. When the combination won at a later meeting with the same Judge on duty, Ginger, as he was known, shouted something like 'How's this, you blind b———d.' The case, without his utterance, appeared in the *Racing Calendar*.

When the Victoria Cup was run at Hurst Park there was a dog-leg which meant the field was out of sight for a furlong. One year it included a horse who was just as likely to refuse to start or lose many lengths. It came to my knowledge that a man would be stationed by the dog-leg and give a pre-arranged signal if the horse started with the others. The recipient of the signal stood near the bookmakers on the rails ready to place his bet. The animal did start and win but its name escapes me but it may have been Princelone.

Sir Gordon Richards is probably the only Derby winning jockey to have done so wearing a truss. He was a wizard when it came to starting quickly and was not in favour of starting stalls. Gordon also started a fashion of challenging in the centre of the course at Brighton.

Pre-war jockey Jimmy Hickey fixed a rattle to his whip when riding a horse that did not do his best. The Jockey Club subsequently banned such contraptions which included a probe powered by a battery to produce a shock.

The only professional jockey that I have seen with a moustache was George Burry who rode under National Hunt Rules, some sixty-five years ago.

In the not so distant past you never saw jockeys wearing gloves let alone goggles. Had a jockey worn goggles he would have been ridiculed as looking like a motor-cyclist or a driver at the Brooklands car racing circuit. More than one pair of goggles are sometimes worn so that they have a clean pair if necessary. Surely they are preferable to having clods of mud bombarding your eyes. Not only can it be painful but often most of the race can be ridden with a diminished vision. I have often wondered how much the horse can see when conditions are bad.

Many parade ring observers watched for horses wearing heavy exercise shoes rather than racing plates. It was similar to the difference between hobnail boots and plimsolls. I know a case when a big gambling stable came unstuck because they had not reckoned with the jockey – Sir Gordon. It was thought that the heavy shoes were enough to prevent him winning.

When trainers and pressmen were given luncheon tickets the favourite, in the south at least, was Gatwick. At the winter fixtures there was always steak and kidney pudding on the menu. It was also the course with the stiffest fences apart from Aintree and the Grand National Trial was the natural stepping stone. The National was run there during the First World War.

The bottom weight in handicaps used to be 6st 7lb and there were several fully-fledged jockeys able to ride at that weight. A. (Midge) Richardson, Kenny Robertson, Johnny Dines and Benny Lynch were among those sought after. 'Midge' Richardson was a popular little man whose stature was usually heightened by wearing a bowler hat.

Tommy Farr, who went 15 rounds with the World Boxing Champion Joe Louis, was a frequent visitor to Lewes to see his horse, Trapani, which was trained by Tom Masson. On one visit he asked if I would work in his turf accountants business in Brighton. When I said I was awaiting call-up for war service he told me he knew someone who swallowed chewing gum which showed up as a stomach ulcer so he failed the medical. I would rather have been killed on active service.

It was boxing of a slightly lower class when the stable lads tournament took place at the Corn Exchange in Cambridge. The intended opponent for a hefty farrier in the heavyweight contest opted out and an appeal for a substitute was broadcast. I was with Peter Crouch, a lad with Don Butchers, who stepped forward. There must have been a difference of around 3 stones, but the house erupted when Peter KO'd the farrier after only a few seconds of the first round. Peter made it a double when leading-up Be Patient to win at Newmarket the following day.

That fine sportsman Billy Shand-Kydd did not box to my knowledge but took part in powerboat racing and steeplechasing. I asked him which thrilled him most and he declared it a no-contest with chasing a clear winner.

Amateur races on the flat were not too plentiful and the riders had to be members of the Racecourse Club. It was different for National Hunt races. Any man or boy could simply turn up and ride without a licence or qualifications. Lady riders did not enter into the equation in those days.

Bert Bray, long-serving head lad to Tom Masson following service to Lord Lonsdale, was first on the scene when the vet came to castrate a horse. He would take the testicles and devour them at the first opportunity. Bert described the eating of this delicacy as 'having a ball'.

When I read that Ann Edgar from Minehead had died I wrote to her daughter Fay expressing our sorrow. It came as a shock when our one-time neighbour rang to say she was in good health. It was a lady with the same name and from the same place that had died. A rare coincidence.

The mighty Golden Miller won five successive Cheltenham Gold Cups but was ridden by four different jockeys. In 1932 it was Ted Leader, then Billy Stott and the next two years Gerry Wilson and finally Evan Williams. When beaten the following season by Morse Code he was ridden by Frenchie Nicholson.

At a Sandown meeting when there was a match between British and USA jockeys, Marian and I were given the pleasant task of hosting Telly Savalas (Kojak) at lunch. He was a gentleman.

Finally, I have always been a DIY nut. My most satisfying jobs were over-hanging the exterior of a house with tiles and turning a flat roof into a tiled pitched roof plus unblocking a fireplace and turning a completely empty space into a handsome marble affair. I made the throat of the fireback so smooth that it burnt coal more quickly than I could afford to buy it! It occurs to me that I probably made a better job of that than I have of this book but if you have enjoyed reading it a fraction as much as I have enjoyed writing it I would, if I knew, be very happy.

INDEX

References are to page numbers.
Figures in bold indicate that reference is to a picture caption.